For Paige.
I know the love of the divine
because of the way you have loved me.

For Sawyer and Finn.
May knowing my secrets
help you make peace with yours.

WHY

SECRETS

HOLD YOU BACK

HIDDEN

AND LAUNCH

YOU FORWARD

KRIS LOEWEN

First Edition published by
The Work of Kris Loewen

ISBN: 978-1-7377788-0-6

Visit www.krisloewen.com for more about the author's work or to order additional copies of *Hidden*.

Cover design © 2021 Kris Loewen,
designed by Adam Newbold - *anew.hk*
Internal design and layout by Kristopher Loewen Marketing and Design.
Produced with Adobe InDesign, Microsoft Word, and Scrivener software.

Developmental editor: Samir Selmanovic - *samirselmanovic.com*
Copy editing and proofreading by E.E. Loewen

Hidden was funded by 188 backers through kickstarter.com.
View the original campaign here:
www.kickstarter.com/projects/1704908600/hidden-a-book-about-secrets
The Kickstarter video was produced by
Christian Bell at CMBell Company (cmbell.com)

Disclaimer: The advice and strategies found within may not be suitable for every situation. This work is sold with the understanding that neither the author nor the publisher are held responsible for the results accrued from the advice in this book.

TABLE OF CONTENTS

AUTHOR'S NOTE

August, 2021—This book has been at least seven years in the making. I'm not sure I would have embarked on such a writing journey had I known how much time, energy, and plain hard work would go into making it a reality. Because of the delay of its completion is the proverbial elephant in the room, I want to share a few words of explanation.

My youngest child was born in 2014. I took "paternity leave" in the months following his birth in the form of a sabbatical. During this time, *Hidden* also came into existence. My family was gracious enough to allow me a few hours of work in the wee hours of the mornings, leaving me time to spend the rest of the days on vacation with them. Each day, I started at 4am in my makeshift office in the garage before migrating to the Starbucks in downtown Walla Walla or Whitman College's library. I made much less progress than I had hoped during that season of life. This would materialize into a theme throughout the project.

By the time 2017 rolled around, I was still working full time at the

Walla Walla University Church as Worship and Communications Pastor, and had slowly managed to church out a first draft of the book. A number of trusted friends reviewed the manuscript, agreed it was solid, but encouraged me to seek out professional editing before taking the next steps. At that time, financing editorial was a challenge for my family and so I turned to crowd-funding for support. Christian Bell and his family's company, CM Bell, was kind enough to help me producing a video for the Kickstarter campaign. When my community successfully funded the project, raising all ~$18,000 needed to finish it, I thought I was close to the goal-line. Little did I know that the work had really just begun.

Samir Selmanovic, a PhD author, former pastor, and now my friend, took on the challenge of doing a thorough developmental edit of all 12 chapters. Every week for three months in early 2018, Samir and I met on Zoom to discuss in detail how to make the book better. Carefully noting his wisdom was like drinking from a firehose. He offered so much to me, and with incredible generosity. While the original manuscript was solid, Samir helped me see that much of it deserved a rewrite in order to say what was really on my heart.

Pastoral transitions at the church along with my own soul-searching regarding my employment situation led to repeated delays in working on the rewrite throughout the rest of 2018. During the 18 months following the Kickstarter project, I interviewed for 3 different positions along the west coast, ultimately accepting an invitation to become the Lead Pastor at the Redlands Seventh-day Adventist Church. Predictably, I found it difficult to wrap my mind around writing while also focusing on job interviews, my family, and my ongoing full-time job at the University Church, which became increasinly stressful during its search for its own senior pastor.

I arrived in Redlands in the spring of 2019. This was the first major move of my life; away from family in Walla Walla along with the majority of my support system. My new community was warm and lovely, welcoming my family with open arms. As is the case with all new jobs, however, the learning curve for my new role as the primary leader was steep. I stepped in as the administrator of a team of five full-time ministers at the Redlands Church. I learned quickly that even the most wonderful appearances can belie stressors underneath. Within six months of arrival, I was faced with some of the most daunting leadership challenges I had faced in my 15-year career. This was capped off by the beginning of the COVID-19 pandemic in March of 2020. Needless to say, I was able to get very little done on the manuscript after my arrival in Redlands.

For reasons that I am now keeping private, I resigned from my position as lead pastor in July of 2021. I had only served for 26 months; time that was filled with incredible joy, unavoidable confusion, and understandable pain. As I shared with my congregation at the end of my ministry there, this was not how my family and I had planned it to go when we moved south from the Pacific Northwest. And yet, I felt a strange sense of peace, confident that the Spirit was leading in the process.

One of the silver linings of stepping away from full-time pastoral ministry for a time has been the space now afforded to me for finishing *Hidden*. Finally, after all these years of churning away, I'm excited to share the wisdom and beauty contained in these pages.

Obviously, I'm a different person than I was when I started *Hidden*. I've learned an immense amount about secret-keeping through my research, conversations with colleauges about the book, and via all the life experience that has come my way during the writing period. Admittedly, I chose an enormous topic with endless twists and turns. Even limiting the scope of the conversation to individual secret-keeping left me with a massive reservoir of possible directions. Inevitably, I left a great deal out. I also recognize that my voice has shifted some over the time that it took me to assemble *Hidden*. I have found that I could endlessly review material I wrote months or years ago and revise it to better suit my current self. But at some point we have to set our lyrical horses free to roam in the world, however inexact or dated they might be. I can say without reservation that every word in this book was heartfelt at the time I wrote it!

In the end, I am a better person for having done this work. I am more confident about the parts of myself I still keep private; and I am at peace about the aspects of my life that self-protection compels me to keep secret. In the months and years to come, my hope and prayer is that I will appropriately guard my privacy while also risking vulnerability in wise and life-giving ways.

Grace and peace to you as you dig through this ragged collection of words. Please know that I hold you in my heart with love.

-Kris Loewen,
Redlands, Calif.

> *"Nothing is covered up that will not be revealed, or hidden that will not be known. Therefore whatever you have said in the dark shall be heard in the light, and what you have whispered in private rooms shall be proclaimed on the housetops."*
> — *Luke 12:2-3*

"I have secrets." Those three words launched the Kickstarter campaign for this book project. On camera in a makeshift studio cobbled together in the church basement, I apprehensively stared into the lens, yearning to project confidence. "You have secrets," I said next. It's a claim that has only strengthened in the years since. Gilbert Wells writes, "The man who has no secrets from his wife either has no secrets or no wife." Truly, concealment is ubiquitous.

A decade and a half of pastoral ministry has taught me that everyone expends energy hiding things. No matter the subject and no matter the reason, we all keep secrets. Usually, the word itself carries a negative connotation: hidden crimes, shameful habits, or embarrassing medical problems. But what I've come to discover is that self-concealment is neither exclusively good nor bad. Depending on the circumstances, it can hold us back or launch us forward into the best life has to offer.

Hidden is a book about how secrets affect our lives both individually and collectively. It explores how Secrets are at once gifts and Trojan horses. They shape family systems for generations, create unspoken cultures, shed light on otherwise inexplicable behavior, and even nurture toxic shame. And yet, they set the stage for confession, intimacy, and therefore community itself.

I grew up less than 100 miles from the Hanford Nuclear Site in Washington State. Originally constructed as part of the Manhattan Project of the 1940s, Hanford is home to the world's first full-scale plutonium production reactor. Radioactive material from Hanford was used most notably in the bombs that exploded over Nagasaki, Japan, during World War II.

Seventy years later, Hanford is still a site of harried activity. As a "superfund site," the American government spends millions of dollars employing engineers and construction workers to clean, store, and dispose of the radioactive waste left behind. Even 80 years later, the environmental impact of the Manhattan project is vast (and that is to say nothing of its emotional, relational, and political effects). The fallout, if you will, continues to impact life on many fronts. I grew up in the small town of Walla Walla to the Southeast of Hanford. I can't count the number of times I mused with friends and family members about how the remnant radioactivity of Hanford could be affecting our health through the Columbia River fish we ate, the water we drank, and the air we breathed.

While nuclear technology has undeniably been destructive at times, it also is responsible for good. It certainly has laid waste cities, but it has also powered them with clean electricity. Atomic energy can mutate cells that become cancerous, but it can also be used as treatment. Radioactive material is what makes household smoke detectors work, helps detect diseases in PET scan machines, and is the technology behind glow-in-the-dark products. Not unlike secret-keeping, nuclear reactions can neither be classified as good or bad, right or wrong, pure or defiled. Most of us at some time in our lives risk the clear dangers of radioactivity in order to grab hold of its certain benefits.

Something similar is true for keeping secrets[1]. In our lives, communities, and families, secrets can yield monstrous fallout. Yet, they can also be leveraged to create such unspeakable gifts as intimacy and healing. The things we hide can ravage entire generations but also building unbreakable human bonds. Little has the capacity to hold us back in life as our secrets do. At the same time, our best contributions to the world sneakily emerge from the wise application of the hidden.

The thesis of this book is that secrets both inhibit and catalyze personal maturity. Hidden asks and answers questions about how our secret-keeping affects us and those we love and the world beyond us. Much has been written about the power dynamics of secrecy employed on the governmental or business level. While I will refer to some of these in Hidden, the scope is intentionally narrowed to the individual and their direct relational systems. But before I outline the way in which each chapter explores a different facet of the central axiom, I want to provide six definitions and disclaimers.

(1) Here and throughout the book, I define the quality of "personal maturity" very inclusively. When I use it or one of the many other synonymous phrases throughout the book, I mean forward progress toward achieving the very best version of our individual or even collective humanity. For some readers, this will take on a religious or spiritual tone, as in, "becoming who God made me to be," or simply, "virtuous." Others might rightly hear it as "achieving my full potential" or "living my best possible life." No matter the life experience you bring to this book, please allow the central thesis to include your worldview.

---

1 - I am indebted to Sissela Bok, a psychology researcher who introduced me to the parallel metaphor of fire for understanding secrets. Check the resources in the back for more information on her work.

(2) For the first fifteen years of my adult life following my undergraduate education, I worked professionally as a pastor in the Seventh-day Adventist Christian denomination. Although I am no longer employed as clergy, I still consider myself to be a spiritual leader. I work to create a more inclusive world through deep caring, wise teaching, and courageous confrontation. While I still follow the teachings of Jesus and see beauty in the Bible, I also recognize that the spirit of God has been, still is, and will continue to move in and through people who exist both inside and outside formal religious structures.

I wrote Hidden with genuine respect in my heart for my home tradition. I also wrote it believing that any claim to exclusive access to Truth is silly. This book isn't about convincing you to become religious. I think its principles are true, regardless of their diverse sources. Readers do not need to be Christians, or religious, or spiritual to find value in Hidden. My hope is that while I enthusiastically draw on the milieu I have marinated in for 40 years, you will understand that I do so because of familiarity and esteem, not as a value judgment comparing other traditions. Thank you for your grace as I express my faith; I write in hopes that you will interpret the message within your own frame of reference.

(3) There was a time when I believed all secrets to threaten the best in life. But as I suggest in the thesis, I no longer believe that axiom to be true. While I will often make strident claims about the phenomenon of secrecy in this book, I am decidedly not making the argument that no one should self-conceal, far from it. Many times, hiding parts of ourselves (and sometimes even later revealing it) can be truly life-giving. This was one of my great surprises in setting out to write this book.

(4) Another important discovery I made over the course of this project is that there are significant differences between secrecy and privacy. Colloquially, we sometimes use the terms interchangeably. In Hidden, I treat them as distinct dynamics.

Secrets concern things we willfully[2] hide in order to avoid something undesired should it be uncovered. Privacy, on the other hand, concerns hidden matters that do not carry anything near the emotional charge s secrets. Bradley Nelson, a playwright from my hometown and a former classmate, penned a brilliant line that highlights this distinction between private and secret. In his play about fundamentalist church culture and the LGBTQ+ experience, one character announces, "I may not always choose to disclose...but I no longer fear its discovery."

Most of the time, private things in our lives are relatively banal: bodily functions or features, sexuality, beliefs, and/or personal property. Thus, by keeping the balance of my banking accounts concealed, I'm not hiding a secret; I'm protecting boundaries. If I choose not to share my weight or the frequency of daily bathroom trips, I'm holding them in privacy, not secrecy. My central argument in Hidden is that it is secret-keeping (not privacy) that holds us back and launches us forward.

Anita Kelly, a Ph.D. psychologist and expert on secrecy, delineates the two parallel concepts like this: privacy is "expecting to be free from unsanctioned intrusion," while secrecy "involves active attempts to prevent such intrusion." In other words, our motive for keeping something hidden deeply impacts its very nature. Intention transforms the private into secret and secret into private. When privacy is threatened, and we begin expending energy to protect that part of ourselves, the thing can functionally become a secret and therefore carry with it both consequences and benefits. Every act of deceit necessitates secrecy, but all self-concealment isn't intended to deceive.

"Being able to keep personal secrets may even be seen as a sign of maturation," Anita Kelly continues. I couldn't agree more. For most children, it takes quite some time to develop an appreciation

---

2 - Sometimes, as we will see in chapter six, it is the unconscious ego expending the will-power and not our conscious selves.

of either privacy or secrecy. At age two or three, my kids had virtually zero capacity for shame or modesty. They naturally didn't have a discrete sense of identity outside our family system. But as they continued to develop, their capacity for hiding (and its many impacts) has increased. This highlights the fact that not only do secrecy and privacy dance with one another, but the human capacity to conceal is also highly individual and is predicated upon (among other things) maturity.

(5) Secrecy (and privacy) only exists within the context of community. Each group, tribe, family system, and culture uniquely defines what ought to be in the sphere of the private for its members, and therefore what becomes secret if it is withheld. In many ways, we surrender privacy in order to exist in any community. For example, when people join conservative churches like I grew up in, they make an agreement to be personally accountable for their adherence to the belief system. This is an implicit disavowal of some privacy. Thus, some behaviors that would be considered private[3] in the broader culture become available to scrutiny. As it happens, because my tradition has something to say about every sphere of life, the organization functionally intrudes on much of its members' privacy. Predictably, this yields a culture with a great many secrets, and a lot of people are stuck spinning their wheels.

In some settings, collective secrecy becomes the means to trust. Deborah Coehn writes about 19th Century British family culture in her book Family Secrets, "It was not only expected that the family would conceal its affairs from outsiders. As a testament to familial solidarity, secret-keeping was also praiseworthy. Well into the twentieth century, secrecy forged the bonds of trust." If what might normally be regarded as private actually becomes a

---

3 - Drinking alcohol, smoking, entertainment choices, money spending habits, and the use of free time.

secret within a family system, very tightly connected[4] community can be formed around it. Truly, secrets are the birthplace of intimacy.

This point is in part why cults are able to engender so much power. Confusingly, in the context of these sorts of communities, even very motivated people can struggle to make an exit. As exposed in the HBO film, Going Clear,[5] the Church of Scientology wields great power over its membership by requiring from them nearly absolute transparency. Once this organization "has the goods" on its people, it can manipulate behavior via threats of blackmail. In short, Scientologists are allowed to have precious little privacy within the club, but some of the content of that privacy would be considered secret in other social circles. Thus, the organization can utilize their adherents' desire to keep secrets concealed as a means to their own ends. It's a vicious cycle that has led to death.

(6) Each one of us manages a complex patchwork of expectations regarding that which we hide. As we move through different environments, our system of secrecy and privacy adjusts according to the limits imposed by each community. This defines what is secret or what is private. My family has one set of wishes regarding my private life, my coworkers have another, my doctor's office has yet another set, and the government has even more yet. Sometimes they overlap from group to group; other times, they are unique. Regardless, most of us move from one context to another, unconsciously shifting our boundaries based

---

4 - A similar dynamic is true in technology. A friend of mine who owns and operates a technology company talked with me about secrecy and trust as it applies in the virtual world. Computer networks have developed webs of trust, where if one server farm or Internet provider is deemed trustworthy by one company, a second company may deem it the same by virtue of the judgment of the first. If I trust you and you trust George, I also trust George by proxy. The web of trust is efficient, but its complexity can also bring unforeseen consequences.

5 - And the book by the same title.

on these formal and informal agreements. What might be a secret one minute can, in the next minute, shift into the realm of benign privacy. Renowned short story author Anton Chekhov writes, "The personal life of every individual is based on secrecy, and perhaps it is partly for that reason that civilized man is so nervously anxious that personal privacy should be respected."

(7) The scope of my formal training and professional experience is limited to religious leadership. I am not a psychologist, psychotherapist, or licensed mental health practitioner. I believe the advice and observations I make in Hidden to be true. This doesn't mean that they can substitute for professional psychological advice. Some readers may be well served to seek assistance from the aforementioned experts, just as I have done throughout my life. Please do not rely upon Hidden as a replacement for actual medical professionals.

(8) Hidden is not an academic exploration of the subject. My goal here is pastoral, spiritual, and inspirational. As often occurs between members of the community and me, my motive is to be helpful. I want to point people in the right direction, to embody light in the darkness. I'm an expert because my life experience has taught me so much, and yet I have so much more to learn.

What's more, I have done my best to provide a breadcrumb trail leading back to the thinkers and artists who influenced me. Each chapter of Hidden has a corresponding list of resource items in the back of the book. When I directly quote an author in the text, I have done my best to correctly identify them and their work. I'm sure my thinking has been influenced by a great many other beautiful people to whom I have not given credit. For this, I am truly sorry.

Author John Sowers said, "Writing is reaching into your deep soul and being brave enough to put those words on paper." The experience of putting this book together has been exactly that for me. It flows from my soul and drips from my wounds. Processing many of the observations and disclosures I make throughout the book has often proved destabilizing for me in the best of ways. Hidden has been an exercise of confession; I am a better person for it.

(9) A brief outline of Hidden follows here. The first four chapters of Hidden primarily demonstrate how keeping secrets has a detrimental effect on personal growth. Chapter one explores the heaviness of secrets: how our unavoidable attention to them keeps us from growing and developing in ways we otherwise might. The second chapter acts as an introduction to the truly massive topic of shame. It argues that shame and secrecy are interrelated, one playing off the other in a destructive spiral. But it also suggests that shame exists on a spectrum, some of whose forms are actually helpful. Third, the chapter on family systems takes a look at how secret-keeping can have a generational impact through family culture. Chapter five is about how keeping ourselves hidden from those who might otherwise support us is a recipe for delayed maturation.

Chapters five through nine begin to demonstrate some of the nuances that arise when we talk about keeping secrets. "Secret Wisdom" explores how the selective curating and sharing of certain secrets actually aids in personal growth. Chapter six digs into the psychological phenomena of repression and self-deception; in essence, our body's way of protecting itself from trauma. Secret goodness in chapter seven becomes the first strong argument in favor of personal secret-keeping. It often pays to hide virtue. The eighth chapter represents the broadest look at secrecy in this book. It describes the important balance that leaders[6] must strike between authenticity and privacy. Finally, chapter nine examines the power of judgment for good and bad. Sometimes an empathetic critique can be useful, but withholding it can cause more damage than good.

---

6 - And in particular, spiritual leaders.

The final two chapters of Hidden form a two-part appraisal of disclosure. Chapter ten outlines confession's intrinsic value to personal growth, and eleven dives into relational dynamics: how confession can be leveraged for building trust and community, and at times damage it. Benjamin Franklin is credited with the saying, "Three may keep a secret, if two of them are dead." This final pairing attempts to describe the substantive risks confession brings while also suggesting guidelines for doing it safely.

As you will notice, each chapter along the way ends with a series of questions intended for group discussion and dialogue. While this book will be a useful tool for individual reflection, because of the theme, I think it will be most meaningful in the context of a trusting community of friends. The questions, in fact, are intentionally not exhaustive. Instead, they are created to be jumping-off points for small groups, church study classes, and family dinner tables.

A few years ago, a close friend of mine casually observed that secrecy is the theme of my life. It took me a while to grasp what he was getting at, but I now believe that he was right. My life has traversed the rocky paths of surviving a house fire, burying my brother, enduring through my parents' family turmoil, suffering the trauma of addiction and abuse, and resigning from my pastoral career in part because of private matters. In each of these and many other experiences, I have kept secrets. At times, self-concealment has become my modus operandi for life. I have learned to cope with threats of abandonment through clandestine consumption and scrupulous self-presentation. Mired in dysfunctional family patterns inherited through generations, entire swaths of my life have been driven from the back seat by an unseen chauffeur. I didn't realize it as a younger person, but my secrets eventually became an emergency brake on my growth as a human being.

Transparency and confession were not magic wands that instantly brought me to wholeness. However, they did prove to be essential in the process of maturation. The same has been true for many hundreds of people I've worked with as a pastor over the past 15 years. Whether through retreat experiences, personal counseling conversations, or small-group processes, I've witnessed scores of people gain new confidence in who they are as humans, shuffle off toxic shame, and embrace unconditional love. While our secrets might conspire to keep us from embracing all that God has for us, confession is a key first step to healing. As people living our true identities, secrets become the best assets for creating intimacy.

Secrets are radioactive. They're like a nuclear power plant seething with energy when well tended and a disaster in the wings when disrespected. Beware. An enormous reservoir of energy is stored up in that which is concealed. If you begin tinkering with your secrets (or your family's or culture's), things will not stay the same. Exposure is a sure-fire way to throw a stick into the spokes of the status quo. But the truth is that your hidden life is already costing you far more than any deconstruction can. I believe that a better life is waiting on the other side of facing our secrets.

One final note. If you are currently satisfied with your life as it is today, I encourage you to stop reading. Seriously. If you put into practice even 20 percent of what I have to say in Hidden, life will undoubtedly change for you and your friends or family. Some of these changes might be unpleasant (I think they'll be ultimately life-giving, of course, but not necessarily easy or fun along the way). So really, if life is comfortable, calm, predictable, or successful, and you'd like to keep it that way, this is not the book for you[7].

---

7 - I'll even give you a refund!

1 | THE WEIGHT OF SECRETS

Sometimes we think we're keeping a secret, but the secret is that it's actually keeping us.
-Frank Warren, PostSecret

Some years ago, I came across a story I'll never forget. *The Teacher Who Couldn't Read*, a memoir by John Corcoran, paints a picture of what it feels like to incubate a secret long term.

Corcoran begins his story in elementary school. He remembers being repeatedly ushered into the "dumb row" of classrooms. This was painful for a socially aware kid like him, who could feel the mocking looks and giggles trickle over his hunched shoulders. As early on as second grade, John began to lag behind other kids in reading. By the time he reached junior high, his literacy hadn't improved. At all. In fact, it might have regressed.

Corcoran recollects being able to keep pace in mathematics and PE during those early years in school. He even wonders if his aptitude in those subjects made it easier for his teachers and parents to miss his underlying problems. As more and more subject matter required reading for comprehension, an increasing proportion of coursework went over his head.

Year by year, school officials allowed him to advance through grades without batting an eyelash. This, despite the fact that his reading hadn't germinated — let alone grown! John passed under the radar for more decades, finally graduating from both High School and college, utterly illiterate. Astonishingly, the absence of this essential life skill didn't prohibit him from being hired as a high school social studies and English teacher soon after college. In fact, he would work for 17 years in that role, all the time keeping his secret tightly under wraps.

In his memoir, John Corcoran writes about devising a wide variety of elaborate smoke screens, ruses, lies, personality characteristics, and manipulation tactics — all deployed to keep his secret under wraps. Corcoran reports how he used his athletic aptitude in high school to deflect scrutiny away from his academic problems. He describes skimming through dozens of classes by cheating, relying on the work of friends, and circumventing conventional evaluation to suit his needs. Rather than writing papers or taking tests, for example, he shrewdly schmoozed teachers to grant him alternative options.

While in college on a full athletic scholarship, Corcoran once convinced a friend to break into a professor's office in the middle of the night. The plan was to steal the filing cabinet with test answers contained inside, copy the key, and return the cabinet undetected. Shockingly, the two pulled off the caper with perfect cunning. John passed the test by rote memory of its multiple-choice answers.

He even manipulated his girlfriend into writing papers for him or dictating as he spoke them aloud. The whole time she remained ignorant of his disability. This, despite the fact that she had become a survival tool in the hands of her boyfriend. By the time his years of schooling were finished, John Corcoran had "earned" both a bachelor's degree in Education and a Master's in Business Administration without the ability to read or write.

Once in his first career as a high-school teacher, Corcoran's deceptions continued. He writes about how he circumvented discovery in his classrooms by using creative "alternative teaching" methods to instruct his students in the given subject matter. Seemingly unavoidable tasks for teachers like filling out grade books, taking rolls, or scoring schoolwork were all farmed out to unwitting students or colleagues. He justified these dubious delegations at the time by arguing that they had beneficial educational value as "life skills." The more elaborate his lies, the weightier his secret felt. But it still didn't come out.

Despite the far-fetched nature of his story, Corcoran managed to live with these skeletons in his closet deep into middle age. Only his wife knew of his illiteracy – and only then because of the unavoidable tension it had created in their marriage. In fact, he writes about how she enabled his secrecy, becoming a codependent player in the game. It wasn't until he was nearly 50 years old that the concealed truth finally slipped through his facade. And it was only then that he began to step into his life's purpose.

I have to admit my admiration for John Corcoran's guile. I can hardly imagine what it'd feel like to have even a fraction of his wit and social dexterity. No doubt, my reaction is related to my own struggles with building a strong sense of identity and living confidently from that.

As a child, I never felt like I had a destiny. Instead, my dreams meandered hand-in-hand with the books, films, and music I happened to be absorbing at the time. While in the thick of a John Grisham phase, I imagined myself clad in a 3-piece suit before a judge and jury, dazzling the courtroom with my genius and theatrics. When 1990s alternative rock music enthralled me in high school, I envisioned myself on stage with my electric bass head-banging with the crowd. Later, Albert Schweitzer's autobiography inspired new dreams of travel, scholarship, and a life of service.

I couldn't have identified it then, but my shifting sense of direction was connected to my need to feel worthy. A number of adverse childhood experiences had left me feeling abandoned, unwanted, and unlovable. In response, I subconsciously schemed to vindicate my value by way of personal achievement. Leveraging my natural talent for schoolwork was a natural approach. Through straight A's on report cards, I would announce to family and friends, "SEE! I'll make something of myself yet!"

My plan seemed to work. I earned a reputation for my intellect and felt confidence from my perch atop the class. As high school continued, I doubled down on this strategy, setting my sights on the most prestigious and lucrative career I could envision: becoming a medical doctor. Never mind the fact that I had no special interest in science or the human body, my goal was pragmatic. "With the letters, M.D., behind my name, everyone will know that I'm good enough."

As long as unexamined motivations drove my choices, my destiny would remain elusive. The same is true for any of us. Whether impulses, beliefs, talents, wisdom, habits, tendencies, or disabilities (as in the case of John Corcoran), that which is hidden shapes our world. Secrets are incredibly powerful. That's what this book is all about. The things we conceal, no matter the reason or the detail, have an enormous impact on whether or not we'll live the life we were born to live.

Once I entered college, my inner tone had shifted. Through a series of painful experiences, the anxiety to prove myself worthy had gilded into a clarity of purpose. I doubt the change was obvious to my classmates and teachers at the time. Perfectionism still shaped my approach to school, after all. But deep in my heart, a sense of destiny had sprouted. I wanted to become a pastor. The more I practiced this art of caring for people, teaching them what I knew about the human soul, and creating moments of spiritual transcendence, the more I fell in love with it. The drive to have my value corroborated by friends or family was replaced with calm confidence.

John Corcoran's early manifestations of self-confidence didn't come from this clear sense of destiny. Instead, they appeared out of a hidden feeling of insufficiency. While the prospect of pulling off a gambit like John Corcoran's might seem exhilarating in some ways, the cost was high.

Writing about his experiences, John Corcoran describes the abject fear his scheme caused him. Throughout his 17-year teaching career and later as a real estate investor, he recalls living day-by-day in a state of perpetual "flight or fight." We are all familiar with this primitive human response to stress. It happens when we sense significant real or imagined threats. In John's mind, if his illiteracy were to become publicly known — everything in his life would be torn apart. He felt stalked by this embarrassing problem, as if by a lion ready to pounce at any moment. Imagine living with that tension all the time!

No part of Corcoran's life survived untouched by his secret.

He writes that some of his old behavior patterns remind him of someone deep in addiction: compulsively responding to fear or shame with damaging decisions but never knowing where to find a real solution. Corcoran's life became a continual string of winces and overreactions to even the slightest threat to his status quo. Paying a bill at the utility company, filling out a form at his real estate firm, or corresponding in any way other than by telephone or face-to-face, would produce otherwise inexplicable behavior. Feeling trapped in these ordinary circumstances, his stress would transform into bullying, blustery attacks, or self-righteous grandstanding. Something as straightforward as being asked to fill out a medical history document at the doctor's office could trigger an angry tirade. Corcoran describes how, in a single day, he could swing several times between dishing out threats and manipulating through pity. All this became second nature,

29

automatic.

Far from true confidence in his identity, John's web of lies created a false public self, as if he were an actor on a Hollywood movie set. He constantly managed this invented persona every moment of every day. The more he shaded and avoided the truth, the more he had to juggle different identities to keep his professional life afloat. The deeper down the rabbit hole he went, the more compelled to do the work of acting, scriptwriting, and building sets, scenery, and costumes. The more he acted, the more complex his life-movie became.

Secret-keeping is very hard work.

When I was in high school, I was privileged to go on a tour to Europe as the bass violinist of my area string orchestra. One of the destinations was the composer Wolfgang Amadeus Mozart's hometown of Salzburg, Austria. At Mozart's family home, the tour guide told us a spurious story from his childhood. Each morning, his mother would rouse him from slumber by playing on the piano the first seven notes of a major scale, always omitting the eighth and final note that would complete it. This created terrible tension in the young musician.

Mozart was so drawn to the conclusion of the scale that his continued sleep became impossible. He categorically could not focus on anything else but the expected resolution. So the story goes, his mother's trick worked like magic. Each day, Mozart would dash out of bed and down the stairs to play the final note himself.

Just as the unfinished scale grated at Mozart, keeping secrets demands our attention. It's hard to focus on anything with much intensity when our minds are incessantly pulled out of bed and down the stairs by the seemingly inevitable moment of exposure.

This ceaseless guarding consumes resources.

In fact, spending energy is *the* critical factor that defines secret-keeping.[1] It's not *what* we hide that determines whether or not the thing is a secret for us; it's *that* we're intentionally hiding it. The reason doesn't matter. If we try to conceal something (no matter how inconsequential), its nature begins to shift from ordinary privacy to secrecy. And along with that mutation comes the many benefits and drawbacks this book explores. The secrets that have the greatest impact on our lives, good or bad, tend to be the ones that we consciously acknowledge and consciously make an effort to conceal.

With tongue firmly in cheek, I'll illustrate the dynamic with cat ownership. In most circles, owning one or two cats isn't something to hide (shocking, I know). In fact, the majority of people wouldn't think twice about allowing family, friends, colleagues, or even strangers to know that they have such a furry pet at home. Cat ownership certainly *could* be a matter of privacy but isn't something most people work to keep under wraps.

However, it's entirely possible that for some people, cat ownership rises to the level of requiring closeting. Perhaps the person doesn't want to be identified with certain stereotypes that may come with cat ownership. Perhaps the person wants to avoid the ridicule of co-workers who dislike cats. Perhaps, more realistically, she is hiding the cat from her landlord! Regardless of the motivation behind keeping the cat secret, this person's choice to expend energy hiding it is what makes it a secret for her — not something inherent in cat ownership itself.

The consumption of mental energy is the linchpin that defines secrecy as opposed to privacy. So, something as benign as owning a cat could present the many consequences or benefits that come

---

1 - See the work of Anita Kelly, a Ph.D. psychologist who has written extensively about the science of secrecy.

along with secret-keeping.

This is key. We can spend our energy (our lives) investing in thoughts and activities that will make us better people and the world a better place. But we can also squander it. Wasting energy is wasting the gift of life. We only have one chance to become who we will become, and many secrets are not worth the toll they take on our maturity. Obviously, none of us would consciously trade a secret like cat-ownership in exchange for our life's destiny, and yet this is the deal we sometimes unintentionally make.

Ph.D. psychologist, Dan Wenger, writes,

> "Secrets prohibit us from growing because the thing is always on our minds. If I tell you not to think about white elephants, all you can do is think about white elephants. This is exactly the nature of secrets. The secret must be remembered, or it might be told. And the secret cannot be thought about, or it might be leaked."

If exposing a certain secret feels like a threat to our very survival (as it did in John Corcoran's mind), the need to keep it hidden requires even more energy! How are you supposed to develop good character if you subconsciously believe you're about to be attacked by a lion? What's the use of developing altruism if you're not sure you'll make it through the day? Why dig into your personality, habits, or generational wisdom if you feel your life is imminently at risk? Those who keep a lot of secrets siphon a corresponding amount of attention away from other important things, even their destinies.

Conversely, people hiding little don't tend to carry the weight of the world on their shoulders. As a consequence, those with few secrets wind up with a good amount of extra energy to spare on more fruitful (and fun) pursuits. Feeling the freedom to make mistakes, for example, those hiding little have access to the unspeakable gift of learning from failure instead of avoiding it at all costs. Instead of spending their lives manicuring false selves for public consumption, people with few secrets have extra energy for increasing self-awareness and emotional intelligence. Instead of scheming contingency plans for the moment of revelation, those with little to hide spend their energy on becoming excellent in art, business, service, etc.

Although his coping methods were quite extraordinary (and his public confession in the memoir praiseworthy), John Corcoran really did cause some significant pain in people's lives. For nearly two decades, this teacher modeled master manipulation, circumvention, and deception to his students. He indirectly showed them how to get what they wanted by leveraging false personas. Kids in his classroom who were the neediest of excellent instruction (e.g., those most like John when he was a child) were neglected. Paralyzed from taking responsibility for his situation, admitting the truth, and getting help, he duplicated a cycle of dysfunction that he had inherited as a student himself. Just like him, John's own under-performing students were forced to teach and cheat their way to "success." Just like him, they were swindled.

As I read, I had a difficult time sensing the degree to which John Corcoran recognizes himself in the education system he critiques. His scarcity of remorse grew to become the elephant in the living room. Instead of contrition, Corcoran's memoir tends to take the tone of either pride for his undeniable ingenuity or blame for the educators that without a doubt failed him. On more than one occasion, he even goes on the offensive: attacking teachers, schools, and administrators for botching his schooling. Although he does acknowledge (and takes some responsibility for) the way he cheated his students out of quality education, he largely seems to excuse his behavior as unavoidable, nurturing the mantle of victimhood. Instead of fully owning his complicity in the system, he hides, still insisting that his unique teaching style gave his students valuable life skills they couldn't have developed anywhere else.

I don't condemn John Corcoran. I don't judge him as evil.

I am him.

We all are him.

We make choices; some wise and others unwise. Choices have consequences, and sometimes it's difficult to face them. This is part of why we keep secrets. The world will be a better place when we all have more compassion for each other in the struggle of living authentically.

With that being said, it's difficult for me not to interpret some of John Corcoran's attitudes in the book as indicative of stunted maturity. This shouldn't be surprising. For someone who had spent a lifetime redirecting energy away from personal growth into self-concealment, we'd expect character cracks to show up in one way or another. John Corcoran's memoir illustrates how the weight of secrets can sabotage even the best of us.

If you've spent your life hiding, you will not have made space for growing. A tragedy!

But don't lose hope. While the picture does get a little bleaker under the weight of secrets, it will become vibrant before we're through!

———————

Keeping secrets doesn't just hold us back from personal growth; it impacts our physical bodies in tangible ways as well. Many research psychologists[2] have studied self-concealment in the lab and in the field, especially in the past three decades. Their findings tend to indicate what we sense intuitively. Heaviness isn't just a

———————

2 - In addition to Anita Kelly's work, check out published articles by Drs. Ahmet Uysal, Helen Lee Lin, and C. Raymond Knee.

metaphor for how it feels to hide things. The weight is concrete.

I can't begin to list the ways how secret-keeping has cost me good health. I'm not alone. Research indicates people who self-conceal are more susceptible to cancer, certain infectious diseases, heart disease and hypertension, increased cortisol secretion and therefore weight gain, anxiety and depression, extreme shyness, loneliness, and even chronic pain. Secrets feel heavy because it's not just our minds doing the work. Remember the "fight-or-flight" type response John Corcoran describes in his book? That was a substantive physiological response to human experience. Our bodies experience secret-keeping as stress. No matter how much endurance or inner calm we have, sooner or later, our flesh and bone will tell the tale.[3]

The more we conceal, the sicker we get.

This is not a new idea. Cultures and religious traditions from east to west, across centuries, have taught on the impact of deception, encouraging people to live with integrity. From Plato to the Bhagavad Gita to modern science to the Bible, we see a shared thread of wisdom repeatedly emerging. Even classic literature points to the physical impact secret-keeping has on our bodies.

Nathaniel Hawthorne's classic novel, *The Scarlet Letter*, illustrates the dynamic well. One of the major characters is a Puritan pastor named Arthur Dimmesdale. In the story, he has made a grave error: as an unmarried spiritual leader, he's become the father-to-be of an unborn baby carried by a local girl (and the book's protagonist), Hester Prynne. Because Pastor Dimmesdale is not only a leader but earnestly committed to his religion, he suffers under the weight of guilt for his actions. Over the course of the book, he compensates for these feelings in part by compulsively

---

3 - Much has been written about the physical effect of stress on our bodies. A quick google search will give you scads of research and journal entries about the phenomenon.

repeating physical self-harm as public spectacles of humility.

About one such display Hawthorne writes,
> "Mr. Dimmesdale was overcome with a great horror of mind, as if the universe were gazing at a scarlet token on his naked breast, right over his heart. On that spot, in very truth, there was, and there had long been, the gnawing and poisonous tooth of bodily pain."

Hester Prynne was the one forced to wear an actual red "A" on her clothing as a symbol of the community's judgment against her illegitimate pregnancy. But Dimmesdale carried the same symbol emblazoned on his soul.

Over the course of the story, Pastor Dimmesdale's health deteriorates until he succumbs to death by the illness of self-concealment. Even overcompensating with added acts of holiness, the pastor still couldn't escape the weight of his hidden life. The old saying, "we are only as sick as our secrets," is more than just an axiom; it's rooted in reality. We've known it for generations. The longer we hide, the heavier the weight, the more substantial the impact.

We sometimes deal with this reality as we deal with our money. You might be familiar with the "sunk-cost fallacy" of *Freakonomics*[4] lore. Economists Stephen Dubner and Steven Levitt introduced the common myth to millions through their book, *Think Like a Freak*. The sunk-cost fallacy describes how many of us are inexplicably pulled as if by gravity, to continue investing in ventures or assets that objectively have become liabilities.

Economists theorize investors reason to themselves, "I've already

---

4 - If you haven't yet discovered Stephen Dubner and Steven Levitt, you are missing out. Their books, films, and podcast are absolutely brilliant. While not directly related to personal secret-keeping per se, there is distinct overlap with the phenomenon. The tagline of the show is "The Hidden Side of Everything."

THE WEIGHT OF SECRETS

got so much riding on it, what's a few more dollars at this point?" As the project circles into increasing degrees of financial disaster, an inner voice ceaselessly reminds them how much they've spent to get this far — and pleads, "Don't give up! Go a little further! Put a few more bucks in!"

Dubner and Levitt write in their book that this thinking, however, is a myth. According to research, it's almost always financially advantageous to let an unprofitable project, car, house, or business go when it becomes an albatross around our necks. Wise investors, they summarize, tend to take the financial hit for selling (even at a loss), and start fresh with a better bet somewhere else.

The vicious cycle of investing in a dark secret likewise only snowballs over time, putting on extra weight in rhythm. As it does, the threat to our status quo increases. A troublesome secret held for a few hours will bear less fallout than the one held for a few years. We might be tempted to continue investing in it despite the immediate consequences. But as John Corcoran and Pastor Dimmesdale discovered, the more they dumped energy into protecting their alternate lives, the more they felt lashed to it. The more we ante up, the higher the stakes.

The question is whether or not we will have the courage to count the cost and begin anew.[5]

_____

Sometimes, long-term self-concealment leads us to see how the pain of maintaining the status quo has become more intense than the pain of getting real. When our hidden life is more burdensome than the consequences of an exposed life, we hit what is sometimes called "rock-bottom." In these moments, it becomes clear that

_____

5 - The final two chapters deal specifically with the "when, where, and how" of disclosure. Remember, sometimes keeping secrets has invaluable benefits for us becoming the people we most want to be. No one should jump into willy-nilly disclosures without careful reflection.

what started as a dainty pendant hanging loosely about our necks is an anchor. This is why rock-bottom, while agonizing, is also a relief. What many of us have learned in these experiences is that while the weight of the secret might've appeared to be sinking us, in the end, it keeps us afloat.

Others of us, however, will carry our truths tucked away for life, taking them to our graves. For some of us, the things we hide will become framed artwork on the walls of our hearts, symbolic of all the beauty we've missed. How many opportunities, relationships, and destinies would we nurture if we only had the courage to admit the truth?

Life passes us by when we spend it in hiding.

My work as a pastor sometimes involves visiting people who are nearing life's end. I remember spending time with one such man early in my career. We hadn't met before and only crossed paths at that moment because a family member had called my church, asking a pastor to visit at his request. Dale[6] was in his late 70s and gravely ill, in the final stages of heart disease. But on the day I stopped to see him in the hospital, he was alert and talkative. Sun streamed through the shades in the low-ceilinged hospital room.

After several minutes of pleasantries, he asked his family to leave so we could be alone. As soon as the door clicked shut, Dale's voice broke the silence once again. He cut right to the chase, speaking frankly about his rapidly approaching death, his happiness with the life he had led, and his willingness to let go — except for one thing.

Dale proceeded to disclose a long-held secret. Years prior, he had been in a sexual relationship with a woman who was not his

---

6 - As is the case with most personal stories in the book, I have changed details (including real names) to maintain anonymity.

wife. This was strictly out of the boundaries they had agreed upon for their relationship. It was also against his sense of Christian morality.[7] Even though his decision had been detected at times by friends and colleagues, he had never been "caught" per se. When accusations arose over the years, he had vociferously denied the allegations. Apparently, his loved ones had always swallowed Dale's lie.

He went on that sunny day, describing how he had been unable to be intimate with his wife continually over the course of their marriage. Overwhelmed by shame, anxiety, and guilt, Dale would become paralyzed in those times of sexual connection, swamped with his past indiscretions. The two had always blamed medical causes for Dale's problem. But he believed in his heart that it was rooted in his secret. He acknowledged his sadness and regretted how his wife had languished in confusion, rejection, and unworthiness all that time. The weight of his secret had been sinking them both.

Dale went on to describe how his unworthiness had led him to shrink away from attending religious events at his church, joining service organizations in his community, or even reaching out a helping hand to someone in need. Over and over again, he said, he ran from whatever the opportunity because of his shameful skeletons lurking in his closet.

As Dale lay in the hospital bed that fall afternoon, earnestly looking me in the eyes as he spoke, he cried (I got the impression this was a rare event for him). Palpable regret welled up from his soul. He was deeply sorry for his choices and for causing so much pain. He believed he could have lived differently, better. But nearing the end, he felt helpless to fix it.

---

7 - In the Christian tradition, people tend to view their behavior primarily through a moral lens (virtue/vice) as opposed to pragmatic (constructive/ deconstructive), wellness (healthy/unhealthy), philosophical (coherent/ incoherent), shame (honor/dishonor), or relational (connecting/disconnecting) lenses.

He was right. But only partially.

Dale had indeed missed out on some of what he wanted most out of life. He plainly had wasted precious energy on hiding his mistake. He certainly could've spent more emotional resources investing in his own personal growth. But the reason he didn't wasn't that his errors were too horrendous for redemption, as he assumed. No, Dale missed out because he had kept it hidden until his final breaths. By the time the truth was out, the opportunity to capitalize on and learn from his mistakes had passed.

At the end of our conversation, Dale asked me to pray with him. He felt the need to ask for forgiveness from his God. We prayed, and when I left, the room felt a little lighter. Dale smiled.

Looking back, I can't help but wonder, what if Dale had been more like John Corcoran? No one is perfect, as we all know. Clearly, they shared the experience of making questionable decisions and then subsequently hiding them. But the arcs of their life stories finished in wildly different places. In contrast to Dale, after coming clean, John Corcoran made it his life's mission to counteract the problems that led to his mistakes.[8] He has dedicated himself to fighting illiteracy, improving teaching methods, and reforming the system that had failed him.

You could say that John's secret led him to his destiny.

Secrets are heavy. They sap our energy. They fill us with anxiety. They hold us back from becoming the kind of people we want to be. And yet behind them, on the other side, are the lives we always wanted.

---

8 - Corcoran is still living, and since publishing "The Teacher Who Couldn't Read," has published his second book, "The Reading Gap: Journey to Answers." Find out more at www.johncorcoranfoundation.org.

Imagine living more directly, with more vitality, with more direction. Imagine stepping out confidently into your sense of calling. Imagine being proud of the life you've chosen. Imagine feeling free.

What if your secrets are the path to getting there?

————

QUESTIONS FOR DISCUSSION

1. Every secret has its cost. For John Corcoran, it was peace of mind. For Dimmesdale, it was his health. For Dale, it was relationships and even his life's calling.

Think about a secret you have kept for a long time. It doesn't have to be grave or dark like those mentioned in the chapter. It could be as simple as a secret dream for your life, like the one the author kept about his career choice. Whatever comes to mind first, grab it.

Now, think about how much it has cost you so far? What might it cost yet in the future?

Take an inventory of loss due to the secret that came up. What are the opportunities, relationships, experiences, or character traits that have been impacted by holding onto this secret? What things (potentially even positive) have you staved off by continuing to keep it?

2. How does it feel to think about these losses? Notice for a couple of minutes what comes up for you emotionally. Is it sadness?

Anger? Blame? Self-pity? Indifference? Depression? Regret?

Reflect on these reactions and why you might be having them.

3. Spend some time thinking about what really is at risk for you (or others) to allow your secret to become known? What might it cost you to tell the truth? It's possible to under-appreciate the toll. But it's also easy to blow out of proportion — and as such is part of what contributes to the weight of carrying secrets.

Do your best to be as realistic as possible: what might you really lose by revealing your secret?

4. Name some manifestations that "the weight" of carrying your secret has produced in your life. How has the pressure to keep it hidden affected you? If you're not sure, how do you think it could be impacting you?

5. What do you know or believe about your destiny? How did you discover yours? If you don't identify with having a particular destiny, why not? How do you feel about this?

2 | SHAME

"Secrets are pillars of the house of shame."
-Greg Loewen, *The Unexplored Room*

Do you remember the first time you felt ashamed?

My earliest experience with this overwhelming emotion was at age six.

The principal of my small private Christian grade school insisted that every person on campus participate in daily calisthenics, rain or shine. Our routine concluded with a lap around the dirt-patched playground (a marathon-like feat in my young mind's eye). As every child and teacher plodded along, I inevitably would slip to the back of the pack in what my classmates and I mentally transformed into a competition. With kindergarten reputation on the line, I almost always crossed the unofficial finish line in last place.

This poor race performance left me feeling exposed, as if the whole world was glaring at me in judgment. My underlying athletic deficiency was out in the open for all to see, and my little heart smoldered in on itself. I couldn't have put it into words back then, but as the experience repeated each morning that year, my self-talk began to sound like: "I'm slow. I'll never be a winner. My body is pathetic. I'm disgusting. I'm not good enough. No one would want me."

Shame's accusations are harsh, absolute, and perpetual.

It's the feeling of self-loathing. Fiercer and more durable than embarrassment or humiliation, shame is also subtler. Shame is the emotion that guides us in berating ourselves as intrinsically defective, declaring something wrong with our very being. It's sometimes referred to as a social emotion because although it points inward, it grows from pre-applying the imagined judgments of others as a kind of inoculation against them. In shame, we condemn ourselves before they get the chance.

Although shame is simple enough for children to experience, it is yet a complex phenomenon.[1] In fact, shame is a paradox. While the first part of this chapter explores how secret shame holds us back, it finishes with an invitation to see our shame transformed into an experience that can feel similar but actually serves our good.

Your first experiences with shame, like mine, might have been rooted in traumatic exposure. Something private, secret (or even secret to you!), was taken or laid bare outside your control. This is trauma, even if that which was revealed was as inconsequential as a slow-paced lap around the grade school playground. Maybe your introduction to shame came when your sister cut your hair, leaving you sulking into school with burning red cheeks. Perhaps a teacher held up your paper in front of the class as an example of shoddy work, actively shaming your performance. It might've

---

1 - In the "resources" section at the back of this book, I've suggested a number of companion titles that dig more deeply into the experience of shame. I recommend any of them for further exploration into the subject. Several, but not all, of these are referenced in the footnotes within this chapter.

been the feeling that surfaced after discovering you had been adopted as a baby. Perhaps it was when he pressured you to take off your clothes. Whatever the circumstances, you likely had limited means to cope — resulting in shame's all-too-familiar sense of vulnerability, inadequacy, and self-condemnation.

Our intuition and anecdotes match the science. The self-help genre is littered[2] with books and articles about how shame impacts mental health and how to get out from under its weight. From therapists to researchers, the consensus is clear: shame is associated with depression and anxiety, addictions and obsessive disorders, aggression and abuse, defensiveness and denial, narcissism and perfectionism, dysfunctional family systems, and the list goes on. It works by turning our original messages of unworthiness into automatic scripts, triggered like a computer program given the right input. Some people just beginning to explore healing their shame have discovered that even the threat[3] of a repeat exposure can prompt a host of otherwise unexplainable reactions.

---

2 - Interestingly enough, focused study on shame is relatively new in psychology and self-help. Only beginning in the mid-to-late-20th century have scientists begun intentionally researching it. We have a great deal yet to learn.

3 - I don't recall if I was *actually* overweight at that early age (my elementary school pictures don't hint at obesity). But I know for certain that within just a few years of that early experience with shame, much of the groundwork was laid for how I would relate to my body, food, exercise, and weight in the years to come. Although I loved sports and admired athletes as a middle and high-schooler, I ballooned up in size further inhibiting my ability to be competitive with my peers in most athletic spheres. Batting last on my little league team, being relegated to second string lineman on football teams, and getting picked last on the playground basketball court all served to reinforce that inner narrative characterized by a sense of unworthiness. Critical comments from classmates and friends about my size or eating habits, harsh evaluations of my health by physicians or employer health evaluators, and the myriad experiences of seeing my heaviness hold me back from the physical activity I wanted, each have continued to touch on and add to my underlying sense of shame. In chapter nine, I discuss further my experience being overweight and how I have worked through some of those challenges.

Exposure that leads to shame is an injury; not unlike a broken bone or a bruise. The bit of our souls, damaged in its subjection to public scrutiny, is chafed raw. It becomes desperately afraid of repeat exposure. We guard our shame from re-injury just like we might with an external injury. It happens without thinking. This hair-trigger protection can come off as strange behavior. The dynamic is not unlike the way John Corcoran coped with his hidden life.

This is how shame can become most pernicious. Keeping it secret is second nature. We unconsciously reason to ourselves that to admit it would be to go through the original violation anew. "Why allow for another round of pain if I can otherwise avoid it, right?!" So, instead of a transient painful zing, shame kept in secret becomes an even more serious threat to sanity.

I love to tinker. I always have. By the time I reached five years old, my curiosity for mechanics repeatedly drove me to tamper with almost any domestic item I could get my hands on. Even though I left a litany of destroyed clothing, small engines, electronics, and household furniture in my wake, my original naive inquisitiveness hasn't faded in adulthood.

Recently, a button on my family's washing machine quit working. We have one of those computer-controlled, electronic, front-loading kinds that looks as though it'll bake you a loaf of bread in addition to laundering your socks. Now, the failing part didn't simply control a minor function. No, it was the "start" button that had turned belly-up. The machine had to be fixed. I relished the challenge.

After studying a YouTube video and subsequently tearing our machine apart, I didn't expect what I discovered. Inside the back of the soap dispenser and running down some of the tubing, I found a thriving colony of slimy mold! Yuck!! My ultimately successful do-it-yourself-repair ended with several extra hours of disassembly and cleaning with bleach and vinegar.

Oxygen, warmth, and moisture form the magic ingredient list for growing mold. When those factors come together in one place, it's only a matter of time before the fungus follows. Typically, it develops in the dark: behind walls or tucked away in cabinets. But sooner or later, it is discovered. Surprise! MOLD!!

The relationship between secrecy and shame is similar. Given the environment of hiddenness, shame is as predictable as clockwork. Keep something secret, and you'll feel ashamed of it in time. Feel shame about something, and your first impulse will be to hide it.

We can carry on with life: raising kids, managing budgets, improving health, studying for a future career, or scurrying up the ladder of success. But then the wheels come off the wagon-train; we lose control, dysfunction erupts from nowhere, compulsion takes over. Everything appeared to be working; everything was clean. But mold was growing underneath. Secret shame was at the reigns the whole time.

Shame in itself can be very problematic, but secret shame is toxic.

Not only does it grow in the dark, toxic shame, unlike mold, also malignantly works to keep itself hidden! Shame and secret-keeping are self-referential, building upon one another. Secrets grow shame, and shame grows secrecy. So linked are the two experiences that the English word "shame" finds its roots in an ancient word that means "to cover, veil, or hide." Hiding is inextricable from shame, even in language itself.

"Secrets are the pillars of the house of shame," a wise friend has often remarked to me about this relationship. As we hide it (and its initiating source), shame's narrative of self-loathing only grows louder in the echo chamber of our minds. Unchallenged by a counter-narrative of truth, we become our own worst enemies. People can go on for decades living out layers of life-threatening behavior, never realizing the cause. Hiding in the shadows, whispering threats laced with self-hate, shame is a Trojan Horse, promising our worst fears if re-exposed.

When it comes to shame, the very thing that kills us is out of sight.

So what now? That's a pretty bleak picture!

Well, as I've hinted, there is a silver lining to shame. It can be transformed into a life-giving source of power. But in order to explore how that happens, we must first take a glimpse at three alternative responses to this problem: oblivion, outright rejection, and masking.

First, oblivion.

My three-year-old son is just on the cusp of developing the ability to experience toxic shame. But at this point, he's not even able to feel modesty[4] or even embarrassment[5]! Sure, he could parrot back self-loathing if people in his life abusively seeded those messages in his head, but he's not yet capable of generating them himself. It won't be until he transitions into adolescence that his self-awareness will be developed enough to support this destructive form of shame.

His oblivion to shame is reaffirmed when I witness him, after helping him out of his car seat, dashing out to the middle of the front yard to pee in front of passing cars and walkers on the sidewalk. In these moments (and there are many as any parent can testify), it's his father who struggles with embarrassment!

Eventually, my sons will be able to look back at these silly stories and recognize their behavior as normal for kids but less than ideal for adults. In fact, they might be nonplussed that I shared them in my book! But as our sons mature, my wife and I hope to guide them not toward the toxic experience of shame per se but toward modesty. Modesty is about self-protection; knowing our limits.[6] Modesty seeks to prevent boundaries from being violated in the first place. Shame is our response to those boundaries already having been violated! The two experiences are related but different. But because both are dependent on self-awareness, our capacity to feel them develops in tandem.

As such, just as modesty is a sign of maturity, in a primitive way,

---

4 - See below.

5 - I define embarrassment or the stronger synonym, humiliation, as a short-acting and episodic version of shame. This emotion is tied to specific events and actions, go as quickly as they come, and do not carry the same toxicity or drive to conceal as the shame we have discussed so far in this chapter.

6 - Unfortunately, this term has taken on a negative religious connotation that I do not intend in this case. (See John Bradshaw's illuminating work on Shame for more on this very useful concept of modesty. Details are in the resources section at the back of the book.)

so is shame.

When my boys develop the ability to feel embarrassed about peeing in public, loud tantrums in the grocery store, and crashing their bicycles into the back of my parked car for the fourth time in the same session[7], they'll also hopefully have developed the modesty needed to prevent future episodes! So, crudely speaking, certain forms of shame for immature people can be a temporary tool for protecting against destructive behavior.

Some people's capacity for shame is permanently stunted. Because of environmental factors, genetic propensities, or even medical conditions, these individuals grow up to be oblivious of shame, even as adults. It is a tragic and sometimes dangerous combination.

The Washington State Penitentiary is in my hometown of Walla Walla. Imprisoned there are a number of notorious criminals, including infamous serial killers Robert Lee Yates, Kenneth Bianchi (the hillside strangler), and Gary Rigeway (the Green River killer). Something that unites the stories of many famous serial criminals is sociopathic personality. While certainly, not all offenders share this trait, the combination can yield a person who commits heinous acts without a drop of remorse. Of course, it's also irresistible to America's tabloid culture.

Clinically speaking, sociopaths lack the ability to empathize with other people. They aren't able to love. Unlike the majority of us, they can't imagine what it'd feel like for someone else to lose a family member to cancer, be unjustly detained by the police, or fear injury in a car accident. Because of this, they are likewise oblivious to shame. Sociopaths possess none of the innate social awareness that leads the rest of us to feel embarrassed or guilty when we step out of social or ethical norms. Impervious to social judgment, they can rape, kill, lie, or steal without a twinge of

---

7 - My sons, I'm sorry, but I couldn't help myself!

shame.

If you read social media comments on articles about sociopathic offenders, you'll find iPhone juries declaring them "animals" or worse. Demonizing one another is always corrosive to a community's health, yet I think commenters are touching on the speck of truth underneath. The presence of some shame is one of the traits that make us human. When it's completely absent, people are surviving in a state that is below them, less than their human potential. None of us want this for ourselves, for our kids, or for our neighbors!

———————

The first alternative to toxic shame is oblivion, not a state anyone strives for. The second alternative is rejecting the very basis for shame.

When I was preparing to become a pastor, I had field training in "evangelism." In the Christian world, this term means convincing people who are not Christians to become Christians. On more than one occasion in this instruction, I remember being taught the importance of persuading people of their intrinsic wickedness[8] as an essential element of the conversion process. Loosely, my instructor's reasoning went that "if people understand just how bad they are, then they'll be open to hearing how Jesus and the message of Christianity can fix them!"

On the surface, some people might not take issue with this philosophy. But you're not alone if it sticks in your craw!

One metaphor for human evil wedged in my memory from this education was "skunk odor." Just as this horrendous smell is incredibly difficult to remove from its victims (we were taught to

———————

8 - Some Christians use the culturally-charged words "sin" or "sinfulness" for this concept.

say), so is wickedness impossible to remove from humanity. Hot water, soap, bleach, or even tomato sauce can't completely take away all the residues in a skunk's spray. Once it is on the skin, clothing, or hair, it's gonna stick around for a while! Likewise, neither can any scheme cure the innate depravity within humanity. Nothing, except Jesus.

In short, the message was: "You are helplessly stinky, fundamentally foul (and not necessarily by any fault of your own). Your filthiness has yielded a chasm between you and the divine... but we can tell you about the way across." You might already see where I'm going with this. I was taught to strategically use shaming to coerce conversion.

"Just beat them down enough; feed their self-loathing enough; help them believe the voices about their unworthiness enough. Then, when we start talking about Jesus and His love and forgiveness, we'll have them eating out of our hands!"

At first, I have to admit falling for this reasoning. It seemed so efficient. Poetic. And in truth, it worked. But "it worked" for what? And at what cost? Is the point of the human journey really as trite as picking "the correct" spiritual clique?

Ehhrmm, no.

Neither this method nor its message[9] is good for people or for

---

9 - Certainly, we all experience brokenness in our lives — sometimes by our own mistakes and other times by decisions of others. But I believe the central arc of Christian teaching is that humans are fundamentally good, not vile. I believe the personal or spiritual journey for any of us is to discover the greatness lying latent within us, see what is blocking that, and to fully step into our best life through compassion and community. This is echoed in the first book of the Hebrew scriptures, which tells the story of a Creator being incredibly pleased with the world they had made, people in particular. Instead of starting with the shame-laced assumption that humans are profoundly inadequate, I think it's more helpful to begin believing that we are of infinite value, full of good and possibility and wonder.

the universe. I feel sad and embarrassed thinking of the collateral damage done over the years by this unexamined use of shame. Those of us who identify as Christians can and must do better.

Toxic shame isn't our friend. Building a life philosophy on the assumption that, at my core, I am inferior is asking for trouble. You may have been on the receiving end of such conversion techniques at some point in your life. You may have embraced the message. But you equally may have dismissed it out of a sense of self-protection. I affirm this impulse.

Shame's massive capacity for damage behooves us to "guard our hearts.[10]"

Wide swaths of American culture[11] at large have picked up on a similar impulse when it comes to shame, sometimes in reaction to the intentional shaming promulgated by religion. "With the obvious damage shame causes," some of us have reasoned, "why tolerate it in any form, from anyone, anywhere (let alone succumbing to it by becoming a Christian!)?" Instead of merely resisting toxic shame, some of us have "super-sized" the effort, pressing to the opposite extreme.

Warriors in this cause have attacked social expectations to eliminate shame at its source. Their implicit reasoning goes something like this: "It's cultural norms that make us feel ashamed of ourselves. It's how we feel judged by other's assumptions about right and wrong. What we need is to do away with those standards

---

10 - To borrow another phrase from the wisdom of the Hebrew Scriptures.

11 - I am writing to a decidedly Western audience, and so my use of shame follows. Many Eastern cultures, in contrast, intentionally use shame as essential tools for societal structure. Much has been written comparing so-called "shame-based" and "guilt-based" cultures.

most associated with shame. If we expose ourselves[12] as often as possible, in our full misalignment from popular standards, we'll be pushing back against shame's pull to conceal. We need to 'live and let live.' Stop voicing your judgments and ignore everyone else's! Universal validation of every person's behavior is the only effective way to keep self-hate at bay!"

Except, that doesn't sound exactly right either. No communal standards for behavior at all?! What about sociopaths who violate the rights and boundaries of others indiscriminately?! What about teachers who lie their way into classrooms? What about sexual predators? What about terrorists?

No matter where you're at on the political spectrum, no matter your religious or spiritual point of view, no matter how you'd like to see American values be shaped, you probably don't openly advocate for the complete abandonment of every "code of behavior" as such. In fact, communities are held together by these shared values, whether well-founded or fickle. It is these standards that form the basis for shame. Outright rejection of all shame can only be done with an outright rejection of entire ethical systems.

When I visit my favorite coffee shop but fail to order a drink before taking a seat, I have committed an offense in that subculture. It might be arbitrary in terms of morality, but it never-the-less is a sign of vice in that setting. Right or wrong, people taking up table space without patronage are judged as disrespectful of the establishment's owners, as well as to paying customers. If I behave outside of these social norms in that space, I risk triggering shame.

I learned this the hard way one day. I entered the cafe and walked

---

12 - I think of social media avenues like Facebook, Twitter, and Instagram that while sometimes are avenues of building shame, also often serve to legitimize what only might've been shameful if left in the realm of the secret.

straight to a table instead of the ordering counter. My intent was to take home some pastries after my visit (honest!). I didn't want anything to drink just then. A shop employee, outraged by my rudeness and disrespect, marched over and loudly confronted me. "USUALLY, we take orders at the COUNTER. What would you like to eat or drink today SIR!?!?" Everyone turned around and looked at me as if to say, "WELL??!"

I felt embarrassed (which was her goal) but certainly not ashamed[13]. If anything, my gut reaction was judgment for their persnickety hipster standards! But in that situation, shame was entirely possible. Another person with different experiences or frames of mind might've easily had shame stoked at that moment. Embarrassment is a cousin of shame. It doesn't feel good, but it isn't as corrosive. Embarrassment is a short-acting tool for shaping behavior, and it's particularly potent for training the immature or inexperienced.

So, even in the uber-liberated environment of a trendy coffee shop, we find a moral code as such. It's normal. Really, we wouldn't expect anything less. Spoken and unspoken codes of conduct hold people together. Despite the fact that these systems form the basis for the experience of shame, we need them to form community. Outright rejection of all standards isn't a plausible solution to dealing with shame any more than oblivion.

The first alternative to shame I outlined above is to be oblivious to it. The second is to eliminate the customs that form the basis for it. Before we move on to how to transform it, let's look at a third (and more nuanced) alternative to shame. Instead of addressing this troubling emotion directly, it's possible to cover it up or pretend it's not there in the first place.

---

13 - Because I love the coffee so much, I still regularly return to the cafe — but I've not made the same faux pas twice! Embarrassment doesn't feel very good. It isn't as corrosive as it's cousin, shame. But it's an unrefined (albeit hazardous) tool for unconsciously shaping behavior, particularly in the immature or unexperienced.

The ostensible opposite of shame is narcissism or excessive vanity. One of the ways we mask shame is by over-compensating in the opposite direction. The human ego is a valuable part of our personalities. It sets the edge for our identity. It helps us make decisions and draw boundaries. It gives us a backbone as we move through life. But problems emerge if we allow our raw ego to run the show (that's more or less how the aforementioned toddlers operate)!

Unrestrained, the ego can create superhero caricatures of ourselves who announce, "I am the BEST! I couldn't be better! I am perfection! It really is all about ME!" Of course, these unbridled sentiments aren't any more true than the objectively false narratives that characterize toxic shame. The unchecked ego is just a mask. And in the age of social media, this mask is all-too-popular.

Love 'em or hate 'em, many politicians, athletes, and performers are case studies for this kind of posturing. Twenty-something singers filling stadiums with crazed fans don't become pop-icons by acting demure or telegraphing the truth of their emotional landscapes. No, they, like many in the public eye, create a grand persona to leverage for likes, follows, and dollars. The latest wide receiver's cocky self-congratulatory gesticulations on the football field (on the surface) are the antithesis of insecurity. The latest politician's "call-it-like-I-see-it" Twitter volleys are not fed by modesty or healthy boundaries. Instead, by becoming "shameless[14]," the celebrated personalities in our culture hope to parade confidence and authenticity instead of underlying insecurity. We are rightly suspicious that these folks might just be compensating for something; perhaps self-hatred run amok.

---

14 - Colloquially speaking, "shameless" doesn't mean the absence of shame, but rather the opposite! We typically use the term derogatorily. Calling someone shameless is a way of judging their behavior (or the ethical system that allows such behavior).

Please hear me. I don't mean to condemn the famous or those in the public eye, but simply to call our attention to a nearly universal human trait. Just as I am the teacher John Corcoran from chapter one, I also am a public performer like these. I am guilty of covering up my insecurity by projecting a grandiose persona. I am guilty of allowing my ego too much leeway.

The truth is that as entertaining as "shameless" behavior might be, most of us don't respect those who navigate life like this. In many swaths of American culture, we tend to look down on it as immature or even immoral. Most of us don't want to live in a world that is "every person for themselves," where we all self-promote our friendships into capitalistic oblivion. Instead, we admire a little bit of modesty. We admire humility. We fall back on the axiom, "pride goes before a fall." Even in Hollywood movies, the arrogant guy is the first to be humiliated (or eliminated) on screen!

A runaway ego isn't a realistic alternative for dealing with toxic shame. Let's look at an even more common example of masking shame before we move on.

A&E began airing its Emmy-award-winning reality show *Intervention* in 2005. My wife and I were immediately captivated. Productions about addiction and recovery like this always run the risk of exploitation[15]. But they also have the capacity for introducing healing by sharing unflinching stories of human pain and recovery.

---

15 - The protagonists of each episode agree to be the subjects of a 'documentary' about addiction. However, because of their addictive state, I could imagine some not fully appreciating the scope of that consent. It's possible that once sober, some might feel as though their private lives were exposed beyond their comfort zone. Regret in general is probably not unusual for participants in reality TV, this seems like it could be particularly sensitive however.

Through interviews, each episode of *Intervention* chronicles a unique person's descent into addiction. Some of the most poignant moments feature unvarnished depictions of the behaviors accompanying chemical dependency. Some of it appears brazen, what unsympathetic bystanders might write off as "shameless." The show portrays its protagonists manipulating, shaming, or bullying family members (even elderly grandparents) to get their next high, often without any external sign of remorse. It pictures them flaunting their lifestyle, bragging about its freedom and pleasure, openly getting high on camera. At the same time, the program also depicts its subjects' decrepit living conditions and battered physical bodies the disease of addiction has caused. These visceral manifestations can make the show difficult to watch.

Intervention is a portrait of people living far below their potential on the one hand but also sometimes occupied by inexplicable grandiosity on the other hand. A hidden truth in addiction is that although the person might appear to lack self-judgment, toxic shame is sitting just below the surface. It's actually the fuel that runs the whole machine. The main subjects on A&E's program almost universally describe how they began using their drug of choice in order to cover up the pain of early wounds (often wounds dripping with shame). Chemicals can be an effective stop-gap for masking the unpleasant experience of shame. At the same time, active addiction causes new secret shame to develop. While simultaneously snuffing out shame, addiction stokes the coals underneath. The "shameless" behavior associated with addiction is only stage smoke. Instead, a cycle of shame thrives underneath: "I use because I feel so horrible about myself, and I feel so horrible about myself because I use." When kept in secret (or repressed by the addict themselves), the dynamic is deadly.

Addiction temporarily masks shame.

The show's climax is always its namesake – (usually) a carefully planned intervention by mental health professionals and the main subject's family and friends. These intense conversations invite him or her to accept help, start recovery, and find healing. Often, people in addiction miss out on the love and wisdom their community has to offer. This can be because their community has rejected them or cut them off. It can also be due to an addict's dismissal of the community (along with their ethical systems) as a way of fending off shame. Mired so deeply in bottled-up self-hatred, it can be hard for someone, in addition, to believe themselves lovable. The intervention gently but firmly pushes back against these impulses.

In the best examples on the TV program, the *Intervention* seeks first to reinforce an atmosphere of unconditional[16] love. Loved ones tell their suffering partner and friend just how much they mean to them unequivocally. The *Intervention* holds up a rhetorical mirror to help the addicted person see him or herself clearly. "You are the beloved. You are wanted. You are precious. You have meaning and purpose, and identity. You have a place in this world."

The same family members and friends also describe how their loved one's addiction has negatively impacted them. They talk about the suffering they've observed in their treasured son or daughter or brother or sister, as well as their own. The point isn't to shame him or her into change ala, "You really are a horrible person! Just look at yourself! You are as smelly as a skunk!" Instead, the goal is to help them glimpse the truth, perhaps for the first time, "You are loved exactly as you are, despite the

---

16 - The definition for "love" varies widely. Here, love means "unmerited favor" — wishing well for the other, manifested in action. This love cannot be earned. "Trust" is disginguished from love in that it is earned, and can be lost. Loving someone does not mean we must trust them. It is possible to love to someone who has deeply or repeatedly wronged us, and yet simultaneously deny them access to our vulerabilities.

Victims in abusive situations should not feel obligated to hold *Interventions* for their abusers or continue the relationship in order to be "loving." Instead, this definition allows conscientious victims to protect themselves, get help, and never trust their abuser again, all while acting in love.

imperfections you share with the rest of humanity. There is hope for you yet." This new narrative challenges the refrain of shame. It invites him or her to love again, beginning with him or herself.

As you might expect, these revelations often trigger highly reactive behavior in the main subject. Sometimes the underlying source of shame is touched or unmasked in the process. Their reactions run the gamut from violent defensiveness or counterattack to doubling down on learned coping mechanisms or to heart-rending expressions of unworthiness. It can feel desperately exposing to hear the truth, especially when you've lived for such a long time acting as though it wasn't there or amplifying it into a grotesque parody.

The intervention seeks to crack this façade, to help addicts see themselves truthfully. It can be painful, but it can also be transformative. The most beautiful and hopeful moments on *Intervention* are when the main subject sees this sight, sometimes for the first time in decades (or ever). They reach out and accept help saying, "I'm so far from who I want to be; please help me get better; help me find myself..."

This impulse is far from the masks of ego-grandstanding or self-harm. It's also the polar opposite of toxic shame created by traumatic exposure. It's a more nuanced self-evaluation. It's calmly seeing clearly. We often call it humility[17].

Without doubt, shame is poisonous to our health. It's also inescapable from the impulse to conceal it. We are right to fear and respect this pernicious threat and the traumas that inflict it.

---

17 - Humility is seen as an essential trait of the mature human in every major religion. From Buddhism to Judaism, Islam to Hinduism, the value of seeing oneself clearly in relation to the universe is second to none. It is an indispensable experience for sensing the divine, touching transcendence, and simply becoming the best version of ourselves.

We are also right to create safe spaces for people to develop free of destructive exposure that leads to shame in the first place! Yet, as we have seen, common alternatives to this troubling emotion once it's blossomed produce their own problems. Oblivion, masking, and sloughing off socio-cultural expectations aren't particularly life-giving options either! How then do we deal with deadly shame in a constructive way, without overshooting and ending up in the opposite extreme?

I've already hinted at the solution. This chapter concludes with a story from the Christian scriptures[18] that illustrates a turning point for someone mired in self-hatred.

The unassuming story[19] describes an interaction between Jesus and a woman. The fact that the two did not share genders, religious traditions, cultures, or social status helps explain why the story was so compelling to its original audience. Early readers would have sensed tension in the juicy narrative right off the bat. The two characters crossed paths alone, in the desert, at noon, at a village water well. The setting begs the question: Where are the other villagers? Why is the woman fetching water during the hottest part of the day? Why do Jesus' friends run off to town without him? Answers come in short order.

The author tells us that Jesus approaches the woman and asks her to draw him up some water from the well. A dialogue filled with spiritual innuendo ensues about different kinds of water. It's the type of conversation that simultaneously happens on two

18 - In the four biographies of Jesus' life (sometimes referred to as 'the Gospels'), Jesus is remarkably gentle with 'outsiders,' despite the popular cultural reputation. While he routinely is described as coming down hard on the religious establishment, Jesus consistently demonstrates grace and kindness to those who don't quite fit the mold. When dealing with the disenfranchised, dismissed, and disheartened, he seems far more attached to their perceptions of his affection toward them than he does to 'being right'.

19 - Read chapter four of the book of John for the original narrative.

levels. Jesus talks about a spiritual kind of water that yields rich and meaningful living, the woman imagines something like the mythical fountain of youth. The dialogue crescendos when Jesus asks her to bring her husband to the well so that he can offer both of them this special spiritual blessing.

It's at this suggestion that everything becomes real. The woman turns stoney. Jesus has touched her shame, her marital status. This is why she's in solitude. This is why she's out at the village well at the most inopportune. Naturally afraid of re-exposing her underlying wound, the woman is curt, "I don't have a husband."

We can empathize. Here, an isolated single woman in a patriarchal culture is being confronted by a male religious leader from a rival tribe about a sensitive personal matter. Almost anyone's ego would jump in to protect us in such a situation, let alone with the personal matter is filled with ancillary shame. The author reveals that the woman had been through a number of relationships in her life (a faux pas in that culture, to say the least) and that she and her present partner were not married (another faux pas). It must've been terrifying for her to hear this truth named out loud. For many of us, it's our greatest fear — witnessing our darkest secret drug into public view for condemnation.

But the story unfolds differently than we might expect.

The woman could've doubled down on her secrecy and run away. She could've frozen in fear or reacted in violent defensiveness. But she didn't. She stuck with it. Sensing Jesus' goodwill for her, she chose to allow the exposure to run its course. This time, notably, it was her own prerogative to choose. This exposure becomes not traumatic but healing for the "woman at the well," as she is commonly known.

Jesus creates a safe space between them. Rather than validating her inner narratives of unworthiness, he demonstrates absolute unconditional love. He names the truth, the object of her shame, yes. And yet, he does not chastise her or reprimand the behavior in any way. He doesn't judge her. This is a turning point. Rather than hearing the shame-laced jeers that have lived in her mind's eye, she hears kindness. Rather than sensing despair, opportunity crests on the horizon. Instead of another rejection, this unnamed woman witnesses transformation dawning.

The story writer makes it clear that the woman leaves the interaction fundamentally changed: open, full of joy, and eager to share what had been the source of incredible inferiority. "Come meet a man who knew about everything I have ever done," she announces in child-like euphoria back in the village, dragging people with her back to the well. She has stumbled into something holy.

"The truth will set you free," Jesus says in another place in the Christian scriptures. When truth confronts shame in spaces of unconditional love, the result can be transcendence; the gap between the human and the divine becomes thin. In these moments, shame isn't just extinguished, masked, or ignored — its narratives are replaced by reality. The shame death spiral is transformed into the universal spiritual value of humility. This virtue of seeing ourselves clearly is celebrated across religious and spiritual traditions, from secular humanism to Buddhism, to Islam. We were never inborn failures as toxic shame might've declared, and we're not perfect in the abstract legalistic sense as the unbridled ego might posture. When we trust someone enough to be willingly be exposed before them — and experience the safety of their love and acceptance — our souls are reshaped[20]. We witness the truth about ourselves.

---

20 - In my experience, confronting shame like this impedes it's growth, but it's not a panacea. Transformation isn't the work of a moment, but the work of a lifetime. Just as with any other habit or skill, the more we practice this truth-telling, exposing and replacing, the more it takes hold in our lives. As we mature in humility, our capacity for feeling shame doesn't necessarily diminish, but the habit of addressing it before it becomes noxious can become automatic. We can practice living at our best so much that our best becomes our default.

The Bible story isn't Jesus' or the woman's or the author's — it is humanity's. It's true because it's ours. We see ourselves in it when we confront and then re-cast narratives of shame in our own lives. In safety, we acknowledge our darkness, welcome it into the light of day, and see it for what it is. The unspoken is spoken. Its power dissipates. We discover humility.

This chapter opened with a story about me as a runner. The self-judgment that began when I was six lasted well into my adult years. It shaped the kinds of activities I participated in, the friends I chose, and the risks I took. It threatened to sink me[21]. But it didn't. I was blessed with a number of safe spaces where I could uncork what was really happening in my soul. Some of them I sought out (like therapists' offices). Others emerged more organically (like relationships with my wife or other dear friends). Regardless, people's unconditional acceptance[22] of me exactly as I am, despite knowing the truth, was transformative. In these spaces of safety and honesty, I have witnessed shame being transformed into humility. I came to see myself clearly. I am beautifully broken.

In May of 2017, along the beautiful shores of Lake Coeur'd Alene in northern Idaho, I ran my first marathon. All 26.2 miles of it. I was not at my ideal weight. I was not fast. I finished near the back of the pack. I did not look like many of the athletes huddled at the starting line or celebrating at the finish. But as I plodded along beside the sparkling waters, a world of difference had taken place between my ears. I saw myself and the situation differently, even though it was much the same as my childhood playground

---

21 - In chapter nine, I write more about my experiences related with and treating my obesity.

22 - Disclosure in the context of trusting relationships is an incredibly important concept and experience. So much so, that I have devoted two entire chapters on this subject matter at the close of the book. Here, I intentionaly just hint at confession's cathartic energy for facilitating growth. Processing toxic shame is but one way exposure proves therapeutic for those who self-conceal.

exposure.

Participating in this running competition didn't feel vulnerable. I wasn't ashamed of my abilities or body. I wasn't embarrassed. I was honest. I was humble. I was just me.

My inner narrative had been overhauled. "Here I am, imperfect and alive. I'm slow, but I'll finish. My boys will see me and think physical activity and taking risks, and setting goals is normal. I'll soak up the fun and sun along the way. I'll spend 4hrs 59mins in the sun, listening to music and gazing at the gorgeous scenery. "Transforming my shame made it possible.

You can give this gift[23]. And you can receive it. You can be set free from destructive stories that hold you back. You can see it changed into a life-giving powerhouse. You can see yourself truthfully and not flinch, not run away.

The only question remaining lies within. Are you ready?

---

23 - Please don't read this as an invitation to hold impromptu *Interventions* with all those in your life you deem to need growth!! But in the context of a trusting, mutual relationship, unmerited favor and truth-telling together can be some of the greatest gifts we ever give or receive. Almost nothing binds people together like authenticity received with love.

QUESTIONS FOR DISCUSSION:

1. Shame is not pleasant to talk about? Why?

2. Reflect and call up an early memory where you felt ashamed. What was it over? Were you exposed in some unwanted way? Did the feelings or language seem to come up from within you, or did someone actively feed them to you (I.e., shaming you)? Reflect on how this experience might shape your behavior even today?

3. The author suggested that there are times in which something that might resemble shame can serve to stop destructive behavior in its tracks (self-knowledge that is accurate or humility). He argues that neither chronic-toxic shame nor the extreme absence of shame is conducive to spiritual maturity. Using a story from your life, explain why or why not you agree with this suggestion.

4. When shame is welcomed into the light of day, it loses some of its power over us. Why is the prospect of 'naming it' for what it is so frightening? What's at risk?

5. Discuss an experience where, in sharing something, you were ashamed or embarrassed at first but then realized you were not alone. How does it feel to hear, "Oh, you too?" when exposing parts of our lives?

3 | FAMILY SECRETS

"There are no secrets better kept than the ones everybody guesses."

-George Bernard Shaw

No One Knows[1] is a snapshot into the life of Hannah Smith, a pre-teen Oklahoman girl from a conservative Christian family. As the title of the 9-minute-film suggests, Hannah has a secret. In this case, it's a secret she'll go to extreme lengths to protect. By the end of the tale, it's clear that the title leaves out an implied punchline: "No One (outside the family) Knows."

The dominant emotion throughout the film is the young girl's despair. She has been abandoned. Hannah's secret is shared by those who are supposed to protect her. Of course, Hannah's abuser is aware of his habitual sexual assaults. The film makes it clear that despite his stellar reputation in their community, her

---

1 - Directed by directed by Bunee Tomlinson (@buneetomlinson) and Daniel Hoyos (@danielhoyos), the film is difficult to find online. As of publication time for this book, it was available for free at: https://vimeo.com/59137646. It also may be viewed for a fee via www.indieflix.com, an online independent film distributor. You may also contact the directors directly via twitter to learn about current distribution.

father's heinous crimes have become part of the family culture. Staggeringly, Hannah's mother is in on them as well. Instead of being an ally, she drowns her culpability with alcohol, domestic chores, and throbbing heavy-metal music.

Besides shining a light on the atrocity that is incestuous abuse, *No One Knows* also illustrates the indubitable interconnectedness of family. We resonate with Hannah's story not because it's unique but because it's common. Hannah's story didn't just happen; it happens. It's true in a cosmic sense. The film's cinematography is sleepy, telling the audience, "you've seen this before." Indeed. We have witnessed it in our friends' lives and in our own. We are familiar with Hannah's outer calm that conceals abject horror underneath.

After setting the scene, *No One Knows* unrolls the story. One Sunday after church, a classmate of Hannah finds himself playing outside, adjacent to her suburban home. Driven by innocent benevolence, he peers into a window and witnesses a glimpse of an assault in progress. In this unintended violation, a new person has become a party to the family secret. It will change all of their lives forever.

Naturally, the boy empathizes with Hannah. Because of his own past experiences with familial abuse, he takes action. At school, soon after, he offers his support. For Hannah, the exposure of her family's painful secret (even to a would-be friend) does not feel like good fortune. It feels like a threat. Terrified, the young girl takes fate into her own hands.

The balance of the film illustrates the chasms we'll cross to keep our secrets concealed. Hannah murders the unnamed boy in the woods, ensuring that once again, "no one knows." Tragically, this act becomes yet another shame-laced burden for her to bear, still alone. The film's story arc draws to a close where it began: the family's community church, but this time, for a funeral. The tone has not changed. Hannah's bleak existence will march on, hopeless.

On the surface, it might be difficult to understand why people like Hannah (or her mother) would keep such awful circumstances hidden. Indeed, the byline of the story is that: a victim of sexual assault murders her friend in order to keep the abuse under wraps.

Astonishing. Or is it?

Families are more than the sum of their parts. They are interwoven systems of personalities, ambitions, emotions, roles, and dreams. For good and for bad, we are inescapably linked to our families of origin. Your family's secrets are your secrets. And your secrets are theirs.

The research of the 20th-century American psychiatrist Murray Bowen pioneered "family systems theory[2]," which helps explain some of the dynamics animating stories like the Smith's in *No One Knows*. Bowen's theory identifies dysfunction, for example, that can arise when people aren't able (or aren't allowed) to differentiate themselves[3] as individuals within their family system. When age-appropriate privacy is denied, secrecy becomes a coping mechanism for survival, and toxic shame can be the result. As I

---

2 - To read more about the eight facets of Murray Bowen's theory, check out the suggested reading list I provide for this chapter.

3 - I've appreciated the work of Sharon Daloz Parks, who has written about childhood identify-formation in the context of faith development. Her analysis of sociological and psychological research suggests that as young people, our sense of identity rightly is derived from familial connection. We first learn secret keeping in the context of family. Here, it is a tool for sorting out who we are as discrete beings. But there comes a time when individuation is essential for continued growth. Both Bowen and Parks warn against families that prevent healthy and timely differentiation.

described in chapter 2, underlying toxic shame can lead to a wide gamut of unspeakably destructive behavior. Likewise, if people are denied the right to have age-appropriate but divergent moral or spiritual viewpoints, they can grow up with serious doubts about their identities and sometimes develop mental illnesses or detrimental habits.

Bowen's theory observes that adults in family systems transmit their own emotional problems to their children, often unconsciously. These, and their accompanying behaviors, are often transferred generationally[4] so that what passes for family culture might actually be decades or centuries of reinforced immaturity. If you have had experience with sexual abuse, one of your first questions about Hannah's story might've been, "I wonder who dad's abuser was?" We ask this question because families are systems.

The truth is that the abuse wasn't just Hannah's secret or her mom or Dad's – it was also theirs, together. The secret wasn't isolated to an individual. It was systemic. Each of them received something in return for keeping it silent.[5] And without doubt, it held them back their best lives.

It's not uncommon for secrets like the Smiths to be guarded amongst close-knit family members for decades or even centuries. Director Daniel Hoyos gives the viewer few clues as to the specific motives for the silence of the family in the film, and the viewer is left to fill in the details.

Attempting to psychoanalyze family and friends (or even fictional characters) is typically counterproductive. We have a hard

---

4 - We will return to this concept later in this chapter.

5 - Again, this doesn't imply responsibility (which was in no part Hannah's), but rather simply helps to explain how it could've happened (and certainly, how it happens).

enough understanding our own thoughts and actions; how do we presume to know the inner workings of everyone else! But I can't help but imagine that some combination of family roles within her family system explains Hannah's course of action.

Many practitioners and researchers[6] have described how, when within their families, people slip into playing roles or characters as if in a stage production. The scripts they follow often begin as survival mechanisms. Under the threat of chaos or danger, we humans are resilient and creative in how we cope. A person might take on the role of scapegoat, hero, chieftain, enabler, mediator, clown, loyal rule-keeper, or even truth-teller given the right circumstances. Even in relatively stable environments, these well-worn patterns are common. Hannah and her parents no doubt took on their own in the interdependence of family, as do we all.

Roles within family systems can easily become part and parcel to our sense of identity. When we're acting out our given scripts in the context of a family system, we don't think of it as an overlay upon our true selves. [7]Instead, we experience it as second nature.

So, when Hannah is presented with the would-be opportunity to escape her abuse, it also quite literally threatens to upend the structure that has sustained her very existence. As an adolescent, she has conceivably taken on a role (as has her parents and even other family members who may or may not be a party to the secret) that is inseparable from her sense of identity. Even though her family had caused so much pain, it was still hers.

---

6 - I have appreciated the work of Augustus Napier and Carl Whitaker in their vintage but powerful record of family therapy in *The Family Crucible*.

7 - Recent psycho-spiritual teachers have used the term "shadow" to describe a part of ourselves that we deny, repress, or hide. In many spiritual paths, identifying and making peace with our shadow is an integral aspect of maturity. My father's book, *The Unexplored Room*, is an instruction manual for doing this personal work.

They were her people, and she was theirs. When the neighbor boy offers to help, it feels not like a minor inconvenience or fleeting embarrassment but like an existential threat. His observation puts her very identity at risk. This prospect would be terrifying to any of us. It leads many to murder, and worse!

Hannah's story speaks to the tragedy that is abuse within family systems. As children, we can so internalize our caregivers' treatment of us that we can't imagine what it could feel like to exist without it. Our families are all we have, even when they so profoundly injure us. And so we carry one another's secrets, even if confusing and contradictory.

If Bowen's theory is correct, then one person's secrets impact the whole. As I said, your family's secrets are yours, and yours are theirs. The things your parents and grandparents are hiding affect you whether you know the details or not. In fact, your coping mechanisms for everyday emotional triggers are linked to the very things your family elders have kept behind closed doors. Your great-great-great-grandparents' secrets will influence the decisions you will make this week. Because families are systems, no one ever acts or thinks in isolation. Instead, the consequences and benefits of our ancestors' habits and decisions cascade from person to person, generation to generation, often unappreciated. We are integrated beings through and through; there is no getting around it. "Secrecy takes us to the heart of the family's mysterious power to impact our lives," writes John Bradshaw[8].

Within the Smith family, each member was well aware of the secret they collectively concealed. It shackled them together like a prison gang. Hefting along a heavy trailer full of dead weight, they pulled the load in community. Disturbingly, their secret might've even created a degree of camaraderie. Families keep secrets for mountains of reasons. And the phenomenon within family systems can mark us permanently.

---

8 - See *Family Secrets* by John Bradshaw

The first time I saw *No One Knows*, I felt overwhelmed. My anger smoldered against Hannah's father and those he represents. It burned even brighter toward circumstances of such untenable powerlessness. I felt sorrow for the injustice inflicted by the very people who are supposed to protect little people like Hannah. I felt fear about the same suffering covertly replicating itself throughout our communities at this very moment.

But I also sensed compassion welling up for each of the characters depicted on screen. No matter if victim, perpetrator, or bystander, each one deserved better.

We are not meant to be held as captives of abusive family systems. We are not meant to use and manipulate people for our own sense of power or thrill. We are not meant to stand idly by the suffering of those we love. The Smiths deserved better. We all deserve better.

If you want a life full of meaning, you must pay attention to your family of origin. If you long to leave people and the planet better than you found them, to connect consequentially with others, and to be filled with abiding joy, you must account for your family systems. Self-help books, psychotherapy, houses of worship, and spiritual retreats are beautiful pathways to healing and growth. But if we try to pursue health and maturity as disconnected individualists in self-care bubbles, we will hit a wall. There are limits to what any of us can do on our own. The integrated nature of family will eventually catch up with us. Our best lives and our families are inextricably linked.

This chapter is an invitation to the essential work of identifying and navigating family secrets.

———————

As a pastor, I frequently become a confidant for people sharing their secrets. I consider it to be one of the great privileges of my vocation. These are holy moments, opportunities for me to embody unconditional love. The countless interactions I've spent with parishioners, perfect strangers, and everyone in between have convinced me that without exception, every person — and every family — keeps secrets.

Perhaps you disagree. This might especially be the case if you grew up in a healthy, tight-knit family. Consider suspending your skepticism for a moment and walk with me through an old tale told across the globe for generations.

The Danish storyteller Hans Christian Anderson writes of a fashion-forward emperor in a faraway land. One day, two peddlers came to the impeccably coiffed capital city looking to make a deal. The pair received a hearing before the Emperor, and they laid out a sales pitch for the most remarkable cloth. The salesmen explained that the fabric was invisible to anyone beneath the Emperor's lofty status. Swallowing the lure, hook-line-and-sinker, the arrogant leader eagerly negotiated a price.

The truth, of course, was that there was no fabric at all. The sale had been a Ponzi scheme from the very beginning. The salesmen rightly gambled that by playing on cultural taboos, they could pull a fast one on the entire community.

With a deal struck, the fraudsters immediately went to work fabricating the special textile right in the heart of the city. Excitement spread as citizens and courtiers looked in on the progress. Of course, not a soul could see a stitch of the magnificent cloth. Yet, no one verbalized their purported blindness because they believed it to be due to their intrinsic inferiority. Each one assumed him or herself to be the only person suffering from a visual impairment.

When the fabric was finally delivered to the palace, the Emperor responded identically. Smitten with the prospect of grandeur (and terrified of the implications of an inability to see), the Emperor kept his true observations a secret. He pretended to feel its perfectly smooth texture. He purported to smell its fresh aroma of newness. He widened his eyes at the weavers' masterful use of color.

The kingdom's interconnected community yielded an exceedingly strange sight once the swindlers finished tailoring the textile into a marvelous royal outfit. Processing down the cobbled streets of the capital city in a formal parade, the Emperor's servants carried him on an elaborate palanquin, stark naked for all to see. His assistants feigned fluffing the train of his robe and adjusting details of the outfit. Complicit in the charade, the entire city ogled in mock awe at the Emperor's supposed clothing. Citizens shouted adulation as the procession passed them on the curbs of wide avenues and side streets. One person saw no more clothing than the next, but each kept their perceptions to themselves. Everyone pretended together, unwilling to risk the consequences of voicing their communal secret.

Along the parade route, the Emperor passed an ordinary-looking child amongst the crowds. Unlike his fellow citizens, however, he didn't keep his observations silent. Loud enough to hear among the waves of glowing praise, he announced, "But he's not wearing any clothes!!!"

The statement was no doubt accurate. But that didn't mean it would be embraced by those who had much to lose by owning up to their suspicions. And so some looked away in avoidance. Others sought to calm the anxiety by acting as if they hadn't heard the boy's remark. Still, others vehemently defended the status quo. Some citizens mocked his comment, condemning the boy as an idiot. No one realized that they all were in the same boat.

But the boy stuck to his guns (or perhaps his naïveté). He embraced the truth as he saw it. "No! Really! Look at him! He's naked!!"

Because of his innocent recalcitrance, the boy's observations began to take hold among his fellow citizens. What started as a threat slowly transformed into a turning point. People on the sidewalks of the capital city slowly realized that they weren't alone in their inability to see the Emperor's clothing. They began understanding how an isolated lie promulgated by two duplicitous salesmen had turned into a secret affecting the entire system.

The city was not unlike a family first believing itself to be free of hidden mistakes, rules, or suffering, but later discovering that it had been animated by them. Within this family "kingdom," the secret of the Emperor's nudity became "the elephant in the living room" only once the little boy named it aloud. All the while, the strange behavior exhibited by the citizenry were clues to the truth[9] underneath.

When we're living out the story that is our family system, it's possible to miss the forest for the trees. We can be so entwined with what ostensibly are our family secrets that we don't realize they're there — or how we're reacting to them! Like a fish in water, the hidden motivators for our behavior feel like second nature. Sometimes (as was the case with Hannah Smith[10] from *No One*

---

9 - I'll come back to this concept of interpreting "strange behavior" later in the chapter when I suggest some tools for "spelunking family secrets."

10 - Everyone in her family system ended up compensating for the secret, regardless of just how much of it was specifically known by each individual. Hannah's mother apparently compensated for the secret by resorting to alcoholism and potentially competitiveness on the social ladder of her town. Her father compensated for it by hyper-religiosity and continuing the abuse. And Hannah compensated for it (at the very least) by murdering the threat to their systemic secret. Had her behavior been witnessed by anyone other than the boy and the audience of the film, she might've been judged as deranged or intrinsically evil. Alternatively, such behavior could tip us off that indeed, 'the emperor has no clothes' ('we have a major dark secret in our family system').

Knows), we can come to believe that our very survival depends on a given set of coping mechanisms. Our underlying logic may or may not be true. But regardless, the obscured truth gets acted out in choices, habits, beliefs, and adopted deconstructive coping mechanisms.

You might not initially believe your family has secrets. But because every individual keeps secrets, by virtue of our interconnectedness, so too does every family. The riddle is, who in your family will have the childlike curiosity to question the clues that expose them? Each of our family systems needs innocent children to speak up and name what everyone is already thinking.

You can be this child. You can be the one who won't let her puzzlement be put to rest. You can be the one who keeps making inquiries. You can be the one who verbalizes the obvious. You can take the risk of appearing foolish. You can upset dysfunction.

You might already have hunches about what's hidden below in your family. You might've had suspicions for years about this collective habit or that reactionary impulse common in your family culture. Your challenge may not so much be about finding curiosity but overcoming the fear of what could happen if you name your intuition.

Remember, we don't live on isolated islands. If we fail to sort out how our families of origin have affected us, taught us to cope, and colored our interpretation of life, we will hit a wall. We can only grow so much through solo self-help endeavors, as wonderful as they might be.

In Hans Christian Anderson's story, the little boy's naming of his suspicions might've felt like a threat to himself or the entire community — but the truth is that it was a gift. Had you been in that situation, you might've felt scared about losing your place of belonging for voicing your confusion! But in the end, the boy's bold act didn't bring conflict so much as a connection. His entire city came together in new and significant ways. He appeared to be a problem at first, but he turned out to be a treasure. After all was said and done, the city was a much safer place to exist.

Before we dive into some practical steps for spelunking the secrets that animate our family systems, I want to turn quickly to curiosity's essential partner: compassion.

––––––––––

When it comes to family secrets, your challenge might be less about spotting them in the first place but what to do with them after the fact. You might not only be familiar with the hidden aspects of your family culture, but you might also have strong opinions about them as well! This is normal. Judging that which is wrong is actually a sign of maturity. None of us were made to be floor mats for the world. Learning to stand up for ourselves is one of the essential tasks of human spirituality. But of course, there's a balance in this necessary critique.

Condemnation disrupts curiosity.

By its very nature, unequivocal judgment seeks to categorize, divide, and settle questions. Condemnation isn't so much interested in discovery or healing as it is in stability and safety. Instead of helping us be childlike, our disapproval turns us into know-it-alls. If we take the posture of judgment, we're just as likely to wind up blind to family secrets as we would be adopting the persona of PollyAnna. Condemnation isn't an asset when it comes to identifying and dealing with family secrets. In order to see our family systems clearly, our critical eye must partner with compassion.

This doesn't mean that your abusive grandfather gets a pass. This doesn't mean that your mother's addiction must be declared a life-giving gift. Instead, the aim is to see these injuries truthfully. Compassion is like a super-power that gives the ability to take in the full gamut of human experience; rather than writing off family members as flat, two-dimensional villains (or heroes)[11]. Compassion is the pathway to honesty about our loved one's brokenness and their gifts.

In order to understand our family's secrets, we must be willing to forgive.

I don't suggest this path flippantly[12]. It's not easy. And it certainly doesn't mean: (a) pretending hurtful behavior did not happen or (b) putting yourself in a position to be hurt again. Instead, the forgiveness I allude to is the process of naming wrongdoing, accepting the pain, paying the cost of the debt created, and setting the wrongdoer free from obligation to repay. Sometimes forgiveness involves relational reconciliation or even restitution; other times, it does not. In my experience, forgiveness begins with openness and flowers later as a gift. It's not something we can force, but something we can be willing to accept should it sneak in while we aren't looking. Forgiving those who have hurt me has been the work of a lifetime—an ongoing process of noticing, owning, releasing, and blessing. For me, forgiveness often feels like, "Oh, I just wished that person well in my mind, and I didn't even mean to."

Before we turn to a few practical tools for auditing family secrets, I want to share two attitudes that can stoke this spirit of empathy

---

11 - For readers familiar with Rotten Tomatoes or other film-critic outlets, you know that unsophisticated characters are a cardinal sin for audiences. We want to see ourselves in the actors on screen. Anyone who is too good or too evil comes across as fake. We know through our own lives that people often have both darkness and light in them. No one is perfect, and no one is the bane of evil.

12 - This is admittedly a massive topic. One that can hardly be explored in an entire book, let alone a single paragraph. For further reading, I recommend, *Forgiving Our Parents, Forgiving Ourselves*, by Dr. David Stoop, *Helping People Forgive* by David Augsburger, and *A Time to Forgive* by my friend Darold Bigger.

in that exploration.

First, it's helpful to accept the fact that in the absence of definitive truth, we make it up for ourselves.

Life can be like watching a movie where we've missed a few scenes. We do our best to make sense of the larger narrative, but it's never the full picture. The stories we create shape our lives, true or not. A child's belief regarding a given family secret need not be accurate in order for her to develop a host of compensatory behavior[13].

Stories We Tell is a gripping documentary that explores how people can remember ostensibly identical experiences in wildly different ways. In it, director Sarah Polley interviews family members about her deceased mother. They reveal a conglomeration of often-contradictory tales and myths about this influential woman (along with their constructive and deconstructive responses to them). Stories we Tell illustrates how our interpretations of personal history can be fleeting—but always full of influence. Polley observes,

"When you're in the middle of a story, it isn't a story at all but rather a confusion; a dark roaring, a blindness, a wreckage of shattered glass and splintered wood. Like a house in a whirlwind or else a boat crushed by the icebergs or swept over the rapids, and all aboard are powerless to stop it. It's only afterwards that it becomes anything like a story at all, when you're telling it to yourself or someone else."

Memory is inexact at best. Its unreliability has been well known in

---

13 - Psychologists sometimes refer to this dynamic as "projection," interpreting life events or people's behaviors through one's own experiences or past wounds; effectively 'projecting' those issues onto any or all new situations that arise. Projection is often accompanied by undue emotional reaction. When we speak of people being "triggered" by unpleasant circumstances, projection is the dynamic animating it.

the criminal justice system for many years. A single eye-witness testimony might seem to be the bedrock of any trial, but in practice, it's far from objective evidence. The problem is that memory is inherently subjective. From raw input and interpretation of the original events to encoding, storage, and later recollection, every step along the way is easily tainted[14] by our emotions, desires, and needs. Remembering is irrevocably affected by the reason we remember in the first place. It can be hard to find compassion for a family secret if our memory of it serves other emotional needs.

This should give us pause when exploring our family's histories. Our recollections may not be as precise as we assume. We may not be able to bring to mind important details—or unintentionally embellish others. What we might remember as a torture session of knife-fighting in a cage could've been a haircut in a fancy salon. What flashes to us as a judgmental yelling-match over Thanksgiving dinner might've resembled a civil debate from the perspective of others in the room.

I'm not saying we all should dawn tin-foil hats and embrace the conspiracy (many of us have indeed gone through great trauma as young people). But healthy fact-checking can go a long way toward building an empathetic spirit. When substantiation happens in conjunction with eye-witnesses[15] (often our elders[16]), truth rises to the surface. The kind of work Sarah Polley demonstrates in her filmmaking is a model for every person. Stories We Tell is a video record of one woman's attempt to audit her own accounts of

---

14 - Check out the 2015 journal article in *Memory* by Mark Howe and Lauren Knott on the subject: *The fallibility of memory in judicial processes: Lessons from the past and their modern consequences.*

15 - I would add that those who have been abused should tread very carefully with this advice. For some of us, simply being in the presence of our abusers is not safe.

16 - I'll return to this at the close of the chapter.

the most influential person in her life. In a sense, she discovered that the context of community is the most accurate repository for memory, a dynamic known by spiritual communities[17] for centuries.

A second pathway for stirring compassion is learning the backstories of the major players in our family secrets. At the beginning of this chapter, I suggested that an early inquiry some of us might ask of Mr. Smith from *No One Knows* is, "I wonder who dad's abuser was?" His behavior begs the question because secret vices rarely emerge in a vacuum. Family systems theory accurately predicts that they're learned behaviors, adopted roles, coping mechanisms, genetic predispositions, and so on.

Of course, illuminating explanations don't eliminate pain. DNA-driven propensities don't excuse wrongdoing. But knowing backstories can hold back the scorching sun of condemnation long enough for the seeds of forgiveness to sprout. We can't have real compassion if the truth is hiding in the shadows.

What might've driven the characters in *No One Knows*? The animating question of the story is, "why would these people continue to keep the abuse a secret?!"

Mr. Smith did so, no doubt, in order to continue the molestations. But underneath, he was likely filled with fear of being exposed and even guilt for the evil he was embodying. It's possible that Mr. Smith himself inherited the pattern from family members—who likewise received it from their forefathers. A man like him will never be able to understand his wrongdoing until he opens the door to compassion—not only for his daughter but for his elders and himself.

Mrs. Smith's possible backstories are endless. Perhaps past

---

17 - Many of whom still rely upon oral tradition and historic lines of authority to "remember together" the stories of their collective past.

abandonment paralyzed her from taking action on her daughter's behalf. Perhaps she was so co-dependent with her husband—enmeshed in his shame—that she projected her insecurities onto Hannah. Mrs. Smith might've been subject to similar abuse as a child and thus judged it as "normal." Because she had become complicit in the crime, perhaps simple fear of accountability was behind the wheel.

None of these theoretical explanations are excuses. They are way-markers for understanding the characters as more than mere caricatures. They are way-markers for better understanding ourselves!

Hannah's backstory is the most vexing and tragic. No one would want the sort of attacks she endured, and yet when presented with the opportunity to end them, Hannah acted decisively to ensure they'd continue! We might be tempted to "blame the victim," as has been a common cultural habit in America. But hollow quips are neither reasonable nor compassionate for victims of sexual assault.

As I suggested at the beginning of this chapter, it's possible that Hannah received her classmate's offer as a threat. If the secret of her abuse became known, all that she knew in the world (as dark as it was) would be at risk. We could theorize ad nauseam about the motivating factors behind Hannah's choices: from emotional enmeshment or misplaced guilt to shame.[18]

One interviewee in the documentary film *The Healing Years*[19] observes about her childhood sexual abuse, "The main reason people can't understand why kids have shame when they are sexually abused is the reason it happens."

---

18 - As I discussed in chapter 2.

19 - A moving 2010 documentary traversing victims' confessions and experiences with sexual abuse.

In other words, the inability for family members to understand one another's emotional landscape isn't just a circumstantial factor in creating the kind of evil Hannah suffered—it is causal! Family cultures that lack the imagination to explore the triggers, wounds, and experiences of their members are also family cultures that curry and pass down deconstructive secrets. Figuring out what makes one another tick isn't just a pathway to empathy; it prevents suffering in the first place!

An oft-quoted warning repeated throughout the Hebrew scriptures ends with the description of a god who "visits the iniquity of the fathers on the children, to the third and fourth generation." In all honesty, this doesn't sound like a god I'm eager to worship—it sounds more like Hannah Smith's abusive father! But while it's possible to read this text flatly, as predictive of a vengeful god who rains punishment down on undeserving bystanders, there is an alternative. What if these ancient reminders are a primitive way of recognizing the truth of family systems? What if they are descriptive of how the universe works, not so much about a god who is controlling every outcome?

We might instead read these warnings like, "All of humanity is interconnected. This is how the created order plays out. If your parents don't face, accept, and forgive their pasts, consequences will follow; patterns will repeat. If you don't have the courage to face the cracks and broken pieces of your life, your children and their children will inherit them. Life is a benevolent teacher. Lessons return to us until we 'get' them!"

In the next section, I will outline some practical strategies for investigating family secrets. As I've applied these in processing my own experience, one conclusion I've arrived at is that my ancestor's secret shame, dysfunctions, and failures were each (at least) in part inherited from their own parents, grandparents, and great-grandparents. Those people, long passed, made choices that still affect me in significant ways today. No one is born with a blank slate. Not me, not you, not our ancestors. Each of us slogs along through the errors of previous generations (and so will our offspring). I often observe to my friends after confessing parenting defeats, "Well, there's another contribution to my sons' therapy fund!" I'm only partially joking. As hard as I try, my children and their children will discover my blind spots and thereby stumble upon an opportunity for forgiveness and grace.

You might've been injured by family members who didn't seem to be trying, who was unconscious to the suffering in their wake, or who intentionally abused you. You didn't deserve it. And you don't owe them anything. But if you want healing, your path lies through coming to understand them. You're not alone if this sounds scary. And you won't be alone when you come out the other side as a more whole human being.

The question for any of us is not whether living implies suffering. The question is, "Would you like your pain now or later?" Absolutely, exploring family secrets with curiosity and compassion will be uncomfortable. As with the boy naming the Emperor's lack of clothing, it might feel lonely. As with the boy who offered to help Hannah Smith, it can turn volatile. But look at the alternative! Choosing to bury our heads in the sand has dire repercussions as well. You might as well take the chance for a better life.

Choose your pain: now or later?

If you take the courage to face your family's darkness and magnificent beauty, and you will find that it's worth the risk.

———————

In this chapter, I've argued that because families are systems, our family members' secrets are our secrets. This dynamic begs us to practice compassionate curiosity. The following are seven practical tools for how we might go about spelunking our collective family skeleton closets.

A disclaimer: remember that once family secrets are welcomed into the light of day, much will change. The way you see people you love can forever shift, relationships can be altered, unintended consequences can emerge. I think it's worth the cost to dig deeply. But don't expect that life will go on as normal after finding and naming this buried wealth. Remember, secrets smolder like fire, warming your home or rendering the neighborhood to ash. Tread thoughtfully.

1. Elders. Talk with the older folks in your family systems[20]. This might seem obvious, but it will be harder for some of us than for others. Go sit at your grandparents' dining room table, make that cross-country trek to see your great-aunt Pat, take your grandma's cousin out for coffee or lunch, accept that invitation to attend your long-lost-family reunion. Sit with your elders and converse about the past. Ask them to tell stories about their experiences, relationships with other family members, and how they came to be who they are. Ask them to tell you about the funniest, saddest, or scariest things that ever happened to them (or to their parents or siblings). Ask them about the things they feel (or felt) the most pride in. Ask about their moments of greatest embarrassment. Ask, ask, ask.

Then shut up and listen.

Take on the posture of a student. These conversations shouldn't be some kind of formal investigation or trial by interview[21]. Relinquish agendas, control, and assumptions. Be the humble

---

20 - Parents & grandparents, aunts & uncles, great-aunts and great-uncles, third cousins twice-removed, everyone who has had connection with your "tribe" is valuable.

21 - Of course, for family members with whom you have no relationship, such conversations might feel more formal. It's worth it no matter what. But I'd expect that relationships will almost universally deepen after these sorts of explorations.

little child on the street corner who doesn't know any better than to ask, observe, and learn. Not only will you discover a great deal about the secrets that drive your family culture, but you'll also likely deepen your relationships with these beautiful humans as well.

2. Taboos. This strategy overlaps a bit with the first (as they all do). Explore the unspoken rules in your family culture. What could you NEVER say to your mom or Dad? What types of questions or points of view are off-limits? What are the circumstances or topics around moments when everyone seems to be walking on eggshells? What would someone in your family have to say or do in order for everyone else to get really, really quiet (or really, really charged up and animated, as the case may be)?

In your interviews with elders, what observations would you like to make but can't because you know they'll react poorly to it? Take note! Taboos, or unarticulated boundaries, are very valuable entry points to secrets lying underneath. This is especially the case when the supposed reasons for a given taboo don't quite make sense.

3. Unusual Behavior. About how family systems influence us, John Bradshaw writes, "The paradox is that at some mysterious level of consciousness, the secrets are not really secrets." Kids are famous for accidentally "acting out" family secrets for all to see.

A father's secret gambling addiction can influence a child to lack the discipline for delayed gratification as an adult; what might look like a credit-card problem likely has deeper roots. A mother's secret mental illness can contribute to her grown child feeling deconstructive anxiety; what might initially appear to be a personality quirk could be best explained by old family patterns. An unspoken and unexplored alliance between one parent and child can create "emotional incest," where the child is weighed down with private concerns from the adult world.[22] This dynamic yields a myriad of life-sucking adult behaviors that could be judged as simple dysfunction but is actually more pathological. Some parents might even keep secrets from their children that are "known" to one degree or another, but about which no one speaks. An adult sibling's drug addiction might be covered up or enabled by them, well-known by other members, and yet still never discussed.

Family roles, habits, patterns, atypical behaviors, and coping mechanisms are the material evidence for what persists in the shadows. In fact, the more we deny our secrets in the first place, the more they leak through in observable action. Just because we don't realize they're there doesn't mean we're not acting them out! The crowds in Hans Christian Anderson's tale fawned in adoration over a naked emperor, an exceedingly odd sight. The more the truth was pushed under the surface, the more amped up their strange behavior became. Only after understanding the full picture are we able to accept the citizens' adopted roles as natural given the context.

You might need the help of trusted outsiders to tell the difference between typical and atypical. When it comes to seeing our family systems clearly, we often end up like fish in water: because we're swimming in it, we can't be objective about family culture. Your job is to notice the unusual behavior and then ask, "why[23]?" But beware! This line of exploration can produce some particularly colorful fireworks.

---

22 - I am most familiar with the work of Dr. Kenneth Adams on this subject. One of his books, Silently Seduced: When Parents make their Children Partners, is regarded by some as a pioneering work in this field.

23 - ACOA, "Adult Children of Alcoholic Parents" has some great resources for helping people who grew up in abnormal circumstances understand what "normal" is. Their "Personal Bill of Rights" is an invaluable tool for anyone who grew up with trauma.

4. Traditions. A more mundane strategy is to take a look at family traditions. Obviously, some of these can be inherited with little meaning from the surrounding cultural milieu; but sometimes, traditions are adopted as a way of remembering something without saying it explicitly. Over time, these traditions can become encoded into family culture without their original causes being obviously connected.

What is something your people do every single year on a particular date or weekend? Do you have a weekly or daily habit giving shape to your lives, that if missing, would make everything feel strange? Traditions can be both constructive or deconstructive in nature. An example of a family tradition with loaded meaning might be celebrating a deceased loved one's birthday on a certain date by eating out or having some other family gathering. Another example might be a regular trip taken together on a certain weekend. I will close this chapter by describing just such a pattern from my own family culture.

5. Fears. Sometimes within families, fears can be passed along or promulgated without a second thought as to their basis. Something happened to someone in the tribe at some point in the past, but the only thing that remains is the rule. "Swimming is too dangerous." "Doctors in this town are incompetent." "Never eat a fast-food taco[24]." Wherever you find irrational fears or unreasonable ultimatums, you can count a secret living underneath.

One way of trying to identify such fears is to compare the kinds of activities or habits common in your family system with those of others. Comparison isn't always the most helpful practice, especially when value judgments or jealousy are in the background. But in this case, the point is to ask, "what do we consider 'normal' compared to the 'normal' of our friends or strangers? Why might these differences be? What happened that makes us a family that is afraid of, e.g., dogs, accountants, guacamole, etc.?"

---

24 - Okay, okay. Some fears aren't as irrational as others!

6. Repeated mistakes and successes (and "Black Sheep"). Take a broad look across your family tree, and in particular, the complete life stories of a few individuals. Do you see any themes? What patterns can you discern among people in your system? Are there many successful entrepreneurs with large bank accounts and impressive financial smarts? Has more than one of your family members gone to prison? Is there a certain level of education (extensive or limited) that seems to be the general "rule" for your family? Why?

Reversing this line of questioning is also useful. By identifying those who stick out like a sore thumb, otherwise indiscernible patterns can begin to take shape. Who is the black sheep in the family? Who doesn't fit in? How have they intentionally or unintentionally crossed cultural norms to become pariahs[25]? Who doesn't come to family reunions, holidays, or other gatherings? Answers to each of these can be clues to secrets, even generations old.

7. Identify family roles. Finally, I once again recommend the work of Whitaker and Napier in The Family Crucible. A casual read of the book will get you thinking about the dynamics within your own tribe. Identifying the different roles (scapegoat, clown, golden child, etc.) various family members might play in your family system can provide really useful information about what is going on underneath. While an initial review from a personal perspective can be useful, this probably cannot be most effectively evaluated by someone within the system themselves but rather by an outsider. As I have before in this book, I recommend seeking out a mental health therapist who can be a sounding board and resource for sorting out why your family ticks the way it does.

---

25 - Sometimes, departures from established patterns evolves on a cultural level and thus is difficult to distinguish within a family system. For example, many more women have careers outside their homes in 2018 than they did in 1910, or 1810. Observing a pattern like this in your family culture might have more to say about broader society than it does about underlying secrets.

When my Dad's parents were still living, they traveled to Palm Springs nearly every year for Christmas with my grandfather's extended family. As far as I can tell, it was a tradition in every sense of the word. Despite the fact that my grandfather's siblings, their children, and grandchildren attended the gatherings, my Dad (an only child) was never invited. My two sisters and I, likewise, were never invited. As children, we didn't know any different. It was something we knew our grandparents did with "their family." But as we got older, it began to imply to us that we were not seen as equals to the others in our family tribe. To this day, I don't recall an explicit dis-invitation or explanation as to why we weren't included. It just never came up as an option. The underlying dynamics were the substance of a family secret I have yet to fully decipher.

Because the question remains, I, my Dad, and my sisters each developed our own intuitive judgments explaining the situation. These became narratives by which we operated. They informed our behavior and influenced our feelings. They shaped the way we interpret the world, even to this day.

Here's the story I told myself. Growing up, my grandparents often referenced the fact that they had adopted my Dad when he was an infant. It wasn't a secret. I knew it all too well, perhaps a little too well! As I grew older, I began seeing myself and my sisters as adopted by my grandparents as well. We were not true members of the family as so often inculcated by their remarks about my Dad's story of origin. Even though they never explicitly named it, I internalized a sense of inadequacy or shame because of my second-class status. This was hammered home in my little mind when they abruptly moved from my hometown of Walla Walla, without explanation[26], to spend their retirement with distant relatives in the American south. I was six at the time and had grown attached to them. They had been caregivers and playmates and, well, my grandparents! Their decision and the way they went about putting it into action devastated me.

While I couldn't have described it at the time, I felt utterly cast aside. Unwanted. Abandoned. This singular event has affected me profoundly over the years, as it does to this day[27]. My inner narrative began to sound something like, "They chose their real family over me. I won't ever truly belong to them." When eerily similar feelings emerged for me in response to my grandparents' Palm Springs holidays, they weren't surprising. In fact, it took me many years to come to the place where I found it curious that I had never been included! The facts fit so tightly with my inner story that I was hardly capable of making such a judgment. Why would

---

26 - The two of them had well-established careers at my future alma matter and were well-loved within the community. After more than 20 years at (then) Walla Walla College, their retirement was cause for a celebration. I found out about their impending departure while attending a large retirement program in the church planned in their honor. When I asked why people were saying so many nice things about Papa, the truth sent me into heaving sobs that came on and off in waves for weeks.

27 - As a kid, my confidence was on life support all the way into adolescence. Even as an adult, it is still a regular struggle. This, despite excelling in quite a number of externally observable aspects of life. As I introduced in the first chapter of this book, underneath my academic successes was a little boy who unconsciously believed he wasn't good enough; who believed that those who "loved" him most would leave him if he didn't perform perfectly, or did anything to embarrass them.

In adolescence, I became a performance junkie – doing everything in my power to keep those in my tribe from leaving me in embarrassment. I lived almost every day terrified of being alone; of being left, despite outward signs to the contrary. While I appeared to be very well adjusted and making good decisions, my locus of morality was entirely outside myself; I only did 'the right thing' when the spot light was on or I knew there would be accountability. Fundamentally, I think I thought myself unworthy of love.

I—a non-priority in their lives—expect to be included in that?

My parents' divorce amplified my chosen narrative. In my religiously devout grandparents' faith community, divorce was seen with skepticism and sometimes contempt. Dissolving a marriage for any reason other than a known extra-marital affair was especially reprehensible. And even then, it was still taboo. When my parents split up just before my first birthday, it was ostensibly because of the onset of my Dad's addiction (not generally an acceptable basis for divorce in their spiritual tribe[28]). Addiction in any conservative religious community isn't generally a celebrated pattern. My impression is that my grandparents were embarrassed by my Dad's disease[29]. So I ended up with a double or triple-whammy (who's counting?!) of a story on top of the adoption narrative.

I was the visible reminder of some of my grandparents' greatest sources of pain; an unsightly snaggle-tooth of a branch on the family tree. I did not possess their blood. I did not belong. I was the outcome of a failed relationship that itself had dissolved

---

28 - Letters written to my Mom by my religiously devout Grandmother and Great-grandmother during the period of my parents' estrangement give legs to some of my assumptions. Each of them intensely implored my mom to reconsider her decision to separate, begged her to move back across the country; to "stick it out." More than one of these notes I've read are littered with Bible texts and veiled shaming. When my Mom eventually chose to go through with finalizing the divorce, she recalls an immediate emotional cutoff from both of her former in-laws. What had been two of closest and most significant relationships in her life became essentially non-existent overnight. This consequence probably isn't surprising except for the fact that my Grandmother in particular had been my Mom's most important mentor (and one of her closest friends outright) since high school. In any case, the experience indicates some of my Grandparents' early disapproval of the divorce.

29 - The shame/guilt model for addiction is well-recognized as a broken one within the psychology and recovery communities. A much more helpful model for thinking about and helping people who struggle with this is that of 'the disease'. It enables us to have compassion both on ourselves as well as others – a key step in sobriety and recovery.

because of their son's mistakes (and, by extension, their own). Of course, they wouldn't want to stick nearby.

Here's the real tragedy in this twisted jungle of overgrown thorns and vines. When they were living, I never had the courage to explore this wilderness of a family backstory. I never asked my grandparents, "Why?" The opportunity to take their hands as tour guides, hearing their perspective, and learning from their wisdom, is lost to me (as it is to my children and their children).

How might my relationship with them had shifted by hearing a more nuanced story? How might my ability to live out my sense of purpose be more effective had I understood the full truth? How might the world be a better place? I will never know.

Your story doesn't have to play out like mine in this regard. You don't have to be left wandering in the jungle. You don't have to be left wondering, "why?"

You can be brave. You can spelunk your family systems for the gold hiding underneath. You can ask the questions begging to come out. You can be the curious, innocent child who doesn't know any better than to notice the obvious. You can wonder aloud at your family taboos. You can ask about failures, or oddities, or rules. You can compare backstories. You can be the stick in the spokes of the wheel of dysfunction. And you can have compassion on the inheritances of your family's past. You can be the problem that opens the door to transformation.

You can do this. Take courage. The life that you always wanted is waiting on the other side.

QUESTIONS FOR DISCUSSION:

1. Reflect on a characteristic or quality you inherited from your family through genetics or culture. How did you learn about it? How has it helped you? How has it held you back?

2. What role(s) did you play in your childhood family system(s)? How do you still fill it/those today?

3. Reflect on the first time you regretted curiosity. Perhaps it was because it revealed your ignorance, or earned scorn, or named the elephant in the room. What did you learn from that experience? What keeps you from curiosity today?

4. In what ways do you suspect hidden prejudices against your own family system; where do you anticipate you'll need compassion as you look at family secrets?

5. Which tools for spelunking family secrets calls out to you like the first one you'd like to experiment with? Why?

6. If you knew today was your last day to live, what questions would you ask family members? (Why not start today?)

4 | ISOLATION

"The first great intimacy is when secrets are told.»
-Jonathan Carroll, Bathing the Lion

From the perspective of my 18-year-old self, the night I lost my brother began as the perfect evening. It was my senior homecoming banquet[1] in early November. A delightful classmate had asked me to be her date for the event. My mother's formalwear store had furnished us both with (then) stylish outfits: me an oversized pinstriped Zoot Suit with a tie to match her delicate flowing red gown. We arrived at the local Elks Club ballroom with panache in my great uncle's jet black 1946 Lincoln (with him as our tuxedo-clad chauffeur). After enjoying what seemed like fantastic food, good conversation, and mediocre entertainment, my date and I joined our friends at my family home for a tame but highly anticipated after-party. Hot-tubbing, swimming, karaoke, and other "safe" fun for my religiously sheltered friends and me followed into the early

---

1 - In the fundamentalist subculture of my youth, this tradition is slightly different than what is often experience by many American teenagers in mainstream school cultures. Rather than a dance (dancing was forbidden), we took our dates to dinner with entertainment. For the students involved, it evokes very much the spirit of prom and homecoming in broader culture.

morning hours. Sure, my younger siblings were there to partake and pester – but all things told, the experience had been surreal. As I fell asleep in the basement of my quiet home around 1 am, I was glowing in the joy of possessing a bit of what I received as "the good life."

An hour later, this contented world had turned upside down[2].

I was awoken by my mother's voice – yelling for me to get up. This wasn't unusual. We lived outside of town – not isolated, but most definitely in the country. Routinely we would have critters on our back porch to "shoo" away. As the oldest male in the house,[3] this was simply one of my responsibilities. As I groggily opened the door to exit my basement bedroom, however, I came to the immediate realization that this wake-up wasn't for pest control.

In the darkness, I felt unusual warmth. As I scrambled up the first few carpeted stairs, the heat intensified to the point that I could not advance past halfway. I looked up to see the red glow of a fire. Dashing down and back into my bedroom, I pounded on the window and yelled at my mom that I was awake. She, thinking I was trapped, began to break the small basement window with a metal dog bowl. In the meantime, I exited the house barefoot and wearing only white Haynes briefs through the egress window on the other side of the basement. By the time I ran around the house, she had broken the window all the way and was convinced I had gone unconscious.

To her relief, I made myself known as I rounded the corner to the rear of the house. Not yet knowing the extent of the fire and seeing both she and my sister outside, I asked for my brother.

---

2 - I recount this experience in a speech I gave at Walla Walla University in January of 2018. Find it on my YouTube channel: YouTube.com/loewkr

3 - I will share more about my family circumstances in a later chapter. At the time of the fire, my mother had been divorced from her second husband (my former stepfather) for about 7 years.

"He's still inside," she screamed, pleading with the universe to do something about it.

For me – a kid who already felt quite alone in the world, and with the weight of the "man of the house" mantle on his shoulders – those three words were equal parts gut-wrenching, terrifying, and maddening. My emotions at that moment would haunt my dreams for many years in the aftermath of the fire[4].

Clad in little more than my birthday suit, I furiously attempted rescue of my brother. Despite breaking his window; dousing the room with hose water (and then myself, for the heat); cutting and burning my arms and chest just trying to lean into his scalding hot room; inhaling enough smoke to develop acute asthma; and screaming until I could no longer speak, Kasey, my brother, did not come to his window. The firemen found him a short time later, tranquil in his bed. He still rests peacefully today. He was only 12-years-old.

Perhaps it goes without saying that this was (and has been) the most painful experience I've ever navigated. When C.S. Lewis writes in A Grief Observed that "no one ever told me that grief felt so much like fear," I recognize precisely the feeling of that grotesque discovery. The pain of traumatic loss billows like dark thunderclouds building on the horizon. The threat heaps upon itself to a breaking point, and then it keeps growing.

Nineteen years later, I still grieve Kasey.

As if the fire itself hadn't been surreal enough, the dreamlike nature of this experience continued. Just minutes into the crisis, I found myself inexplicably surrounded by an empathetic community of friends and family. In my shock, loved ones seemed to appear out of thin air, multiplying by the hour. The warmth of

---

4 - And to some degree, continue to do so.

their embraces in those moments is as seared into my memory as the heat of the flames.

Aside from the continually shared hugs and tears, which stretched for months following the fire, loved ones found practical ways to support my mother, sister, and me as well. Old acquaintances organized a wedding shower (sans wedding) where hundreds of people gifted us appliances, furniture, clothing, and other household necessities destroyed in the fire. Church leaders showed up for weeks to our rental home to mop floors, fold laundry, cut the grass, and feed animals. Teachers and classmates stopped by with casseroles and cookies for more than a year following the disaster. My family's tight-knit community was an unspeakable gift that not everyone traversing loss is lucky enough to enjoy. I remember back on these tangible expressions of love with embers of gratitude still warmly glowing.

But as beautiful and supportive as the majority of people were, I also had many painfully poignant interactions of insensitivity, ignorance, shaming, and even betrayal[5]. I don't resent those who didn't "show up" in the ways I wanted or needed at the time. We all do the best we can with what we have. It's not surprising that many of us witness our own insecurities and issues arise when faced with other's pain. Suffering has a way of confronting the worldviews and pat-answers that work well for navigating ordinary inconveniences. When these platitudes are shared in the context of debilitating loss, they come across as hurtful rather than encouraging. Ill-equipped but more socially aware friends choose to distance themselves rather than risking saying anything at all. For those recovering from loss, this too can be mystifying and painful.

---

5 - I tread carefully here for the next four paragraphs because the last thing I want to do is alienate or judge my loving and beautiful home church community. One of their greatest traits is the positive and healing way in which they respond to crisis. I'm forever grateful for their many gifts of love — and I also can't tell the story honestly without acknowledging the rough edges.

I vividly recall a teacher haranguing me in my high school hallway about some missing assignments (a new experience for me as I had been an A-student at the top of my class before the fire). The instructor repeatedly reiterated that they were not going to give me grace on a deadline, despite the circumstances, ending with an exhortation that the real world wouldn't stop turning to accommodate my pain and that it was past time for me to "move on."

A few months after the fire, I was asked to speak in front of the student body of my Christian high school ostensibly about how I had integrated losing Kasey into my spiritual life. As an adult looking back, that task seems like a lot to expect from an 18-year-old! But at the time, I relished the opportunity. For many of my classmates, however, it was uncomfortable hearing me speak so frankly about my grief. More than one approached me in the days and weeks following my presentation, saying something to the effect, "It was good; I just don't know why you always have to talk about that subject when you speak up front."

It's disquieting to see someone we love in pain, an unpleasant irritant reminding us that things are not the same. Empathy fatigue is real—none of us can take on the full gamut of emotion for every human experience we learn about or even encounter. We all have limits for how much we can engage in the world's suffering. I understand why my friends might've subtly shifted over time from asking me how I was doing to whether or not I had yet achieved "closure." I understand why acquaintances who had not experienced the same trauma wanted me to return to "normal" with them. But everyone who has personally tangled with loss (and everyone else, who eventually will) knows that there is never a return to normal. Trauma doesn't give us that luxury. What loss yields is an unrelenting new reality that, if you stick with through the pain, will eventually reveal new joy, gratitude, and hope.

For me, Kasey's death isn't an obstacle to "get over." Rather, it represents a wholesale reordering of reality around which I have learned to adapt. In the years following my family's great loss, we have felt it unavoidable to process and integrate the experience as opposed to suppressing or denying it. Pressure to get back to normal felt then and still feels now like anti-empathy incarnate.

But mixed up in all these complexities, in the early years following the fire, I accommodated people's empathy fatigue by keeping my grief secret, pretending that I hadn't already entered a "new normal." Instead of continuing the process of healing through reflection, contextualization, and storytelling, I buried much of my pain out of sight. My instinctive secret-keeping led me to a place of dark isolation and loneliness. This chapter is about that dynamic.

The first time I read Jon Krakauer was as a young high school student on summer vacation at my grandparents' rustic cabin in Northern Idaho. I plowed through *Into Thin Air*[6] in a single evening, instantly becoming an apologist for the author and outdoorsman. Later that summer, I devoured his earlier book, Into the Wild, a true tale of a young man's fateful journey into the Alaskan wilderness. Using Christopher McCandless's own journals as the backbone of his research, Krakauer retraces the young man's trek across America, chronicling his accidental death by food poisoning in the Alaskan bush. The story's themes of survival, self-sufficiency and absolute freedom enchanted me.

---

6 - The book tells the tale of the now infamous Mount Everest climbing disaster of 1996 wherein eight people lost their lives. My fascination with the premise of the book is ironic given my averseness to risk in general and heights in particular. My very first experience with rock climbing was at summer camp. During the outing, I had gotten stranded 20 feet up on a rock face. The camp hadn't told some harrowing story of death regarding the sport; the leaders hadn't put the fear of heights into my mind. I brought it myself. I clung to the ledge, frozen in fear. In the end, it took about a gallon of tears and my counselor scaling the rock face without ropes to bring me safely to the ground.

I wasn't the first to idolize the archetype of the "rugged individual"[7] (and I certainly wouldn't be the last). A great swath of American culture is enamored with the idea of the "self-made person," the one who, sequestered in their own world, achieved success without an iota of help from anyone[8]. We celebrate people who "pulled themselves up by their own bootstraps" to grab hold of their success. Steve Jobs and Oprah Winfrey are our totems:[9] shining examples of how we alone control our own destinies.

Malcolm Gladwell's 2008 book *Outliers* sets out (among many other things) to debunk the philosophical foundation of this fierce American self-determinism. He calmly argues that no one achieves high heights in a vacuum. Rather, he says, each of us (no matter how isolated we may seem) has immense outside contact; each of us benefits from the support or detriment of our wider communities. "The people who stand before kings may look like they did it all by themselves. But in fact, they are invariably the beneficiaries of hidden advantages and extraordinary opportunities and cultural legacies that allow them to learn and work hard and make sense of the world in ways others cannot."

---

7 - A term coined by president Herbert Hoover in a speech celebrating the American Spirit, downplaying the importance of the Federal government, and attempting to motivate the populace to work harder. This speech was given in the very early days of the great depression in 1928.

8 - From John Wayne and the Lone Ranger, to Batman or Superman, to Michael Jordan going 5 on 1 against the 'Space Jam' aliens, or Will Smith eking it out alone in the post-apocalyptic world of *I am Legend*.

9 - We love hearing the story of Steve Jobs, who, from his parents garage singlehandedly innovated his way to creating Apple Computers from the strength of his own will. We love listening to the music of Susan Boyle, who through the amateur talent show called *Britain's Got Talent* became both a household name as well as an international chart topping singer. We love how Oprah Winfrey overcame a childhood of sexual abuse, a pregnancy at the age of 14, and continued bouts with her bodyweight, to become one of the wealthiest and most successful women on the planet.

The self-made person is a myth.

In fact, isolation (far from a yellow-brick road to our personal panaceas) actually tends to hurt us. While legendary lone-eccentrics tantalize us with their successes, their biographers tell the nuanced story: shipwrecked relationships, gratuitous pettiness, disastrous physical and mental health, and on and on. Isolation is risky. We know this. Spend 5 minutes in the leadership aisle of any Barnes and Noble, and you'll be battered with warnings about the trap of "the lone wolf."

Our best selves can only be found on the other side of collaboration, mentorship, accountability, rebuke, and encouragement. I love what psychologist and theologian David Benner observes, "We were never intended to make the life pilgrimage alone. And attempting to make the spiritual journey on our own is particularly hazardous."

Grief is complex. And it's unique to each individual mourner. Although I certainly kept my process secret because of empathy fatigue, looking back, I now know that my motives were multi-faceted. The truth is that I didn't know what to do. Isolated, I felt ashamed, scared, and confused. I didn't want to become a prima donna. And so, I wrapped myself in the embrace of self-concealment. In the midst of community, I became hidden. And while my isolation didn't literally lead me "into the wild" like Christopher McCandless, I never-the-less found it hazardous, just as David Benner predicts.

Nineteen years have passed since the fire that took my brother. I still wrestle with symptoms of PTSD: nightmares, hyper-vigilance, catastrophic thinking, and bouts of rage. This condition for me was compounded by the strained relationships it sometimes caused: inexplicable behaviors are easy to judge, but when contextualized by authenticity, empathy is born. My isolation in grief contributed to unconsciously seeking unhealthy coping mechanisms for my unpleasant emotions. I lost out on a treasure trove of wisdom from would-be mentors[10] who, if they had only known the depth and darkness of my grief, would have jumped at the opportunity to help. Self-concealment allowed me to coexist, anonymous in plain sight. My personal growth was the casualty.

As a pastor, I can't count the number of times I've witnessed parishioners suffering disasters because of secrecy-induced isolation. Whether hiding an unpleasant medical diagnosis, financial disaster, or moral disappointment, the results are predictable. Resources and support that might've otherwise been available were left untapped because no one other than the person in crisis knew the need. I've seen teenagers exploring their sexuality without the support[11] of healthy education, ending up with STDs, unwanted pregnancies, or in abusive relationships. I've seen young adults experimenting alone with treating underlying pain via illicit chemicals only to wind up in addiction. No matter the specific application, isolating oneself from community prunes human potential.

This destructive dynamic also applies to communities as a whole. Alisa Williams' 2014 contribution to the Adventist journal "Spectrum," entitled "A Community of Loneliness," describes the Seventh-day Adventist religious community in the U.S. as

---

10 - An absolutely essential practice for anyone wishing to experience personal growth is robust and diverse mentorship. I am indebted to Robert Clinton, who researched and wrote extensively on mentorship in the context of leadership development. His work lays out an inclusive model that includes counselors, coaches, teachers, historical figures, and even fleeting chance encounters. It's challenging to overstate the importance of this ingredient to spiritual maturity.

11 - In the following chapter (Secret wisdom), I will discuss the other side of this equation: how withheld information can be both beneficial and damaging to young people in their development.

being deeply isolated despite common geographical[12] proximity and tightly upheld cultural norms. Unable to nurture frank conversations about divergent beliefs[13] or behavior for fear of reprisal, stated doctrine and policy become frozen in time[14]. Drawing hard boundaries doesn't magically change our stories, philosophies, or feelings. It only delineates what is safe to admit in pleasant company. Of course, this dynamic isn't unique to the Seventh-day Adventist denomination or even religion in general. During the American civil rights movement of the 1960s, many of our relatives lived through a powder keg of polarization. A white person in the south who agreed with the cause for Civil Rights would have found an easier path by keeping her opinions private, feigning allegiance to dominant voices, and waiting it out.[15] But until a diverse wave of citizens drummed up the courage to step out of this isolation, the entire country was held back.

---

12 - The Adventist Church's education system has produced a number of "Meccas" such as Loma Linda, Calif., Walla Walla, Wash., Berrien Springs, Mich., or Collegedale, Tenn., where the per-capita density of believers is substantially higher than across the country as a whole.

13 - In 2014, I circulated an informal and non-scientific survey on social media that ended up with more than a thousand participants who are currently or were formerly members of the Seventh-day Adventist Church. It indicated that the overwhelming majority (80%) do not believe everything the denomination officially teaches. Fascinatingly, respondents reported being three times more likely to lie about their differences when amongst Adventists than they would be amongst the general population.

14 - Interestingly enough, the Adventist Church originally grew from the fertile soil of honest dialogue. For nearly a century, leaders resisted the urge to even write down a statement of beliefs. These pioneers didn't want to lose "present truth", the assumption that human understanding is progressive over time. The philosophy is still reflected in a preamble to the church's current 28 stated beliefs where it proclaims that revision is expected over time.

15 - Kathryn Stockett's celebrated novel, *The Help*, highlights some of these dynamics, I highly recommend it.

Isolation is risky. But all forms of aloneness aren't therefore suspect. For centuries spiritual leaders have regarded solitude as an essential ingredient for personal maturity. Jesus himself routinely retreated to "lonely places" for prayer and reflection[16]. Authors like Dietrich Bonhoeffer have even argued that being alone is an improbable yet necessary component for living well in community: "If you refuse to be alone you are rejecting Christ's call to you, and you have no part in the community of those who are called.[17]"

Susan Cain's excellent book *Quiet* explores some of the benefits of aloneness by exploring personality. In the book, Cain challenges the stereotype of introverts as anti-social Neanderthals. She writes that introverts aren't automatically lonely or distressed or somehow a liability because they enjoy spending time by themselves. Introverts enjoy satisfying relationships and often more deeply than their extroverted counterparts. Beyond that, Susan Cain discusses how introverts' circumspection, concentration, critical thinking, creativity, and concern for their fellow humans are enormous assets in every sphere of life. She argues that many of the world's greatest models of success or virtue, in fact were introverts[18].

The danger in solitude is found in distressed aloneness: isolation that is a product of fear, abandonment, prejudice, trauma, or pain. The story of Samson in the Old Testament book of Judges

16 - Luke 5:15-16

17 - From Bonhoeffer's spiritual classic, *Life Together.*

18 - Abraham Lincoln, Rosa Parks, Bill Gates, Laura Bush, Nelson Mandela, Albert Einstein, Guy Kawasaki, Eleanor Roosevelt, Dr. Seuss, Frederic Chopin, etc.

is a case study for this truth. Samson's tale isn't a triumph[19] if it is explored through the lens of isolation. Instead, it's a tragedy ending in suicide. He wasn't a hermit, a loner, or a survivalist like Chris McCandless. As a young adult, Samson simply cut himself off from the community that had looked out for him previously. Perhaps his story might've ended without suicidal revenge if he had taken advantage of the resources no doubt available to him through trusted mentors. Instead, he wandered through life, blind to his repeated patterns of lust. Unable to assuage his rage, he was likewise unable to hear the *Intervention* of would-be advisors. Samson was physically present and yet adrift. Something similar may be true for all of us. His story is our story.

It's possible to be physically alone and yet not distressed; it's also possible to be surrounded by people and yet alone. As I illustrated above by my observations regarding the Seventh-day Adventist community, destructive isolation doesn't hinge on the presence or absence of people but rather on the intangible connections between them. On the title page of this chapter, I quoted from Jonathan Carroll's cerebral novel *Bathing the Lion*, "The first great intimacy is when secrets are told." The full passage is brilliant:

> *Forget that first kiss, the first sex, the first tears of misunderstanding, the first fight. Forget the first amazing gift from them that says they thought long and hard about you and what you love. Here is physical proof they tried as best they could to get you something concrete, in the hand- there that shows some of the intensity of their feeling for you. Forget it. Forget it all. The first great real intimacy between two people begins when secrets are told. The time you stole the money from the candy drive when you were a girl scout. The time you slept with your brother in law after their marriage dissolved. The lie you told your boss that*

---

19 - In Christian circles, Samson is frequently regarded as a praiseworthy Biblical hero who avenged his betrayal with glorious bloodshed.

changed everything and burned every bridge you had at the time. The secret about your parents you thought you would never, ever tell anyone. But suddenly you do—to your new partner. No matter what happens to you two after that, they know these things now. You can never take them back. They have the goods on you and you on them. At that point your life together shifts on its axis permanently. You have begun to let them into your soul and often we don't even know ourselves what the result of *that* will be.

Likewise, when none are told, loneliness is inevitable, regardless of proximity. Even in the midst of community, it's common to be hidden.

A theme I will repeatedly visit in this book is the incredible power of disclosure. My life experience has taught me of its incredible knack for sparking positive change. Centuries-old spiritual wisdom has reinforced my belief. Modern scientific inquiry has also verified the connection. Brené Brown's masterful material on vulnerability argues that while self-concealment can ostensibly keep people safe, it won't lead them to their greatest triumphs. In her viral TED talk, she says, "Vulnerability is not weakness...[it] is the birthplace of innovation, creativity, and change." I couldn't agree more.

Looking back on my experience with grief over the death of Kasey, I absolutely kept aspects of my process secret. At the same time, I also did reach out to connect. It wasn't a binary affair. I know first-hand how isolation can hurt us, likewise how confession can conjure support.

Through disclosure, I discovered that when people go through untenable circumstances, they frequently discover thriving communities of survivors just like them. Drawn together by common suffering, these "clubs" live just under the surface of polite society, something like metaphorical subterranean mole people[20]. Unless a person has endured similar challenges, he wouldn't even know such brotherhoods[21] exist. Sometimes they meet in musty church basements. Other times they gather on hidden internet forums. At their best, these clubs support the most vulnerable through the darkest of life's valleys. They surface through knowing nods, a smile at an inside joke, or an out-of-the-blue encouragement card in a mailbox. If you've personally discovered such camaraderie, you know that something as simple as eye contact with an ally from across the room stokes the flames of courage like nothing else.

But with that said, disclosure isn't a cure-all[22].

If you're anything like me, you've shared your secrets to people who didn't treat them with the gravity they deserved. And if you're anything like me, through authenticity, you've also discovered unspeakably beautiful connections. And even still, if you're anything like me, you've also continued to experience moments of isolation and loneliness despite meaningful relationships. Discovering common ground didn't automatically produce the kind of healing, growth, and maturity I wanted.

This is normal. It's common in the wake of vulnerability to continue experiencing aloneness, straddling both recovery and

---

20 - A term I first encountered from Jennifer Toth's 1995 book, *The Mole People*, describing homeless people living in abandoned subway tunnels under New York City.

21 - I'm not a member of the clubs for survivors of cancer, bankruptcy, active combat, racism, suicide, alcoholism, incarceration, robbery, or genocide. But I know they thrive because I am a member of the one for survivors of the traumatic death of family members (not to mention those for survivors of obesity, children of divorce, alcoholic parents, etc.)

22 - In the final two chapters of the book, I'll discuss this dynamic in greater detail.

distress simultaneously.

Self-exposure is powerful, but it isn't a panacea. It's magic. But it's just the first step in becoming our best selves. The truth is that even in the discovery of a like-minded community, I was still all by myself. I still had work to do. In short, I still had to learn non-distressed aloneness.

How then do we become more like Jesus, who was able to use his inevitable aloneness as a tool for good rather than succumbing to it as a liability? How do we arrive at a place where loneliness isn't damaging but rather an opportunity?

The key lies in learning to be at peace with our secrets.

I've learned that secrets are similar to grief in this sense. When it comes down to it, there is no escaping grief. It's like a black hole. No matter the loss, the reason we find it so gut-wrenching and painful is that there is absolutely nothing we can do to fix it. I cannot escape the finality of Kasey's death. He is gone. And the losses have only compounded since the fire; 21 years of missed memories, experiences, and depth of relationship. There is no way out.

What do you even do with that?

Well, there are only two options. Sidestep the loss via distraction, codependency, addiction, fantasy, etc. — or learn how to be alone and at peace with it.

And how do we do that?

Therapy. Lots of therapy.

I jest. But it's true to a degree. Becoming untroubled by secrets that once put our lives at risk is certainly a spiritual endeavor. Clergy, spiritual directors, and mentors are undeniable friends to this task. I've been unspeakably blessed by a diverse squad of guides over the years — and a number of those included skilled therapists. Truly, for anyone struggling with isolation in secret-keeping, a licensed therapist is a great place to start.

But aside from making that first phone call, let me provide a couple of additional practical strategies as I close this chapter.

———————

I grew up watching Disney films. Perhaps you did too. Looking back, I can't help but notice repeating themes through the most vivid movie memories in my mind's eye[23]. One of the most prominent themes that pops out is identity: in which a character's struggle is to discover or affirm who they really are. While it's less present in some of the original classics[24], it's hard to deny in Disney projects from the 2010s forward[25].

Moana discovers that she is a new kind of queen. Buzz Lightyear comes to accept that he is indeed only a toy and yet still has a purpose. Nick Wilde and Judy Hopps discover and pursue their callings as police officers despite cultural prejudices. It isn't an accident that storytellers worldwide and throughout history repeatedly return to the motif of identity. We resonate with a hero's process of discovery because we're all on the same journey[26]. Every single person has work to do, discoveries to make, and transformation to welcome. On the other side is gold,

———————

23 - *The Little Mermaid, Toy Story, Mulan, The Lion King, Aladdin,* etc.

24 - *Snow White, Bambi, Sleeping Beauty, One Hundred and One Dalmatians, The Jungle Book, or Dumbo.*

25 - *Tangled, Brave, Wreck-it Ralph, Frozen, Zootopia, Moana, Coco,* etc.

26 - You might be familiar with Joseph Campbell's influential work *The Hero's Journey,* which proposes a metaphorical template for the universal tasks found in being human.

including the ability to be alone with our secrets peacefully.

Perhaps the most important affirmation I came to embrace in my journey is that "as a child of God, I am enough, exactly as I am." It might sound trite, but this simple switch in identity changed everything for me. Your work will no doubt produce different affirmations. Adopting new beliefs about identity might seem straightforward. But you already know from personal experience that on the soul level, truth and lies are complex. We can say one thing using reason and intention while at the same time emotionally believe the exact opposite. For me, accepting belonging in God's family was[27] a life-altering gift that allowed me to be alone and at peace.

Now a second practical strategy.

Like me, you may have conscientiously witnessed the #metoo movement develop in 2018. You may be a part of that movement. One of the abiding themes of the #metoo conversation has been far too often what should have remained secret[28] was illicitly wrenched into view, grabbed, touched, or otherwise violated.

There is violence to all forms of sexual assault, even when there are no bruises. There is unspeakable injury, even when it takes place in the calm of a doctor's office or the apparent safety of a family living room. One small reason for this (of the many) is that something private became public against our will. If you are in recovery from these kinds of wounds, you know that part of healing sometimes involves revisiting the egregious wrongdoing and reasserting the truth over the situation. Sometimes healing includes reaffirming and protecting healthy boundaries.

One of the most surprising discoveries I've made in studying

_____

27 - (And IS still because the hero's journey is a continual process.)

28 - I touched on this in chapter two.

secrets is not the power of confession but the power of resisting forced exposure. Willing disclosure can bring catharsis, but so can protecting autonomy. The age of social media has taught us that our personal information has incredible monetary value[29]. What I hope we also learn is that our private lives have incredible spiritual value — and we are right to protect them.

For those of us who have been involuntarily exposed, there is something life-giving about later saying "NO" (even if it happens decades later in therapy). Drawing boundaries can highlight a well of strength we may not have known we possessed — and once we start, the resource only deepens. Not unlike the work of affirming identity, boundary-making is easy to prescribe and difficult to do. Therapists again can be useful[30] in this process. Scrupulous management of our secrets[31], telling them to some, but guarding them among others, is a second key practice for learning to be at peace while alone.

---

29 -   An adage I like to throw around is, "If the product is free, then you are the product."

30 -   Ironically, it was by drawing a boundary with one of my therapists that I first began to discover the importance of this practice. During one session, I showed this particular practitioner a picture in my journal I had drawn on a weekend retreat. After looking, she casually began flipping to other pages. I hadn't said it, but my intent in handing the book over was for her to view only the one page. I nervously verbalized my discomfort, clumsily expressing a boundary. She apologized and affirmed my courage to speak up.

31 -   This topic is admittedly enormous, one that a paragraph cannot suffice. Henry Cloud and John Townsend's book Boundaries is a classic on the subject. Another I'd recommend is *Emotional Blackmail* by Susan Forward.

A few years into my career as a pastor, I was in placed charge of a weekly youth group. It was a ball. I got to work with an enthusiastic team of college students who put on the program, intentionally designed for lighthearted play with 7-8th graders. And as you might expect, some of the youngsters showing up each week brought with them, shall we say, "challenging behavior patterns."

I remember one kid distinctly. She drove my staff bananas, constantly getting into mischief and orchestrating conflict. The group could be in the middle of singing, and without warning, this student would be doing cartwheels through the crowd. My team regularly reflected in meetings on how frustrating it was to have her in the group because her disruptions made it difficult to connect with and give attention to other students. At one point, I remember a staff member asking whether it might be for the greater good if she just stayed home.

"But she's my favorite kid!" I replied, with a twinkle in my eye.

The team responded with raised eyebrows and sideways glances. Nobody truly liked this particular student. She was tolerated.

The truth is that while I too was often annoyed at her behavior, I also empathized with her. I had done enough of my own personal work to see myself in her anxiety, reactivity, and constant testing. "Do you love me? Do you see me? Do you love me? What about if I do this? What about if I do that? Do you still love me then? What if I'm like this? Do you see? Do you love me? Do you love me?"

Looking back, it's true that I may have been projecting my own issues onto her. I didn't then, and still don't today, know the secret complexes animating her behavior. And yet, so to speak, "the proof is in the pudding." Because I had begun the hard work of sitting alone with my secrets, I was less reactive to hers. Having learned how to be at peace with the things I hide from the public,

119

I was less distressed by the behaviors that signaled her shadows. Instead of wishing her away or responding harshly, I was calm and kind.

My empathy is my superpower. And today, I feel grateful for the many surprising ways that it shows up in my life. It is among the most important gifts I've ever received.

I began this chapter by sharing the most agonizing moments of my life. The horror of losing Kasey in the house fire is still extraordinary. So much so that the first time gratitude welled up in me for my developing empathy, I immediately felt ashamed. Any thankfulness associated with that loss seemed like a betrayal of the highest order. "How can I be appreciative of anything connected to Kasey's death?" This too became a perverse secret for a time.

But as I've sat with it, I've come to be at peace even with this. I think my brother would understand my conflict. I think he'd be proud of my stumbling into healing. And I think he'd offer his blessing over the way in which his passing has given transformation and courage to me and to the world.

QUESTIONS FOR DISCUSSION:

1. In this chapter, the author cited empathy fatigue as one of the reasons for his self-concealment regarding grief and loss. What are some of the reasons you've kept pain, failure, or bad news secret in your life? How do you determine whether your rationale for hiding was legitimate?

2. Which risks associated with (secrecy triggered) isolation most resonate with your own experience? This chapter gave just a few of the many possibilities: mental illness, suicide, lack of access to medical care, abusive relationships, sexually transmitted diseases, etc.

3. The author draws a distinction between aloneness and isolation. When have you found aloneness to be useful for your personal growth or spiritual maturity?

4. What "clubs" have you joined because of shared suffering? Reflect on how discovering or participating in such communities has impacted your life.

5. Is it easier for you to draw boundaries or disclose secrets? Why?

6. What "superpowers" do you possess through learning peace with your secrets?

5 | SECRET WISDOM

*"The best weapon of a dictatorship is secrecy,
but the best weapon of a democracy should be
the weapon of openness."*

-Niels Bohr

Information is powerful. Secret information is more powerful. The greater the secret, the greater the jolt it delivers.

You already know this.

It's why former NSA employee Edward Snowden ended up the focus of an international chase culminating in his exile in Moscow. After leaking thousands of top-secret U.S. Department of Defense documents to the public, he earned equal parts praise and infamy. Snowden's brave (or reckless, depending on your perspective) actions set off an explosive chain reaction of media, legislative, and law-enforcement scrutiny. Regardless if you are persuaded by his profession of benevolent motivation, it's hard to argue with the incredible amount of energy evident in the secrets he exposed.[1] Secret-keeping and secret-telling are so potent they

---

1 - The documentary *Citizenfour* by Laura Poitras chronicles a fascinating conversation between Snowden and reporter Glenn Greenwald that took place in a sequestered hotel room in Hong Kong. A related piece is James Bradford's 2014 article in Wired magazine, "The Most Wanted Man in the World."

can alter entire civilizations.

The truth of this axiom is illustrated in the business world, where trade secrets are vociferously protected to maintain competitive edges. Whether the hidden information is a recipe, chemical formula, engineering design, or line of code, it can represent the very survival of corporations or even economies. Companies spend untold millions of dollars and human hours each year to protect their exclusive knowledge, processes, and skills. They do it because of the great power latent within secret information.

I learned the concept first hand as a teenager one summer while working at my grandfather's antique auction house. He was a shrewd businessman (some of his contemporaries might insist that "unscrupulous" is a better adjective). One of my grandfather's particular talents was remembering exactly what he had paid for each and every one of his hundreds of thousands of items for sale. It didn't matter that his "junk" emporium was packed floor-to-ceiling with merchandise. Each and every box we'd open in preparation for the auction floor would be accompanied by a story about how it had been acquired and at what price.

These financial secrets (as you might expect) were only shared behind closed doors. As with most business dealings, the exact figures are ammunition for battle. Dozens of times as an auction hand, I'd bring items up for sale which supposedly had "no reserve price." And dozens of times, they'd mysteriously sell to "number 32", or "99", or "12", none of which ever corresponded to actual buyers in the audience. Nevertheless, when any of these "bidders" purchased an item, I had been instructed not to carry it immediately to the winning customer as was our policy, but instead to a special room in the back. 32, 99, 12, and so on were my grandfather's own numbers! Deviously, he leveraged his secret knowledge to always guarantee a profit.

Information is powerful. Secret information is even more powerful.

Secret information isn't all bad, however. In fact, this chapter is about how some secret knowledge can launch people forward into becoming the beings they were born to be. We frequently call it "wisdom."

In a 2014 TED Talk titled "Our Loss of Wisdom," Psychologist Barry Schwartz spoke about this familiar and yet slippery concept. He described wisdom as appropriately applied knowledge. "A wise person knows how and when to bend the rules, how to improvise, how to adjust to varying contexts...," he said, "...[they] operate not by rote adherence to rigid standards, but by deeper convictions, principles, experiences, and knowledge." Wisdom is simultaneously obvious and obscure, practical and puzzling.

The book of Proverbs in the Christian scriptures describes how humans come to attain this secret knowledge. The author personifies it as a woman benevolently calling out guidance in public from the street[2] corner. In another breath, the author also describes wisdom as something one must intentionally pursue as a miner in search of valuable minerals[3]. Complicating the concept further, the author additionally presents wisdom as a quality that emerges naturally through life, experienced like blooming flowers in a well-tended garden.[4] How elusive! Wisdom is at once: only attainable by deliberate seeking, naturally growing in its own time, and yet teachable as if from a street-corner prophet.

This chapter focuses on that third manner of acquisition, from teacher to learner. When imparted from one person to another, the factors that determine wisdom's helpfulness or harm are

---

2 - Proverbs 1:21-24

3 - Proverbs 2:1-5

4 - Proverbs 3:1-4

twofold. Bestowed with (a) benevolent motive and (b) good timing, wisdom can unquestionably transform lives[5], launching people forward. But when the reason for sharing such secret information is checkered with selfishness or cruelty, or when it is revealed too soon (or too late), the result is stunted growth and even permanent harm.

Let's first look briefly at the variable of motive.

During my undergraduate years in college, I took an introductory course in philosophy from a professor who became notorious on campus for his pedantic teaching style and ruthless grading. I remember the first day of class when he trumpeted how one-third of all prior pupils had failed the course. The smirk on his face told my classmates and me that he wore this fact as a badge of honor, not a sign of inadequate instruction.

"Half of you have no business being here," he crowed as he dumped a stack of pre-filled university drop slips on his desk, "don't waste my time or yours."

Over the next several weeks, the professor "taught" the remaining students with every intent to confuse and humiliate them. His intelligence was beyond question; probably the smartest person I had ever met to that point. Yet clearly, in my professor's mind, possessing knowledge or even wisdom wasn't about gifting it beneficently to the next generation (as one might expect would be the calling of an educator). Instead, it was ostensibly for increasing his sense of superiority. He didn't use his "secret wisdom" on the subject of philosophy to bless and equip his students. Rather, my professor hoarded it like a miserly broker. Because of his narcissistic motivation, any wisdom imparted came poisoned with shame.

---

5 - The Brazilian novelist and poet Paulo Coelho takes it a step further saying, "Knowledge without transformation is not wisdom."

My memory can't help but call up the contrasting picture of a different college professor that I'll likewise never forget. Instead of philosophy, the subject was research writing. And instead of bleeding self-importance, my writing professor oozed empathy. I remember how he began class sessions with "check-ins," reviewing students' progress and feelings about the material. If he had been moving too quickly or too obscurely in presenting new knowledge, he'd slow down and retrofit his plans to accommodate their needs.

I learned many bits of wisdom from that course, some of which I still tap into today. One of this professor's golden proverbs sticks in my mind, "The truth told with bad intent beats all the lies you can invent[6]."

Motive matters, especially when it comes to sharing or receiving secret knowledge. Information may be the truth, but if its telling is driven by selfishness, egotism, or fear, the outcome of exposure is more likely to be atrophy than maturity.

Now we'll momentarily visit the second variable affecting the helpfulness of shared secret knowledge: timing.

My Dad often says, "the right thing and the wrong time is the wrong thing." It's an axiom I return to again and again when facing important decisions. The principle also applies to the giving or receiving of secret knowledge. Not all information is helpful for every person at every time. Teachers and guides must be careful to meter their wisdom out to the right people, at the right moments, in the right quantities.

I experienced the dark side of this principle when I lost my brother. As I described in chapter four, my community of faith enthusiastically showed up to support me during my time of grief,

---

6 - I've since learned that this line was originally penned by the 18th century English poet and theologian, William Blake.

and early on, some inflicted additional injury that compounded my suffering. On more than one occasion in the aftermath of the house fire, well-wishers approached me sharing their treasured wisdom.

"He's doesn't have to suffer anymore."

"You'll grow from this and become a better person."

"Everything happens for a reason."

I have no doubt that my friends and family were motivated by kindness and empathy. Sometimes their shared wisdom was true. Some of it was even beautiful! But the most helpful moment for expressing it wasn't when the embers of my childhood home still smoldered.

No matter how sublime the axiom, none of us can hear its wisdom if the timing is off. Far from being blessed by unveiled knowledge, such sharing at inappropriate moments is more likely to harm. In my case, it felt cruel and underscored isolation.

Even Jesus, the master teacher, lived by the principle of "the right thing at the wrong time is the wrong thing." As an instructor, He wasn't overly concerned that everyone understands everything at every moment. He was patient. He moved slowly. He knew that time is the difference between transmitting information and facilitating transformation.

The four Gospels[7] repeatedly record Jesus saying, "those with ears to hear, let them hear[8]." Most of the time, he drops it after an ambiguous parable or provocative maxim as if to say, "If you're able to understand this and incorporate it into your life, LISTEN

---

7 - The four biographies of his life, Matthew, Mark, Luke, and John.

8 - E.g. Matthew 11:15

UP! And if not, file it away for later use. You'll be ready soon enough." In another place[9], Jesus complains to his most advanced students, "I have many more things to tell you, but you're not able to grasp them right now...". Isn't that a remarkable statement?! Even his closest disciples (some of whom went on to write the books and letters now known as the Bible) weren't always ready to absorb everything.

So after acknowledging these two cautions, where does that leave us?

Giving and receiving hidden knowledge is part of what makes us human. It's truly an awesome gift. You have much to share, and you also have much yet to discover. We all do. Whether your expertise or curiosity is in the science of communication, the spirituality of generosity, healthy eating, or ethical investing, you are both a learner and a teacher of wisdom. In his spiritual classic, *The Road Not Taken*, Scott Peck writes how "withholding truth[10]" at the wrong time and in the wrong way is universally damaging to maturity.

The remainder of this chapter aims first to equip you as a student; that you can better protect yourself from injury at the hands of unscrupulous brokers of wisdom. Second, it seeks to prepare you as a teacher; that as a caretaker of wisdom, you can share your secret knowledge morally, bringing the most good.

———

All my life, I've been a part of the Seventh-day Adventist spiritual tribe[11]. Until just recently, I worked full time as an Adventist

---

9 - John 16:12

10 - In his words

11 - It's now both a Christian denomination and multi-national corporation with tens of thousands of employees and more than 20 million members.

pastor. Like almost every religious or fraternal community, Adventism has a distinct subculture that brings beauty and good but also annoyances and dysfunctions. And also, like many such communities, Adventism is a custodian of secret wisdom.

One day early on in my career, I found myself on assignment careening through the streets of London in the backseat of a cab. I had inexplicably been invited to present on youth ministry at a church conference[12] for pastors and lay leaders. Accompanying me in the car was another speaker at the event; he was a well-known world leader in the church. As we chit-chatted, the subject turned to the Adventist belief system[13].

"Any Adventist pastor who doesn't support every iota of voted dogma shouldn't be collecting a salary," he confidently announced at one point in our conversation.

As a young pastor, I had already been casually intimidated by our dialogue. But upon hearing this condemnation, my feelings turned to fear. "Could he have said it because he suspects me of being a traitor[14]?" I thought.

For my leader friend, our church exists only because of our differences with other religions, denominations, etc. To him, Adventists are here because of our unique set of secret wisdom.

---

12 - Looking back, I feel a little sheepish about accepting the invitation given that at the time, I had little in the way of expertise on the subject.

13 - At present, the Adventist Church claims 28 "Fundamental Beliefs" but local cultures and working policy extend organizational influence.

14 - I believe that the Seventh-day Adventist Christian church brings some wonderful gifts into the world. And it has also been responsible for horrifying wrongs. I am faithful by refusing to subscribe to every misguided jot and tittle voted into policy over the church's 150 year history. In fact, I think there are official stances that need to change in order for the church to achieve its calling (e.g., ordination of women and the full inclusion of LGBTQ people, just to name two).

It's the source of our identity and the reason for our mission. "We have The Truth[15]," my London car-mate might say, "and we must share it with the world." Because of these assumptions, the thought that a fellow clergy member might espouse nuanced versions of that source of meaning was anathema.

To be honest, there is a part of me that agrees. Every spiritual community, fraternal order, organization, business, or social system is formed around a particular set of hidden knowledge. You are probably a part of some, and in the future, you will likely join others. Giving and receiving secret wisdom is what we as humans do, remember? Each of us has been entrusted with this gold to steward and share. But as we've already observed, information leveraged in immoral ways can cause injury. So how do we equip ourselves as discerning students of wisdom? To draw out this lesson, I want to take you back in time to the origins of my spiritual family.

The Seventh-day Adventist Church grew out of the second great awaking, a 19th-century protestant[16] revival movement in the U.S. that emphasized cultural and religious reform. One particular thread of that awakening was led by an itinerant preacher named William Miller. A self-taught theologian and businessman, Miller preached authoritatively that Jesus Christ would return to earth in person in 1844.[17] "Millerism" caught fire and became a national movement as hundreds of additional preachers joined the chorus and scattered their message across the country. New converts

---

15 - Yes, "capital T" Truth. In my circle, Truth with a capital "T" refers to always-and-forever, a priori truth for all people in all places. This is in contrast to the notion behind truth (small "t"), which is the more subjective variety, temporal, and not applicable to all people in all times.

16 - Especially Presbyterian, Methodist and Baptist.

17 - The group's eschatological (end-of-time) prediction would eventually be pinpointed to October 22, 1844, a day that later became known as "the Great Disappointment".

believed William Miller's interpretations of Daniel and Revelation so thoroughly that many severed ties with their previous spiritual communities to join his movement, and some even left their own families!

One of my colleagues wrote about these fervent proto-Adventists in his book, *The Green Cord Dream*. He generously suggests that they took such extreme actions because of their great excitement and love for the person of Jesus. I think this is true. Adventists are serious about their devotion to Jesus — even still allowing His teachings to disrupt their lives in surprising and beautiful ways. With that being said, I also think that additional motives may have been afoot in the Millerite enthusiasm to share the message.

Daniel 12:4 reads, "But you, Daniel, keep this prophecy a secret; seal up the book until the time of the end, when many will rush here and there, and knowledge will increase." This Old Testament Bible text became a rallying cry for Millerites. They believed they were living in the end times. They believed that their discoveries in Biblical prophecy were no accident. In short, Millerites saw themselves as a people entrusted with secret wisdom and a mission to share it.

Again, this is natural. And it's beautiful. We all want this for ourselves. And we all have it. Everything doesn't come to everybody[18]. Each person has the opportunity of acting as a custodian of secret wisdom. You have contributions to make for the good of us all! It's no accident that early Adventists made the discoveries that they did — and it's no accident that you have as well. We have all been entrusted with secret wisdom, and it must be shared.

Now, for the sake of this conversation on secret knowledge, let's

---

18 - As my friend and editor Samir Selmanovic taught me during the process of bringing this book to life.

pretend[19] that the Millerites were correct in their calculations. What would be the moral prerogative for a custodian of such vital information? Not unlike [20]*The Avengers*' Tony Stark in the classic superhero conundrum, Millerites were faced with the question of how to apply great power, i.e., wisdom. They could jump in the Iron Man suit and save the world (i.e., share the good news) or use it instead for their own benefit. As we already know, sharing is just what the Millerites did...with one caveat.

Again pretending that Millerites were correct in their predictions, some of their preachers lost track along the way[21] of their identities as stewards of wisdom and began employing it as a tool of persuasion for joining the fervor. Instead of sharing their convictions regarding Jesus' soon coming with no-strings-attached, evangelists packaged their wisdom in a matrix of interrelated theological axioms[22]. These would be baked together as a single dish and presented as though it must be swallowed in a single gulp or not at all. Students were led to believe, for example, that in order to accept the (albeit incorrect) interpretation regarding Jesus' October 22, 1844 second coming, they had to leave their existing spiritual tribes, sometimes their families, and adopt a whole new lifestyle. To say it uncharitably: some Millerites exploited their secret wisdom as a manipulation chip in a membership drive.

---

19 - October 22, 1844 did in fact come and go without the appearing of Jesus in the clouds of glory. So it stands to reason that someone was wrong about something!

20 - Please permit me a playful analogy.

21 - Check out George Knight's material on the development of Adventist theology if you're curious to read more on the history.

22 - Some of which would be recognized as standard-fare Christianity: atonement by faith in Jesus, baptism as a sign of commitment, a life of holiness, etc. Other aspects of this new way of being Christian were a little more peculiar: Sabbath keeping, healthy eating, non-violence, denial of belief in hell, etc.

Uff da.

Today, I believe that my church is a caretaker of secret wisdom[23]. I wouldn't characterize it in the same way as my London car-mate, but I think there is profound truth and beauty in my faith system. Some of that wisdom has been inherited from our spiritual ancestors, the Millerites, to whom I am grateful. But as it turns out, they have also passed down some dysfunctional cultural DNA[24] that still lurks around in shadowed corners of the Adventist Church today.

One inherited pattern I have observed among some of my pastoral colleagues, now ministering 170 years later, is the habit of making all-or-nothing proposals to would-be acolytes. Instead of humbly approaching learners as individuals who possess their own sets of secret wisdom (and who almost certainly have something to teach us!), some of my colleagues relate to them as a pushy car-salesperson might to a customer. On occasion, I've witnessed Adventist pastors misuse what could be an unspeakable gift in the service of manipulating people to become members of the church. The secret wisdom is shared, but only on their terms.

In these broken behaviors, the proposition is total assimilation in exchange for secret wisdom or nothing at all. "Take it or leave it! Sign the paper! Make the commitment! Become one of us, and we'll let you in on the benefits of our wisdom. (But reject any

---

23 - For example, I deeply respect my community's teachings on the practice of Sabbath-keeping, the non-existence of hell, theodicy, and healthy living.

24 - For example, as an Adventist pastor, I frequently interact with denominational members who's sense of possessing "secret truth" bleeds over into many quadrants of life. Besides being convinced that they possess unique and secret Biblical wisdom, many Adventists are also taken by popular conspiracy theories of the day. These of course carry a similar feeling of having unique access to an unseen reality.

detail[25], and you'll be kissing your salvation goodbye.)."

I find this misuse of power to be perverse. The collateral damage it causes is immense. Some victims understandably become permanently inoculated to what could've been life-giving wisdom. Secret knowledge is for the good of all, not an individual nor organization[26].

Now, while I find this dynamic particularly maddening when I see it within my own spiritual clan, it is by no means unique to Adventism (or even Christianity). As we've already observed, religious systems like Adventism aren't the only curators of secret wisdom. Narcissistic college professors, hard-pushing merchants, conspiracy theorists, and fake news philanderers each can peddle niblets of truth manipulatively. From alcoholic-turned-vegan-athlete-gurus[27] to attachment-parenting extraordinaires, many segments of the population are unscrupulous in utilizing their particular insights for their own advantage. In many ways, mythologies promulgated through culture as wisdom is what maintains unequal power structures. And in the case of religious

---

25 - Rob Bell writes masterfully about this concept in his book, *Velvet Elvis*, where he draws out the metaphor of a brick wall to explain a common way of holding faith. To those who think of their religion in this way, every piece must be precisely in place, or whole belief system is liable to collapse.

26 - One alternative method is something one of my pastor friends has dubbed "open-source-faith", borrowing from software developers. In this approach, pastors open-handedly ask how they might bless a person with secret wisdom (which may include not speaking at all!), and setting them free to make the world better on their own terms. Such "students" may choose to become part of the spiritual tribe, but they may also spin off and create their own or join others. The wisdom is free to take and build upon without any required system of membership.

27 - If you haven't yet seen the hilarious parody of this dynamic called "The Ultra Spiritual Life," it's worth a look. JP Sears takes on the whole gamut of postmodern spiritual awakenings with devastating sharpness. See www.awakenwithjp.com.

sects like Scientology or the FLDS[28], some even intentionally withhold certain aspects of secret wisdom in order to discourage converts from emptying the pews. Concealing organizational secrets until new subscribers are emotionally, financially, and personally invested is an effective strategy cults use to build inertia against "apostasy."

But besides making us angry, we can also receive these case studies as warnings. You don't have to be manipulated by the misuse of secret knowledge. You have the power to cut off exploiters of wisdom, to vote with your feet, and to quit rewarding them with your money or attention. Each of us are students of secret wisdom. The question is about how we protect ourselves.

I remember one of my students several years ago, who went through a long process of choosing to follow Jesus[29] for himself. Although "Dan"[30] had been raised amongst Christian culture, it wasn't until he was nearly 18 that he seriously considered adopting the worldview for himself. Each week as we got together to talk over coffee or on walks, our agenda set itself organically. Dan asked questions in response to things he had read, emotions of the week, or the religious culture of his family of origin. Sometimes I brought up issues that I considered important and appropriate to his state of growth. Little by little, I witnessed Dan grow in his enthusiasm for the Way of Jesus, eventually making a lifetime commitment.

Now, over the course of our conversations, there were times I responded with concrete answers to Dan's probing. In fact,

---

28 - Jon Krakauer's *Under the Banner of Heaven* is an insightful exploration of the Fundamentalist Church of Jesus Christ of Latter Day Saints (FLDS).

29 - Please permit me one last illustration from my spiritual tribe.

30 - Again, I have changed the name and details surrounding this story.

sometimes my explanations were far more concrete than I actually believed myself! Other times, when I considered the starkest answer to be likely disorienting, I smoothed my response, knowing that it may need revision down the road. In a few cases, I admitted my ignorance on a subject and later found myself researching in preparation for the next meetup.

Here's the thing, had I stewarded my secret wisdom unscrupulously or carelessly with Dan, his process of growth would have been short-circuited. Whether imploring him to "take it or leave it" after dumping it all on him at once or veiling the truth too much by evading direct responses, I was faced with countless opportunities as a mentor to interrupt his development.

Not to toot my own horn, but that's what moral teachers do for us. They aren't motivated by membership drives or particular outcomes — they seek the good of their students. And sometimes, that means slowing down. Other times that means speeding up. If you have a guru[31] in your life who is moving super fast, snowballing your sense of context, beware! If you are being pressured to make decisions NOW, someone might be gaslighting you. If your guru is stalling, it might be that they have not themselves gone where you need to go! If it seems like your spiritual teacher is getting something in return from your acceptance or conversion, they probably are.

Christian missiologist and theologian Richard Peace writes about these dynamics in his book about conversion in the New Testament. "Insight drives conversion," he says, "Without insight, there literally cannot be conversion." Peace goes on to describe how the structure of the Gospel of Mark highlights conversion at its best is a gradual unveiling and integration of secret wisdom. Mark's biography of Jesus focuses on six successive aspects of Jesus' nature as it marches through the story toward his death. As His disciples come to accept these secret characteristics, they

---

31 - Whether in finance, religion, health, sports, parenting, politics, etc.

steadily approach the point of conversion. Along the way, Mark reports Jesus instructing acolytes, "don't tell anyone about what you have seen or heard or experienced, keep it secret!" His goal is progressive disclosure of insights, a steady march from darkness to light.

Slow and measured absorption of secret wisdom is very often the path of spiritual maturity. Not a trickle - but not a firehose either. This implies that down the road, each of us will need to revisit explanations for clarification or revision. If we continue growing, we will find ourselves in a continual spiral of enchantment, disillusionment, and re-enchantment. This doesn't mean that what we once received as truth was false or that past teachers were unscrupulous. It was the right thing at the right time, and in time, we will be ready to receive deeper and more nuanced insights, continuing the spiral. Just because you've advanced past a former teacher doesn't mean they were wrong. It doesn't mean they were out to get you. It simply demonstrates the nature of spiritual growth. Fully developed people integrate their past experiences and beliefs into their worldviews, not jump back and forth between entirely different tracks.

As it turns out, that is something like what we've seen in the Adventist denomination. Its beginnings were characterized by a progressive march of doctrinal evolution—this value embedded itself in the cultural DNA of the tribe[32]. Rabble rousers like myself continually press for broader and truer expressions of faith; agitators like me do so with full hearts because we know the secret of progressive truth.

————

Finally, let's turn our attention to caretakers of secret wisdom.

————

32 - Adventists sometimes talk about "Progressive Truth", acknowledging the dynamic of unveiling secret wisdom. The church's statement of beliefs begins with a preamble embracing this concept: "...we expect God to show up and grow our understanding of truth...".

If each of us has been entrusted with life-giving and even transformative truth (and I believe we have), then we are faced with at least two paths. You can act as a stingy broker, metering out your secrets for personal gain. Or, you can act as a curator, carefully guiding students in making their own discoveries. One track is insecure and agitated, and the other is calm and measured. It takes intentionality and practice to discern which path we're on. In fact, I've found that secret knowledge is more commonly mismanaged by good intentions than corruption.

My home town of Walla Walla is a small sleepy community in Southeastern Washington State. Within this sheltered enclave, Seventh-day Adventists form their own distinct subculture[33]. This is no accident. Many Adventists maintain a tight community as a means of encouraging their values (as I've already indicated, the Adventist worldview is integrated: we believe every part of life to be interconnected[34]). Even though it can be effective, it's certainly a sword that cuts both ways.

Many children have grown up in Seventh-day Adventist families (in Walla Walla or other similar confines) face challenges later in life integrating with the wider world. When I worked as a family pastor in my hometown, I routinely interacted with kids and teens who'd nary been exposed to pop-culture entertainment, adult behaviors like drinking alcohol or sex, or divergent worldviews to their own. Because I was a pastor on the campus of an Adventist

---

33 - As it turns out, Walla Walla county has more Seventh-day Adventists per capita than any other county in the United States (a greater proportion than even the famous Blue Zone in Southern California where I now live).

34 - Adventists tend to be health conscious, fiscally conservative, simple in lifestyle, eschew alcohol and drugs, dress modestly, spend money sparingly, live simply, avoid many expressions of popular entertainment, care for one another attentively, and 'rest' Jewish-style from work collectively as a community each week from Friday night to Saturday night. In part to ensure these (among other) values are passed on to future generations, Adventists have developed nearly the largest parochial school system on the planet (second in size and scope only to the Catholic Church).

college, I also worked with young adults who themselves were once sheltered children just like my primary flock. It was not uncommon to witness some students' lives explode as they enthusiastically explored formerly denied taboos. Smitten by new experiences, sometimes these individuals even became convinced that the worldviews of their youths had been entirely bankrupt[35].

Withholding secret wisdom too long (even with benevolent motivation) can work against spiritual growth. It's true regardless of the topic being impeded: from emotions to human origins, pop-culture to science, prayer to people-pleasing. Scott Peck describes it well in his spiritual classic, The Road Less Taken. Withholding truth (as he dubs concealing secret wisdom) at the wrong time and in the wrong way is universally damaging to maturity.

Now, let's slash the other way with the same sword and briefly discuss premature exposure. Writing in the early 1980s, author Mary Winn was already observing a shift in what American culture considers normal for adult-child relationships. She suggests that we had evolved from a protection model to a preparatory model as we relate to kids, orienting their entire lives around soon-dawning adulthood instead of nurturing the joys of present childhood. Winn advocated for a prolonged and safeguarded childhood more full of innocence and wonder. In her mind, the matters of the adult world pose serious dangers for kids when exposed too early.

Many parents (and certainly not just Adventist parents) rightly see it as their duty to protect their children from premature exposure to the adult world. We know that if children are exposed to violence, explicit sexuality, or even certain foods or drinks at

---

35 - I am one who believes that there are times in which stepping away from a spiritual tribe for a time can represent a step forward toward God. When this happens in a productive manner, the person maintains a sense of gratitude, perspective, and kindness toward the community of their past. Unproductive severing yields uncharitable storytelling and overblown characterizations of faith.

young ages, they can be permanently damaged or stunted in their future growth. This is verified not only by common sense but by a great deal of scientific research[36]. For example, several studies have indicated that (especially if left untreated) childhood victimization of sexual abuse correlates with higher instances of medical problems, addictions, re-victimization of sexual or domestic violence, risky sexual behavior, and psychological disorders in adulthood.

Overzealous sheltering of the truth is unhelpful. But so is irresponsible exposé. The right thing at the wrong time is the wrong thing.

So how do we, as custodians of secret knowledge, share it responsibly? One solution to the conundrum is illustrated by the tradition practiced by certain Amish sects known as Rumspringa, loosely translated "running around." The film *Devil's Playground* provides an engaging window into the diverse practice, which sometimes allows formerly sheltered teenagers uninhibited samples of the real world. After several days of absolute freedom to taste taboos, teens must choose between permanent banishment from their communities or baptism and lifelong fidelity to the Amish way. Interestingly enough, after participating in the rite of passage, many kids return home for good.[37]

While some of us might regard a practice like this as practical ("If it ain't broke, don't fix it!"), others like me consider it a little reckless. If incoherent exposure to secret knowledge is damaging (and I believe it is), then applying the principle of Rumspringa to our roles as teachers of wisdom would be irresponsibly throwing caution to the wind.

---

36 - See two articles cited from the National Institute of Health in the "resources" section for this chapter.

37 - Some sources suggest the rate of return is as high as 90%.

Returning once more to the master teacher, Jesus warns His teachers-in-training with an analogy: "Don't give what is sacred to dogs. Don't throw your pearls to the pigs[38]." In the context of Jewish culture that considered anything associated with swine to be deeply unclean or even offensive, the picture is stark. The wisdom we possess is powerful, and it's also beautiful and valuable. Don't waste it by sharing it at the wrong time in the wrong way. In the famous phrase, He implies, "If you cram your wisdom down the throat of someone who isn't able to appreciate it. They'll probably choke!"

As keepers of secret wisdom, we must learn to be at peace with the fact that not everything is useful for every person at every moment. The more we can accept this reality, the more patient we will be as teachers. I know that for me as a student, I'm profoundly grateful for the forbearing but yet persistent instructors of my past who calmly pieced out their truth to me over time. Heaven knows that God himself is patient in his revelations to humanity. My friend Samir[39] once quipped that God takes a thousand years and a thousand angels to deliver his messages. If the creator of the universe waits for the right time, maybe I should try it as well.

––––––––

Let me paint a picture from my work of what I consider to be an example of good stewardship. "Wildfire" is a rite of passage weekend experience for young men[40] I developed some years ago with a team of colleagues and church ministry leaders. We first

––––––––

38 - Matthew 7:6

39 - Samir Selmanovíc also helped me with the developmental edit of this book.

40 - My team also created a similar experience for young women.

created it to address the vacuum[41] of initiation processes[42] for adolescents transitioning into adulthood. Over the course of a Wildfire retreat, my team of dedicated adult men would carefully pull back the curtain on a number of secrets of the adult world, leveraging them to help younger men grow.

Rites of passage are ubiquitous across many cultures, present and past. They typically mark significant changes in life: birth, adolescence, marriage, leadership roles, eldership, death, etc. Initiations often legitimize a person's new status within a community, pronouncing the change through a set of rituals. Anthropologist Arnold Van Gennep (who pioneered the study of these kinds of experiences) writes, "The life of an individual in any society is a series of passages from one age to another and from one occupation to another. Wherever there are fine distinctions among age or occupational groups, progression from one group to the next is accompanied by special acts."

A key aspect of initiation traditions is the process of unveiling previously hidden knowledge to the apprentice. What had been withheld for his or her own good is now made known through

---

41 - American culture has lost or abandoned virtually all formal initiation processes for young people. Instead, Americans have tended to adopt a nebulous and ill-defined cloud of markers for maturity: driver's tests, voting or alcohol purchasing rights, sexual experience, graduations, amassment of wealth or power, marriage, gang or fraternal memberships, or even baptism have served as pseudo-initiations in the vacuum. While some of these are certainly rites of passage, none of them directly pertain to the process of maturing through adolescence into virtuous adulthood. In a real sense, we in American culture have stepped back and asked teenagers themselves to show their peers the way into the secret wisdom of the adult world. Of course, this is an incoherent task at best, and abusive at worst. According to Chap Clark, professor and chair of the Youth, Family, and Culture Department at Fuller Theological Seminary, this dynamic is one of many signs of what he calls the systematic abandonment of our youth.

42 - For an excellent read on male initiation, I recommend Richard Rohr's book *Adam's Return*.

ritual. Historically, rites of passage have tended to coalesce around three phases: separation from the community, a psychological or physical descent or trial (sometimes but not always painful), and a reincorporation back into the community. As you might imagine or have experienced yourself, it can be frightening to embark on such a journey of discovery. Whether informal, formal, or accidental, the secrets of initiation are only available to those courageous enough to leave home. Learners depart with one social status and return with a new standing.

As generation after generation of American children initiates themselves[43] into the adult world, our cultural confusion about maturity and virtue only compounds. As the blindfolded lead the blindfolded, so to speak, we can't help but get off track. The secret wisdom that ought to have been nurtured and passed down has been squandered, misused, or abandoned entirely. My team and I created Wildfire in order to take greater responsibility for appropriately stewarding the secret wisdom we had ourselves received.

Over the years of Wildfire, I witnessed dozens of young men sitting face to face with older men, who pulled back the curtain on the secrets of mature masculinity. Some of what the initiates took in on the weekend retreat was familiar – signaling appropriate prior exposure to the adult world. Other items were brand new, surprising, and even jarring. The presence of the adult community[44] kept the environment safe and calm, with questions being addressed along the way. In a thorough, metered, and conscious manner, Wildfire leaders equipped initiates for some of the challenges they would face once home. And when they did return, the community at large could see they had changed. Secret wisdom, stewarded well, transforms our lives.

---

43 - Again, check out Chap Clark's research on this.

44 - Wildfire retreats endeavored to establish a 1:1 ratio of young men to old men for this reason.

But even at Wildfire, not everything was revealed. Life itself is an initiation. And as we've seen, sometimes keeping secrets is counterintuitively helpful to growth.

Every person is a keeper of secret wisdom, whether by education, age, gender, life experience, wealth, or expertise. As such, you are a steward, teacher, or mentor. Whether you accept it or not, you have a responsibility to both share and withhold your secret wisdom with beneficence and great care. Hoarding it in arrogance, hiding it in fear, or flippantly spilling it turns it into a destructive force instead of a powerful tool for good.

———————

One of my favorite portrayals of a measured transmission of secret wisdom between mentor and student is found in the science-fiction film *The Empire Strikes Back*. Yoda, a master warrior, teaches Luke the ways of the Force, a mysterious metaphysical-spiritual power that could be used for good or evil. Luke, the series' hero, seeks out Yoda on the planet Dagobah where he asks him to train him to be a Jedi.

The very setting for Luke's teaching sequence communicates Yoda's vast secret wisdom. Dagobah is a misty swamp planet with little light and caves and dark shadows around every corner. Throughout the sequence, Yoda is portrayed as shrouding his identity, the powers of the force, and his own proficiency. He very slowly and progressively opens the doors to what is concealed to Luke. As Luke demonstrates increasing maturity, aptitude, and mastery of the concepts Yoda has taught, he reveals more and more.

At more than one point, Luke is frustrated with the speed at which he's allowed in on the secrets of the Force. He demands to know more – and to know it more quickly. Yet Yoda's stalwart replies as he carefully stewards his wisdom are consistent and firm,

"Nothing more will I teach you today."

In the end, Luke himself becomes a Jedi master and eventually goes on to overcome the evil empire. The shrouding and transmission of secret wisdom in a responsible way brings unprecedented good to the universe.

Secret wisdom is power. May you steward it well.

QUESTIONS FOR DISCUSSION:

1. Do you have a secret family recipe or a secret tradition that is held in confidence by "your people"? What does it feel like to hold that information? What has it felt like to share it (if you've had the chance to pass it on)?

2. Describe a time in your life when wisdom showed up at just the right moment. What was it like to receive that information? Talk about what you have done with it since.

3. The author quoted his father in this chapter, "The Right Thing at the Wrong Time is the Wrong Thing." Do you agree with this axiom? Why or why not? What are the limits of this bit of wisdom?

4. Have you ever been manipulated by the unscrupulous use of secret knowledge or wisdom? What did you learn from that experience?

5. Do you consider yourself to be a keeper of secret wisdom? Why or why not? Discuss whether or not, or in what ways, you consider yourself to be initiated into adulthood.

6 | SECRETS FROM OURSELVES

*"Only when we are brave enough
to explore the darkness will we discover
the infinite power of our light."*

-Brene Brown

One of the top ten movies of all time on imdb.com is there for a reason. If it weren't for the fact that it was released in 1999, a spoiler alert might be in order. David Fincher's *Fight Club* is not only an iconic cult classic, but it also perfectly illustrates a slippery sort of secret-keeping that we've all experienced, self-deception or repression.

A quick plot synopsis goes something like this. An unnamed city-dwelling and mild-mannered insomniac creates an adventurous new life for himself after meeting a happy-go-lucky soap maker named Tyler Durden. The protagonist's life spirals out of control as the pair's fight club devolves into a fellowship of mayhem plotting violence against corporate America.

The grand twist that captivated audiences is the revelation that Tyler Durden is not a second character at all. Instead, the pair of hooligans prove to be two fragments of a single man's personality. Tyler Durden suffers from a form of dissociative

149

identity disorder[1], a self-discovery that both he and the audience make concurrently in the closing scenes of the film. The climax of Fight Club allegorizes well some of the consequences of our most deeply repressed thoughts, feelings, and beliefs. The war within ourselves can sometimes lead to death.

Most people don't suffer the kind of rare psychosis that plagued Tyler Durden. However, every single one of us has things hidden in the basements of our souls that we may not even know are there. Carl Jung called these secrets "the shadow." But many humans have described and experienced them under other names. We all have pieces of ourselves that we deny, repress, or hide, even from our own consciousness!

In this chapter, we will peer down the stairs[2] into the experience of keeping secrets from ourselves.

––––––––––

One of the first times I realized I was keeping secrets from myself was in my therapist's[3] office shortly before my first son's birth.

––––––––––––

1 - A condition formerly known as Multiple Personality Disorder in which a person is controlled by at least two distinct personality states. A form of amnesia accompanies the disorder which renders each separate personality unaware of the others. It is incredibly difficult to diagnose as well as to treat.

2 - My father's book on this very topic captures this imagery well. Titled *The Unexplored Room*, it conjures the feeling of spelunking a basement room that we've never dared to enter. The room is in our souls. And the journey is a spiritual one.

3 - The first time I visited a mental health professional was at the age of about 23. I sought help to change unwanted behavior patterns. What I discovered is that habits are defined by a sea of hidden motivators. During the years since, I have been blessed by a fairly wide array of mental health practitioners who have reached helped me with different facets of my emotional and unconscious self. I highly recommend every person to see a therapist or psychologist at least a few times in their life - if not on a regular basis! These professionals are unspeakable gifts to humanity.

After complaining to her about my frustration with flying off the handle in anger over insignificant provocations[4], she asked me for an example. (If you're reading footnotes, you'll naturally guess that I had a portfolio of stories to choose from.) Embarrassingly, the stuff that winds my clock the most is, on the surface, inconsequential at best.

Sitting in her office, my mind immediately went to a story about installing floorboard molding in my Walla Walla home. I explained how, as an amateur craftsman, I only vaguely knew what I was doing. Yet internally, I fancied myself as an HGTV house-flipping star, expecting perfection. Unfortunately, I wound up more closely resembling Bruce Banner transforming into the Incredible Hulk than Chip & Joanna Gaines transforming living rooms. After mis-cutting the same board for the third time that day, I snapped. Cussing and raving, I broke the molding into pieces on the garage floor and tossed my miter saw down the driveway, where it tumbled into the gutter. My neighbors might've concluded that my home was under attack based on the intensity of my outburst!

I didn't know it at the time, but I later realized that somewhere along my life journey, I had come to equate competence[5] with self-worth. My emotional self believed that life itself depended on me cutting that blasted board correctly!

Having grown up in a religious culture marked by guilt and shame,

---

4 - I think of the time I accidentally pinched myself with a set of kitchen tongs, and I flung them across the room as punishment, leaving the sheetrock with a dent. There was also the time when, late for an appointment, I dislocated my finger slamming the door in a huff. And how could I possibly forget the time when I slung the lawnmower across the lawn, hammer-throw style, after it bogged down in wet grass and refused to restart?!?!

I could go on, but I must preserve some dignity!

5 - Especially competence in tasks often identified in American culture as being essentially masculine, but that's another story!

it took me many years to begin facing up to these emotions, to the harm they caused, and to the driving forces behind them. I wasn't proud of the pain my overzealous intensity had inflicted on people (or appliances). I also intuitively believed that something deeper had to have been going on. But (especially) in the moment of the tirade, I felt powerless to understand why it was happening!

So I started to poke around in my spiritual basement, opening doors and shining a flashlight in dark corners.

Along with therapists[6], I began to discover that my rage was connected to a number of secrets hidden from my conscious awareness, many of which were stored (and still activated) in old memories. Instead of judging myself as an incorrigible rage-a-holic, I grew to have self-empathy by discovering that past wounds were triggering average situations with incredibly intense old emotions. In fact, one of the aspects I came to understand about myself was that I had been suffering from

---

6 - Among many Christians, visiting a therapist is seen as a sign of spiritual failure. For a lot of us, we view seeking out this kind of help to be a last ditch effort when all other avenues have been exhausted. The thought process seems to be, "If only you had practiced spiritual disciplines more consistently; if only you had been closer to God, THEN you wouldn't have such a problem." The stigma our collective culture has constructed around all forms of mental illness is profoundly destructive and multi-faceted. This book isn't about addressing that dysfunction, so I'll just say this: mental health challenges aren't spiritual failures. Seeking out help for problems related to emotional regulation isn't weak or a defeat - it's mature; it's taking responsibility for one's life and actions; it's being courageous.

Sometimes Christians are tempted to equate psychology as one and the same as spirituality — to conflate the fields in simplistic binary dogma. Besides from being a grievous error practically speaking, it's also incoherent philo-sophically. A variety of modes of psychological therapy have a powerful way of helping us see the unseen within ourselves; discerning secrets within us about which we are yet unaware. I am no exception to this rule. For additional reading on the intersection between psychology and spirituality, I highly rec-ommend the work of Dr. David Benner. His book *Spirituality and the Awaken-ing of Self* is a masterpiece in this vein.

symptoms of C-PTSD (complex post-traumatic stress disorder). This multifaceted condition is typically linked to the experience of repeated childhood traumas over a long period of time. One of its hallmarks is responding to normal life stressors with "fight, flight, or freeze" levels of fierceness. All of a sudden, I started to see how my psychological" basement" impacts the whole of my emotional house. As time marched on, I learned that these discoveries were just the tip of the iceberg.

On an episode of the radio show, *This American Life*, the novelist Piers Anthony describes the dynamic well: "One thing you who had secure or happy childhoods should understand about those of us who did not: We who control our feelings, who avoid conflicts at all costs, or seem to seek them. Who are hypersensitive, self-critical, compulsive, workaholic, and above all, survivors. We are not that way from perversity, and we cannot just relax and let it go. We've learned to cope in ways you never had to."

Not everyone has PTSD. But every one of us has been through traumatic events, and as such, we have all repressed painful experiences over the course of our lives. God designed our brains to operate this way. Bessel van der Kolk, a remarkable psychiatrist from Boston University Medical School, was one of the first to do rigorous research on the effects of trauma on the human psyche. In his 2014 book, *The Body Keeps the Score*, van der Kolk writes that when a person goes through a physically or emotionally overwhelming event, their autonomic nervous can take over, rerouting energy away from low-priority functions and into systems needed for survival[7]. But in some extremely intense situations when the trauma proves too elusive to avoid, he writes, our brain can choose the nuclear option as it were and shut the whole thing down[8]. Anyone who's ever 'blacked out' during a car accident, fall, or sports mishap knows what this feels like.

---

7 - We sometimes casually call this the "fight, flight, freeze, or fawn" response.

8 - I've frequently labeled this dissociation.

One minute a person is having a great time, and the next, they're waking up in the back of an ambulance. According to van der Kolk, something similar can happen due to emotional trauma[9] as well (particularly in children).

Beyond immediate impacts, trauma-induced repression can actually change the physical structure of our brains. If you imagine the brain as a vast and complex network of electrical circuits, we could say that trauma rewires the mind. A person injured by past trauma might thus experience hair-trigger responses to present events because their brain perceives them as similar to the original hurt. Even if the event itself is hidden away from conscious awareness, our bodies remember. The brain, assuming an analogous threat has reared its ugly head, will ready us for battle or escape. Our minds know by experience that certain things are too much for us to handle[10], and so does their absolute best to protect us.

Maggie Scarf, in her book *Secrets, Lies, Betrayals: The Mind Body Connection*, describes how these old events can be carried in our bodies as muscle tension, chronic depression, or a myriad of other medical manifestations like as high blood pressure, incontinence, headaches, or unexplainable pain. This echoes van der Kolk's scientific research on EMDR[11] therapy for PTSD, which can result in patients physically experiencing surfacing memories in different locations on their bodies during treatment.

---

9 - This is in part why some perpetrators of violent crimes experience psychogenic amnesia, legitimately having no memory of their own destructive actions. Even when we ourselves are directly responsible for trauma, our brains can step in and attempt to protect itself: even to the whole world's detriment.

10 - This phenomenon echoes a famous old Christian axiom based on 1 Corinthians 10:13 that says, "God won't let you go through something you're not able to handle."

11 - Eye Movement Desensitization and Reprocessing therapy.

Sometimes even being touched in a particular place or in a particular way can bring a repressed memory to consciousness. Van der Kolk describes how some of his patients have recalled theretofore forgotten events right in the middle of therapeutic massage sessions. One moment the therapist will be working a shoulder, forearm, or ankle, and in the next moment, the client will be in tears, reliving a formerly hidden event. Truly, even if we're oblivious, *our bodies keep score.*

Trauma isn't the only thing our minds repress, however. Humans are incredibly creative with our ability to keep secrets from ourselves. Anything in life, whether beliefs or feelings or mistakes or desires, can be subject to repression. Merely the *threat* of suffering can provoke our minds to press even the banalest details into the shadow. Because we are integrated beings, these hidden truths will inevitably drive our lives from the backseat.

This dynamic is painfully familiar to many people in the LGBTQ+ community, who intuitively know that investigating their gender identity or sexual orientation feels risky. Cultural homophobia, transphobia, and misogyny threaten to disrupt the relationships, careers, religion, finances, and health of anyone not fitting the norm. We all know friends and family members, who despite their suspicions of being gay or transgender, pushed it down, got married, had kids, built a career, etc., only to come out later in life. On the surface, it might seem perplexing why a person would "wait so long." But if we look empathetically, we might see that LGBTQ+ people are normal humans, hiding potentially painful parts of themselves in the shadows out of self-protection. Interestingly enough, coming out of the closet (i.e., exploring and exposing repressed secrets) appears to be a remarkably effective treatment for improving overall health[12].

---

12 - A 2013 study by the University of Montreal and published in the journal *Psychosomatic Medicine* found that LGBTQ people who were still "in the closet" had higher levels of stress biomarkers than their peers who were out of the closet.

Now, it's possible that you may be feeling triggered[13] after simply reading this section. You might be fielding internal objections rising up that are rooted in your worldview, personality, childhood culture, or life experiences.

You may think to yourself:

"But if repression occurs for good biological reasons, why disturb it? The original trauma is obviously very distressing, or else my mind wouldn't be hiding it. How could the potential good possibly outweigh the risks of dragging this stuff up?"

"What if ignorance is bliss? Why not just continue on and be (relatively) happy? No one's life is perfect."

"It makes more logical sense to focus on the symptoms (rage, addiction, distressing attractions, etc.). Any underlying causes are inconsequential in the big picture. It's the present that is really at issue."

"Think about the relational or legal implications of exploring secrets like these! My whole family would hate me if they knew! Why not just let sleeping dogs lie?"

The answer to each of these is: Do we want to grow or not? Do we want to stay stuck or not? The journey to maturity requires a courageous walk down the trail of honesty. It's not an easy path. But it is the best one.

As I discussed in the opening chapter, secrets are loaded with potential energy. This is especially true for repressed secrets. I believe the life you've always wanted is waiting on the other side of the things you're currently hiding (even if you don't even know what they are!). But the process of self-discovery must not

---

13 - See what I did there? ;)

be trifled with lightly. John Bradshaw, who I also referenced in chapter two, writes in his important work on shame, "To truly be committed to a life of honesty, love, and discipline, we must be willing to commit ourselves to reality." A commitment to reality is hard work; it's scary, unnerving, and destabilizing. Yet, the potential for growth and healing is worth the risk.

———

Israel's King David is described in the Hebrew Scriptures as a deeply spiritual, artistically rich, and courageous leader. At the same time, the ancient stories are not shy about pointing out his vigorous failures. While David's reach through the centuries is undeniable, his story arc doesn't read like a happy-clappy fairytale. His fame begins with the triumph over the champion Goliath in hand-to-hand combat, but his reputation is punctuated with confusion and tragedy. By the end of his sojourn as king, David bequeaths to his fellow citizens a kingdom in turmoil.

It turned out this way in part because of David's stunning capacity for self-deception, a form of secret-keeping closely related to repression.

The celebrated ruler's life begins to slip sideways long before his waning moments. 2 Samuel chapter 11 reports how, in his early days as ruler, while the ebb and flow of war dragged on year-after-year, David's attention diverted from battle to more interesting matters back home in the capital, Jerusalem. With his army out on tour, the young king settled into an affair [14]with the wife of Uriah, one of his military captains. After ensuring that he would be killed on the front lines in the war in order to cover up Bathsheba's pregnancy, David made her his seventh wife among a harem of concubines.

———

14 - Some commentators have observed that the nature of David and Bathsheba's sexual relationship was one of sexual assault, given the unequal power dynamic between them. I can't help but resonate with this analysis.

David's oblivion to the depravity of his behavior is perhaps the most mystifying aspect of the story. The way the king carries on with his contented life as if the tidal wave of trauma in his wake didn't exist is grotesque. Only Bathsheba mourns her husband's death. Secrecy as self-deception in the hands of the powerful has a unique capacity to destroy all that is good in life.

It isn't until the prophet[15] Nathan confronted[16] David that the king appeared to appreciate the gravity of his mistakes. Even then, his dawning self-awareness was halting and cringeworthy. The prophet used the soft approach of drawing out an allegory with the king: A rich man and a poor man live in a city together. When a stranger visits the wealthy man, he takes the poor man's only sheep and kills it for a feast in order to show proper hospitality to his guest.

In response, David blusters, "As surely as the Lord lives, the man who did this must die!"[17]

Still, in the darkness of self-deception, he missed the point of the fable entirely. Instead, David received it as a literalistic report[18] of injustice within his gates. Of course, his moral infidelity was obvious, at least to everyone without a crown!

It is only after an exasperated Nathan exclaims, "YOU ARE THE

---

15 - In the Bible, prophets bring the words of God to monarchs and rulers, speaking truth to power, often at the risk of their own lives.

16 - If you haven't seen the VeggieTales (yes, also classic 1990's entertainment) version of this story, you're missing out. *King George and the Ducky* is a classic around my home.

17 - 2 Samuel 12:5

18 - Interestingly enough, this is mistake many religious people make with all sorts of other historical and allegorical stories in scripture.

MAN!!!" that the bamboozled king starts to catch on. And once he does, David responds with the kind of spiritual maturity he has become famous for. In fact, Psalm 51 from the Old Testament is a written poetic record of David's repentance in the wake of his profound violations against Bathsheba, Uriah, and the Israelite people.

It's easy to judge David for his apparent idiocy. But the truth is that we're all at risk for similar self-deception. As rulers over our own kingdoms of mind, everyone has the tendency to avoid or deny the truth — even when it remains unmistakable to everyone around us!

Sometimes an out-of-control ego is the key contributor to self-deception[19]. If we buy into the lie that "I am the center of the universe," other beliefs and behavior will follow. Little by little, arrogance can make us impervious to the truth, even if it were to jump up and bite us in the face. From religious cult leaders to political provocateurs, we have all witnessed the dynamic.

Other times, we can slip into self-deception by way of fear; the truth can be more frightening or inconvenient than the suffering caused by living a lie[20]. Others might live in self-deception because of a chronic lack of safety: if you're constantly fighting for survival, it's basically impossible to attend to matters of spiritual or moral development[21]. In a 2012 TED Talk, Michael Shemer[22]

---

19 - I am indebted to The Arbinger Institute, who's book Leadership and Self-Deception helped shape some of my thought on this

20 - Again, I think of LGBTQ+ people who "come out of the closet" later in life after spending decades with repressed sexual orientations or gender identities.

21 - While Maslow's hierarchy of needs has been appropriately criticized, I think it accurately highlights this reality we all know well.

22 - The publisher of Skeptic magazine, he is especially interested in pseudo-science and the nature of belief.

argues that people often end up entrenched in error because of stereotype; we observe patterns in the world or in our lives and overemphasize our ability to analyze that data, drawing broad but inappropriate conclusions that gradually become entrenched.

The late theologian Dallas Willard, who is esteemed for his contributions to our understanding of spiritual formation, warns that self-deception is one of the great threats to people becoming who they most wish to be, pervading every aspect of life. He writes about these secrets hidden from our own minds, "In self-deception the individual or group refuses to acknowledge factors in their life of which they are dimly conscious, or even know to be the case, but are unprepared to deal with: to openly admit and take steps to change. Those factors continue to govern their actions and shape their thoughts and emotions. The further result is that what they *say* they believe, intend, and want is not borne out in life."

So what do we do then? How do we sort out the secrets hiding from ourselves? Great question! As I close this chapter, I'll make some suggestions.

Aside from an environment of unconditional love, the most important element for spiritual growth is accurate and compassionate self-awareness. This universal truth is why Dallas Willard warns his readers so vigorously about the dangers of self-deception.

The dynamic isn't unlike the organic process of unfurling greenery in the garden. If you want to harvest tomatoes in the summer, you've got to pick a spot that gets sunlight, put down good soil, build scaffolding, wait to plant until the risk of freezing is minimal, and water, water, water all along the way. Remove even one of those essential variables, and you're likely to get a scrawny plant with an inadequate harvest.

Our lives take the best possible shape when certain conditions are in place. It is impossible to mature into the people we were created to be absent the context of knowing ourselves fully and empathetically.

Psychologist David Benner writes about spiritual growth from the Christian worldview in his book *Spirituality and the Awakening of Self*. In it, he suggests that the concept of "original sin[23]" would be better described the way I'm discussing self-deception in this chapter: unconscious secrets we keep from ourselves. Benner then takes the next step, arguing that as we uncover our hidden motivations, fears, beliefs, and attitudes, we simultaneously discover how we might be healed on the arc of the spiritual journey. He goes so far as to say that "conversion" in real life feels far more like an awakening (hence the title of the book) to what has been within us all along than a philosophical or religious shift. "Christian spirituality," Benner summarizes, "involves a transformation of self that occurs only when God and self are both deeply known" *(emphasis mine)*.

While I would never argue that self-awareness is the *only* condition needed for us to grow into the people we were created to be (and certainly by itself could devolve into unproductive or gratuitous navel-gazing), it is, without doubt, a foundational component of the trek to maturity. Self-deception, or secret-keeping from ourselves, is a universal barrier on the spiritual journey. Dallas Willard calls the personal process of discovery "prophetic illumination." About it, he writes, "the only path of spiritual transformation today still lies through [it]."

While some of us pragmatic farmer types might naturally lean our attention toward the most observable external signs of growth for achieving progress, spiritual giants like Dallas Willard and David

---

23 - This may be a problematic term for you, and perhaps rightfully so. I use it here simply because Benner does.

Benner warn that this approach can prove detrimental to the overall process. Everything we can see and measure externally is connected to inner motivations, beliefs, emotions, and ingrained neural pathways. Whether the outward challenge relates to disordered eating, substance abuse, outbursts of violence, toxic shame, or self-doubt, the journey toward becoming who we were created to be is far more about inner work. "Above everything, guard your heart," the Biblical book of Proverbs pleads, "for everything you do flows from it."[24] Sorting out what lies buried within can hardly be overstated.

Sometimes strict and narrow forms of religion can become systems of approaching our inner secrets and yet never fully owning up to them. Fundamentalism has a knack for giving a person the appearance of walking the spiritual journey, but in reality, only offering a cheap facsimile. This is part of why fundamentalists sometimes turn up as morally defunct -- they've mastered everything external to them: facts, figures, details, Truth. And yet, they've left unexamined the mysteries within their own souls. Driven by those things in their hearts they are yet even aware of, dysfunctional behavior flows out quite naturally. This is one of the reasons why isolation (whether physical/spatial or secrecy-induced) can be so destructive to our maturity; adrift in our own world, our minds are very crafty at justifying almost anything that flows so naturally from the heart.

The Christian author and mystic Thomas Merton writes,

> The great tragedy of our age is the fact...that there are so many godless Christians. Christians, that is, whose religion is a matter of pure conformism and expediency. Their 'faith' is little more than a permanent evasion of reality—a compromise with life. In order to avoid admitting the uncomfortable truth that they no longer have any real need for God or any vital faith in

---

24 - Proverbs 4:23

Him, they conform to the outward conduct of others like themselves. And these 'believers' cling together, offering one another an apparent justification for lives that are essentially the same as the lives of their materialistic neighbors whose horizons are purely those of the world and its transient values.

The sphere of Christian spirituality isn't the only one to observe this link between self-awareness and personal growth. Psychology and behavioral therapy recognize (and plays into) the connection as well. In Jungian psychology, for example, the part of ourselves that we are unconscious to is known as "the shadow." While there exists vigorous scholarly and practical debate about the technical ins and outs of the applicability of Jung's theory, many hundreds of thousands of people have found it to resonate deeply with their personal work, fueling transformation and wholeness.

In 1955, two American psychologists[25] developed a graphical model (Fig.2) for visualizing the relationship between ourselves and others as it relates to secret and private matters in our lives. It is built upon the central axiom of this chapter: that increased self-awareness is associated with personal growth. Named the Johari Window,[26] Luft & Ingham's model highlights four potential zones of knowledge:

1. *That which is known by both ourselves and others.*
2. *That which known to others but not ourselves.*
3. *That which is hidden from others but known by us.*
4. *That which is not known by anyone (including ourselves).*

---

25 - Joseph Luft & Harrington Ingham.

26 - The creators named it by combining their first names: Joe & Harry.

A universal goal of most therapies[27] (even if not explicitly stated), theorized by Luft and Ingham, is to enlarge the upper-left 'open' window while simultaneously decreasing the size of the other windows[28] (especially the lower right zone, the complete unknown / the shadow). As a client becomes aware of their own secrets, new horizons are opened for exploring the myriad motivations of external behavior. Whether a therapeutic relationship utilizes the Christian worldview and associated spiritual disciplines to process discoveries or if it simply applies standard psychological strategies like CBT[29], the underlying dynamic of change is strikingly familiar.

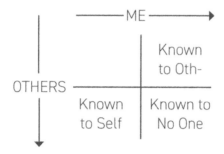

Fig.2

Daniel Goleman and Richard Boyatzis present a similar principle but apply it from the perspective of leadership in the business world. In their book Primal Leadership, they argue that cultivating 'resonance' among followers is the pinnacle of leadership. This

---

27 - If you've never seen a mental health practitioner before, Lori Gottlieb's book *Maybe You Should Talk to Someone* could provide a helpful introduction to the experience. It gives a behind-the-scenes look at what therapy is all about.

28 - It's important to note that the goal is NOT to eliminate all the other windows. The creators make it abundantly clear that there is significant value to maintaining areas of privacy from the outside world or even the therapist.

29 - Cognitive Behavioral Therapy is an extremely common methodology for social workers, psychologists, and psychiatrists alike.

only happens, they say, when a leader is highly in tune[30] with their and their followers' emotional lives. Thus, once again, we see how self-awareness becomes a linchpin for self-actualization. Goleman's and Boyatzis' model calls for a five-step process[31] of discovery to increase emotional intelligence. Check out the resources section at the end of this book for a more detailed description.

The examples are endless for the undeniable connection between self-awareness and personal growth. Anything we keep in the shadows might feel safe, but it will inevitably hold us back and drive life from the back seat. The key is to have the courage to dive into the deep end, even not knowing what will be discovered.

One of the reasons I found the Wachowski's film[32] *The Matrix* captivating as a teenager was its exploration of the nature of reality. The cult following that ensued after its 1999 release is a testimony that I wasn't the only angsty young person to connect with its ontological questions either! *Are we really who we think*

----

30 - Daniel Goleman dubs this "Emotional Intelligence" and has written rather extensively on this concept. It describes a person's intonation with his/her own inner life as well as that of others. Goldman has theorized that people with high E.I. are more likely to have successful and fulfilling relationships, careers, and well, lives.

31 - 1. Who is "my ideal self?" 2. Who is "my actual self?" 3. What is "my learning agenda for closing the gap between the two?" 4. Experimentation and Mastery with continued asessment. 5. Both the outcome and context of this practice: solid relationships.

32 - One impulse I have is to apologize for using two 1990s films as illustrations in one single chapter. But I won't. After summoning up Fight Club, I might as well go all in! (And besides, film is the most compelling art form of the 21st century, full of truth about the human condition and spirituality. We have a lot to learn if we only will listen!)

we are (or who the world perceives us to be)?[33] *What if the truth lies beyond what we tangibly sense around us? What is even real?*

Once again, you'll have to forgive me for spoiling a two-decades-old movie if you haven't yet seen it[34]. The Matrix is a science fiction action flick, and so the premise is equal parts fantastical, intricate, and bombastic. Its plot goes: in a dystopian future, people have been captured by artificial intelligence that uses their bodies for energy by keeping their minds enslaved in a computer-simulated reality (the matrix). The protagonist, a computer hacker named Neo, discovers the truth and joins an insurrection against humanity's mechanical overlords. Explosions and looks of astonishment from Keanu Reeves ensue.

Now, several scenes throughout the movie depict different character's inner conflicts as they are exposed to the secret of the matrix. Such discoveries inevitably lead to a choice: leave the matrix for reality or remain in ignorance. Their decisions become stark and frightening when they consider the fact that embracing the truth will inevitably be inconvenient and even painful when compared with keeping their heads in the sand.

At the climax of the movie's first act, Neo himself is given that choice. And in one of the most famous metaphors from the film (even to the point of becoming cliché), Neo finds himself staring down at two pills, one red and the other blue. Swallow red, and all his self-deception falls away like scales from his eyes; swallow blue and remain in the computer simulation forever.

---

33 - Two years after I penned the first draft of this section of the book, the Wochowski's revealed that that Matrix itself is an allegory of the trans experience. The two, formerly known as "The Wochowski Brothers", have both come out as transgender women and have transitioned publicly to their identified genders.

34 - And if you are familiar with the film, you'll have to forgive me for painting the picture because you already know exactly where I'm going with this illustration.

Of course, Neo chooses the red pill, now a veritable icon in American pop culture.

You have that choice today. The work of digging into our secrets, exploring our own shadows, identifying self-deception is swallowing the red pill. Everything will change if we do it. But *everything will change if we do it*!!

Certainly, to some degree, "Ignorance is bliss," as the film's character Cypher pronounces while willingly slipping back into the computer simulation. In many respects, remaining ignorant in our repression and self-deception is a much easier, lower stress, and peaceful path. No one wants to have relationships, life circumstances, or philosophical assumptions to be destabilized. But remaining unaware of our inner workings, our hidden motivations, our underlying shame, has its own cost, as we all know.

Your secrets are real. Your hidden truth is real. It is shaping your life whether you like it or not. And today presents you with a choice. You might feel scared. You might feel excited. You might feel confused. But you can do this. You have the courage to dig. You have the bravery to see. You can own your dissatisfaction with the status quo. You are not alone. You are not crazy. You can wake up. You have supporters in your corner that you don't yet know about. As you let the Spirit lead your curiosity, you will become the person you were meant to be.

QUESTIONS FOR DISCUSSION:

1. Fear is a huge deterrent for many of us against exploring the unknown in our lives. Sometimes it can feel safer to remain in oblivion than face the truth. Begin this exercise by simply making a list of what you're afraid of. What scares you? What might happen if you dig a little deeper?

2. On the other end of the spectrum is love. What is drawing you forward? What do you have to gain? What is the best that life has to offer? Make a list of the things you love most.

3. In this chapter, the author discussed the way in which self-deception can feel like questioning the nature of reality itself. Another film from the late 1990s on the subject is the *Truman Show* starring Jim Carey. If you haven't seen it, check it out. Better yet, see it with friends and take some time for a lighthearted debrief after it's over!

4. One well-respected and ancient avenue into our unconscious minds is through dreams. In the Biblical/Hebrew tradition, dreams are frequently interpreted as messages from God. In some psychotherapy modalities, dreams are utilized as interpretive windows for our deepest desires and fears. Regardless of the intricacies animating them, people from across the religious and political spectrum and throughout the centuries have found paying attention to dreams as a useful tool for increasing self-awareness.

Consider praying specifically to God when you go to sleep for a week or two — asking for dreams. Keep a journal and pen next to your bed so that you can jot down details the minute you wake up (dreams frequently fade from our conscious awareness seconds after waking). Looking back at specific dreams, consider discussing your related thoughts and feelings with trusted friends.

5. Finally, give some thought to who you have in your life willing and able to be honest with you about what is and is not working? In the story the author shared in this chapter, King David had the prophet Nathan show up and give him difficult but merciful feedback. Sometimes, in order to begin seeing what we ourselves are blind to, we need an outsider's perspective.

If you do have someone in your life who is trustworthy and kind and who is 100% on your "team," consider asking them specifically for feedback. If no one comes to mind, perhaps begin building an intimate friendship with someone who may be able to play that role: perhaps a pastor, an older elder from your church, a parent, cousin, former teacher, or coach. The most valuable "prophets" for individuals are often those who need to be given explicit permission to "speak into our lives."

7 | SECRET GOODNESS

"But when you pray, go into your room, close the door, and pray to your Father, who is unseen."
-Matthew 6:6, NIV

Good things can come from secret-keeping.

You read that correctly. Hiddenness isn't all bad. In fact, some secrets are essential for virtue. Thus far, I have primarily offered warnings about how secrets can hold us back from becoming the people we were made to be. The principle is true. Secrets are heavy and complex, they can lead to toxic shame, and they can isolate us from community or ourselves! But the thesis of the book also highlights how hidden aspects of our lives can be leveraged into creating the very best in life.

The first time I dreamed of writing a book was in college. I had written a position paper for a course, felt very confident about its content and style, and was happily rewarded with positive verification for my feelings with high marks. But even more than that, my professor complimented my work and told me I should pursue writing for publication as I continued to grow and mature as a pastor and scholar. It felt good to be "seen" in this way. I already knew I had something to say to the world, and to imagine that I might have the skill or talent to share it well was deeply affirming. That interaction may have been the first moment I seriously considered setting the goal of writing a book.

It wasn't until I finished my master's degree in seminary that I felt I had the time or energy to throw myself into writing. I began researching for the book you are now reading all the way back in 2013. I had a great deal to learn. It has been a slow and humbling process while also rewarding and energizing. The process of putting a book project together is daunting, especially for a first-time author.

I don't remember the first time I told someone that I was writing a book, but I remember being surprised by how good it felt to share that information. Yes, that's right. I found it somehow satisfying to tell friends or colleagues about this goal I had set for myself — but had yet to achieve. In fact, I'm sure the first time I began yammering on about this book about secrets; I didn't even have a single word down on paper! The second time I shared my vision with someone, the positive "zing" was a little less pronounced. The third time, even less. The fourth, even less, and so on.

I came to discover that talking about my audacious goal (I knew very few people who had tried or even wanted to publish something like what I wanted to write) wasn't a reliable source of that oh-so-familiar dopamine rush.

What I also came to discover is that the more I talked about it publicly, the less motivated I felt to actually do the hard work to get it done. As it turns out, this dynamic isn't unique to me. A 2010 TED talk by Derek Sivers explored this very same psychological phenomenon and described how it had been observed in humans as far back as 1920.

According to the research, when a person shares an aspiration with someone else who appears to hear and understand it, the mind of the goal-setter is fooled into thinking that the goal has already been achieved. The positive rush of dopamine I had experienced as a result of talking about my goals turns out to be almost indistinguishable by our brains from the sense of satisfaction that emanates from actually achieving our goals. Our minds appear to experience sharing our dreams and completing them almost the same. As a consequence, when it comes time to do the hard work of fulfilling the original aim, our motivation is far lower if we've already talked about it.

Strangely enough, keeping the goal a secret is a useful strategy for achieving it. And in the end, it makes for a better story. Part of the reason we are so drawn to a character like Harrison Ford's *Indiana Jones* is because of his endless secret proficiencies. He has confidence and strength, sure, but it's rooted in modesty about his considerable talents. If Indiana Jones were constantly talking about his exploits, describing his goal of surviving a booby-trapped Mayan temple or the murderous attacks of magic-obsessed Nazis, we wouldn't believe him. And we might even root against him. And he'd find himself far less likely to make the unlikely escapes we so enjoy in the movies.

Obviously, there's a balance in this somewhere. We all need mentors and guides along the way; we need to self-reveal in order to gain support and wisdom. But it might be healthiest to regard our deepest callings as being on a strictly need-to-know basis. If your dream is to write a novel, or open a restaurant, or grow a world-changing non-profit organization, you'd likely do well to be strategic about when and with whom you share the vision. If you want to lose weight, quit drinking in excess, or become more generous, not everyone needs to know, and you'll actually be more likely to achieve it if they don't! How decadent does your confession feel? How much of a zing do you get when you talk about it? These are your first clues. In an odd way, it might just be that keeping secrets will make you a better person.

In this chapter, we will explore the importance of allowing some of our good to remain invisible.

The first time I found myself emotionally impacted by Anne Frank's story was as an undergraduate in Walla Walla, Wash. I had previously read her published diaries in high school, but like many of my peers, I failed to appreciate the depth and importance of the tale, which describes her Jewish family in the German-occupied Netherlands going into hiding during World War II. But when the drama club on my college campus put on a famous stage adaptation of Anne Frank's life[1], I began to understand. More than that, however, I was emotionally captivated.

As the play unfolded, I sensed a taste of the constant anxiety that Anne's family must've experienced as Jews living for two years in hiding during the Holocaust. I identified with the anger that sometimes erupted amongst them in the cramped attic space under such untenable stress. I related to Anne's adolescence: maturing, self-exploring, and identity-formation.

Back in class, following the performances, my peers and I discussed some of the underlying ethics suggested in her story. We imagined ourselves as owners of a parcel like Prinsengracht 263 with its "Secret Annex" within which Anne and two other families hid. Someone asked the ubiquitous question, "If you had the opportunity to make such living quarters available for others in a similar situation, what would you do?"

The underlying debate was about deception. When is it morally virtuous to "bear false witness" (to borrow words from the Biblical 10 Commandments)? In the case of the Franks and many others like them, it was only after their secret hiding spots were betrayed that they were subjected to the horrors of Nazi internment camps. Thus, Secret-keeping directly resulted in the preservation of life, indisputable goodness. Further, I will argue in this chapter that

---

1 - *The Diary of Anne Frank*, originally written by Frances Goodrich and Albert Hackett.

good deeds performed in secret produce maturity and character in the virtuous liars themselves!

In considering the possibility of concealment contributing to positive growth, my mind is drawn to one of Jesus' teachings from his famous "Sermon on the Mount," recorded in Matthew chapter 6. He says, "Be careful not to practice your acts of kindness in front of others to be seen by them. If you do, you will have no reward from your Father in heaven." According to Jesus, there are drawbacks to transparency and benefits to hiddenness.

In this saying, Jesus is talking about practices of personal spirituality, things we do to grow as human beings, approach the Divine and settle our souls. Sometimes dubbed "spiritual disciplines," activities like prayer, meditation, generosity, fasting, study, service, confession, worship, etc., have long been considered by leaders of nearly every spiritual tradition as essential to transformation. The late Dallas Willard writes that while God is the one who ultimately forms us into the best versions of ourselves, spiritual disciplines are the means by which we place ourselves into a position for God's gentle chipping away of the rough spots to take place. The change happens behind our backs, outside our control. And yet, we have agency in setting the stage for it.

But that's not all. Jesus' statement adds another layer to this truth. When we practice spiritual disciplines like meditation or worship, our motivations can easily be clouded. If we are "performing" religiosity in order to get something from people witnessing it, the would-be positive benefits are minimized. In the Sermon on the Mount, Jesus goes on to condemn how spiritual leaders of his time were using things like praying or giving money in order to gain social capital among their flocks. According to Jesus, the benefit of these practices are only possible in the context of an "audience of one."[2] Secret-keeping simplifies our motives for doing the right thing.

Now, we could look at this concept mechanistically, drawing a hard boundary, "never do anything good that can possibly be witnessed by other people." But obviously, we intuitively can predict that rigidly applying this principle would create a lot more monk-like recluses and rockstar jerks than mature humans! A better application would be to increase our self-awareness so that we can better discern which "acts of kindness" are most apt to be shadowed by a needy ego.

Am I giving to the local shelter because my heart is touched by the need and feel the Spirit's leading, or because I secretly crave a place at a boardroom table? Do I really love worship, or do I like to be seen worshiping? Am I sharing about my new diet because I'm looking for compliments or because a friend asked for my wisdom?

These are difficult questions. But they're worth asking and answering if we want to become our best possible selves. The reasons animating our behaviors fundamentally shape their meaning. As such, strategic secret-keeping can become a strategy for laying claim to the value and beauty of certain behavior while avoiding the pitfalls of public performance.

———

Will is one of my closest friends. He works as a teacher in a grade school. Will is just about the most generous person I know. Aside from putting his heart and soul into his daily work, he frequently also puts his checking account on the line for the kids he serves too. Serving in the public school system, Will's students run the gamut of socio-economic backgrounds. But because many

———

2 - As a young adolescent, I was greatly impacted by the musician Sara Groves, who sings these words in her song, *This Journey is My Own.*

of them are from homes where resources are scarce, my friend frequently finds himself in a position to help them out with small but significant tangible needs. Whether for a pair of shoes or a set of pencils, basic toiletries, or a winter jacket, Will's generosity is automatic.

And that's why I was so surprised by what he told me one warm June day as we walked downtown toward the sandwich shop we liked for summer lunches. "I have to go pick up a set of tongs for my mom."

"Tongs?" I replied, confused as to why my friend would be doing his mother's shopping for basic kitchen essentials when she lived on the other side of the country.

"That's what she told me to get this year for her birthday," Will explained without missing a beat, continuing to stroll down the sun-blotched sidewalk in Walla Walla.

"Told you to get...like...as a gift?" I inquired, now even more confused.

"Yeah." Will stopped momentarily, looking over to catch my gaze. "My mom always puts in her' order,' and it's easier for everyone if I just go with it."

I was dumbfounded. I had never heard of such an arrangement. How could anything be enjoyed as (or even considered) a "gift" if it had ostensibly been demanded?

Sitting in front of our paninis in the modern cafe overlooking Colville Street, Will explained more about how he and his mother related to regular yearly holidays and birthdays. For just about as long as he could remember, my friend would receive detailed "orders," penciling out what sorts or purchases his Mom wanted, which restaurants she'd enjoy, and the kinds of physical signals of affection she expected. When the given event arrived, whether it be a birthday or Christmas, or other celebration, Will's Mom would make it a habit to speak up and make "corrections" in real-time if her requests were not in order.

As we finished up our meal and strolled back out onto the sidewalk, my friend went on to describe how there have been times when he had already purchased or arranged for a certain gift, but in the interim, before delivery, his mother would grow impatient or afraid he hadn't done as asked. "I hope you haven't forgotten... [insert yearly token item]," she'd preemptively blast away.

"Wow, that must be incredibly difficult to navigate," I replied with honesty. "I can imagine it feeling a little fake between the two of you."

"I feel bankrupted," Will replied bluntly. "Even if I wanted to express genuine love and affection, she robs me of the opportunity." He began to tear up, putting on his sunglasses as we turned the corner toward my car. "Don't get me wrong. I love my Mom. I just wish I could be truly generous, truly loving with her instead of just obedient and afraid."

Will is an incredibly benevolent human being. It's in his nature to give out of the goodness of his own heart and the conviction of his soul. But because of his mother's distrusting and demanding behavior, the joy and connection the two might've otherwise enjoyed were minimized. Instead of signs of endearment, his presents became obligatory obeisance.
Because of her explicit expectations, Will's motivation for being kind necessarily changed on a basic level. And because his motive changed, so did the power of the gifts themselves.

This dynamic is true for all of us. The driving reasons behind our behaviors fundamentally shape their meaning.

Throughout his first years of life, my oldest son witnessed me purchasing flowers for his Mom many times. Sometimes the occasion was a holiday or birthday. But most of the time, it was" just because," communicating love and affection. And as is the case with almost any behavior passed on from adult to child, my boy picked this one up by osmosis. Even today, as a ten-year-old, when strolling by the flower section at the store, he asks to get his Mom a bouquet of flowers to take home.

I remember one day in particular when Finn was around four. I had picked him up at my Mom's house after a visit. As we jumped in my car, my son noticed a large blooming purple lilac bush near the driveway. He insisted that we cut off a branch to take home for his Momma. Even at a young age, my son knew how goodness looked and felt.

I mentally rolled my eyes, thinking to myself, "Look at this Pandora's box I've opened now. Am I in it now, for decades? Of course, I said yes, and cut a small bunch of flowers for him. The picture of him beaming is still one of my favorites in the family picture album.

The truth is that it was a sweet gesture of love, and both my wife and I celebrated it. Finn knew that his Mom loves flowers. He knew that giving her lilacs that day would put a smile on her face and express his love. He wanted to be a good human, to receive love back from his Mom, and he trusted that the exchange would result in feelings of connection and affection. It was pure and beautiful.

As a dad, I was proud to see Finn beginning to express generosity and to recognize the gift of joy that comes from doing good for good's sake. I wanted him to internalize these values. I wanted his life and the world to be better because of his future generosity as an adult.

Now, what if it had played out differently? What if my son had been thinking several steps ahead, calculating what he might get back from his Mom? What if he had been buttering her up? Well, the meaning of his "gift" would have shifted entirely. It would have ceased to be generosity and instead morphed into a cute 4-year-old version of manipulation. And troublingly, the reward of character development his gift might've otherwise created would've been forfeited.

Nearly everyone deals with this dynamic on a daily basis. It is especially true in the age of social media, where we habitually chronicle every detail of our lives for the public to see. Many of us, in fact, curate two or more different versions of ourselves across Twitter, Instagram, Facebook, etc. We tailor our behaviors, good deeds and bad, to suit the expectations of our followers. And as such, we fundamentally affect the reasons why we do what we do, be it ever so subtly.

In the process of putting this book together, I repeatedly ran into this truth. Because of the nature of the publishing industry in the 21st century, authors (especially first-time authors) are compelled to become their own marketing agencies if they want their work to be seen. Rather than simply focusing on the task of composition, writers also must be their own number one fan! One small consequence of this dynamic is that an author's social media presence becomes co-opted in a way. Especially during the Kickstarter campaign that funded the editorial component of this book, my social-networking accounts shifted from tools for connecting with friends and family to implements of capitalism. Each day, I spent a half-hour or more planning outposts, intentionally acquiring followers, and interacting with those I likely wouldn't have otherwise. My temporary mask of online extroversion was a means of getting this material published. As such, my motive forced me to forfeit some of the joy I might've otherwise received from sharing my truth.

Let's return for a moment to Matthew Chapter six, the passage I referenced earlier, where Jesus warns people to keep their personal acts of piety hidden. In it, he doesn't only teach the consequences of performing virtue to build social capital. If we read closely, we can see that He promises a benefit from such grandstanding as well.

"Truly, I tell you, they have received their reward in full," He says in verse two.

Now, there was a time in my life when I read Jesus' teaching here as a thinly veiled threat of destruction. I imagined Him to really be saying something like, "Those altruistic performers have got it coming! God's going to pay them back! All you actors out there, watch out! You're going to get it paid back...in the form of flames!"

And honestly, reading Matthew 6:1-3 this way makes a lot of sense if we don't yet have a lot of compassion for our egos. The truth is that while an unbridled ego can be problematic, all of us need the backbone that ego provides. It's essentially impossible to survive doing good for the public without being paid or appreciated for it. This is part of our reality. We all need a right-sized ego for proper personal development, and praise for good deeds seen by others is a pathway to it. Because of all this, I don't take Jesus' explanation here as a warning of damnation. Instead, I think Jesus' point is quite the opposite of promising retribution. The master teacher is suggesting that there is, in fact, a literal reward for doing good in the public eye. The crux is whether or not it will benefit our souls or our sense of self-importance.

As a teenager, when I held an all-night prayer vigil with my friends and found myself dizzily drowsy at 2 am as we walked through our small town, my motivation for prayer had changed. I was praying *in order to* get my friend's approval, no longer to simply connect with the Divine. I was praying for my ego instead of my soul. For religious leaders of Jesus' time, public performances of scripture teaching and ritual no doubt earned respect and influence among communities of faith, but they might not have produced maturity. For aspiring authors in the 21ˢᵗ century, YouTube demonstrations of piety might produce sales but not necessarily quality work.

Jesus' warning in the Sermon on the Mount is more of a statement of reality than a threat. The soul and the ego dance with one another. Intimacy with God is predicated upon privacy, fidelity, not unlike a monogamous marriage. When we do personal acts of spirituality for public consumption, our ego gets something out of it. There is a payoff. It just isn't spiritual maturity for the soul. The potential reward the deepest parts of ourselves might've enjoyed had we kept those practices private are likewise forfeited. The growth available through practices of personal piety is predicated upon their continued hiddenness. In this sense, secret-keeping is absolutely essential to becoming the people we were created to be.

The question is when and how we wish to see the benefits materialize.

I've only visited New York City on a couple of occasions. One of them took place over "the Blackout" of 2003, and the other was during a 24hr layover en route to Africa. Needless to say, I've not yet experienced the joy of seeing Broadway shows in the city that never sleeps. When I do get the opportunity, however, I hope to visit a little-known tiny theatre that has a minuscule budget, few actors, and an entirely different vision for the dramatic arts.

"Theatre for One" (T41) is a mobile, custom-designed, state-of-the-art theatre made to host a single guest enjoying the talented acting of a single artist. A 2011 *New York Times* review of a performance in Times Square described T41 as "intimate, incredibly intense, and highly personal." Necessitated by the nature of the physical space, the audience and the actor are forced together into a relationship.

Each performance is truly crafted for an audience of one.

When we practice personal spirituality in private, our only audience is the Divine. And the consequences of such "performances" are nothing short of intimacy. For much of my youth and adolescence, a "relationship with God" was touted as essential for anyone who wants to follow Jesus. While I have a more nuanced view of personal spirituality today, I'm still convinced that well-played secret-keeping is an essential path to holy awakening.

The 13th Century Muslim poet Jalal ad-Din Rumi (widely called, simply, "Rumi") is famous for mystic writings in the Sufi tradition of Islam. Most of his written work came by way of dictation and is named by some as being the most popular poet in the world. One section from his most important work, *Masnavi*, highlights how in the end, our good deeds in secret require great trust — that even if no other human sees, God Himself witnesses them.

> *Eternal life is gained*
> *by utter abandonment of one's own life.*
>
> *When God appears to His ardent lover,*
> *the lover is absorbed in Him, and not so much as a*
> *hair of the lover remains.*
>
> *True lovers are as shadows,*
> *and when the sun shines in glory*
> *the shadows vanish away.*
>
> *He is a true lover to God to whom God says,*
> *"I am thine and thou art Mine."*

QUESTIONS FOR DISCUSSION:

1. Bring to mind a goal that you have had (or currently have). Consider how you spoke about that dream prior to its completion. Did you over-share or under-share, and why? It's possible that even discussing it now may present a risk for its future completion; feel free to draw a boundary and decline this prompt :)

2. Anne Frank's story provides a tangible example of a time when secret-keeping is undeniably life-giving. Do secrets and privacy bring up negative or positive, or neutral connotations for you? Why? Tell a story about a time when keeping a secret helped you or those around you.

3. The author discussed in this chapter the concept of "spiritual disciplines," practices that we do in order to put ourselves into connection with the Divine. What spiritual practices have you found helpful in your life? Discuss one practice that you have considered adding or wish to add to the rhythm of your life.

4. What does it feel like to be generous or kind out of an obligation to do so? Explain.

5. Christianity often finds itself stretched between emphasizing two different ends of a spectrum on daily living. On the one hand, the faith is concerned with DOING (behaviors, ethics, religious practices, etc.) But on the other hand, it is also concerned with BEING (identity, humanity, guilt & shame, etc.) Which end of the spectrum do you tend to find your headspace living in most of the time? If it shifts, explain when and why.

8 | SECRECY AND LEADERSHIP

"Looked through the paper, makes you want to cry.
Nobody cares if the people live or die. And the dealer wants
you thinking that it's either black or white.
Thank God it's not that simple in my secret life."

-Leonard Cohen

Pastoral ministry was the only profession I had ever known before, following the Spirit's lead elsewhere, shifting gears at age 40. As such, living and thriving as a spiritual leader is where I learned many axioms I still hold dear. The subject of this chapter is no exception; it flows directly out of my experience as clergy. But because of this, I also found it to be the most difficult chapter to write. The material itself isn't difficult to understand; it just strikes close to my heart. As a leader, I have kept secrets. And I'm certain that they have impacted those to whom I have ministered.

The core message of this chapter is that secrets held by leaders are heavier than individual permutations of the same. In chapter one, we established that all secrets carry "weight," in part because of the energy expended to keep them hidden. As we expand on that concept in this chapter, we will explore how concealment in the hands of leaders not only can hold back individual growth, maturity, and potential but can expand beyond that into the sphere of the collective. When leaders keep secrets, communities, organizations, and networks can be affected by the underlying energy.

In many ways, this dynamic was the defining theme of pastoral ministry for me. I constantly found myself traversing the ridge of authenticity, balancing my own transparency against privacy. Many spiritual leaders [1]are afraid of being too genuine with their flocks for fear of criticism or worse. Their worries are not unfounded. I have believed throughout my walk as a pastor that it's possible to lead by way of vulnerability, to demonstrate a third way of influence. This ideal has been beautiful at times and profoundly difficult at others. While I do not have regrets, I still experience fear for how I may have mismanaged this powerful truth in my years as a pastor. In the same breath, I also respect myself for the way telling secrets has benefited those I've served.

As a child, I spent many weeks of summer vacations in the northernmost part of the Idaho panhandle. In the early 1980s, my grandparents had purchased a small remote cabin on the shores of (the still) pristine Priest Lake. This was a significant upgrade for my blue-collar family, who had spent many summers before that camping in tents on the lake's wilderness island beaches.

The setting is truly enchanting. Priest Lake's waters are crystal clear, its forests are virtually untouched, and people are sparse. As a child (and still sometimes as an adult), the five-hour drive from my hometown in SE Washington State felt like a journey into another world. The unique odor of granite dust and pine mixing even still takes me right back to lazy summer afternoons in this place that became central to a family tradition of yearly pilgrimages to "the lake." It was a private, personal, holy place for many years.

---

1 - Including many family members and mentors who routinely cautioned me about becoming friends with or getting "too close" with parishioners. Many of the "elder states people" hand down advice to be extremely careful about trusting their congregations because of the duplicity and harm they have experienced at the hands of vulnerability.

Each of my five first cousins (along with my sister and I) still carry fond memories of long hours spent joking and playing in the sunshine, swimming and skiing in the lake, and exploring the woods our cabin was surrounded by. We almost never formulated a schedule while on vacation at the cabin; we rarely had so much as an agenda for activities or sightseeing. The most important thing for all of us was "to be," come what may.

On cold days[2] or when the wind blew and brought with it afternoon swells, we spent our time inside or on the deck, voraciously reading whatever book or months-old magazine we could scrounge in the knotty-pine abode. Novels, celebrity magazines, dated newspapers, and home decor journals were all fair game. And of course, it's impossible to think about our summer afternoons at the lake without thinking about The National Enquirer.

I don't remember which aunt or uncle, cousin or parent made it a habit of picking up the gossip magazines from grocery store newsstands and then depositing them on the cabin's large low circular yellow coffee table, but the family always had a wide variety to choose from. The periodicals' outlandish headlines are etched into my mind. Whether announcing the existence of aliens or suggesting juicy nonsense about our favorite celebrities, this kind of trash journalism always had secrets to share.

Categorically speaking, the sorts of salacious stories slathered across tabloid headlines are known as scandals. People in power (no matter if by way of leadership, fame, or talent) frequently project intentional images to the masses designed to maintain influence. When secrets that contradict those projections are exposed for public consumption, outrage predictably ensues. This mismatch between what a given power-broker might say and what they actually do in private is at the heart of all scandals.

---

2 - Temperatures could always drop into the 50's or 60's even in the dead of the summer at that altitude and longitude.

In American culture, our collective appetite for scandal seems insatiable.[3] We crave gossip almost as much as modern media companies crave profiting from it! I think part of the reason we love it so much is because of the way it tips the power dynamic back in our favor. We who are not in leadership, not famous, or not particularly talented can hold their heads a little higher if they know a bit of "dirt" about the prominent people around them. Possessing hidden information can help us feel like insiders instead of outsiders. Knowing the failures of our heroes validates our egos, normalizing our own missteps.

During my pastoring years, I sometimes became the object of a largely anonymous tabloid's hit-pieces written by far-right fundamentalists in the Adventist Church. Through the power of social media, the authors' articles allowed them fleeting fame in their sliver of the Christian political landscape. Not unlike major media, the more obscene the reporting, the more attention their posts would gather. That is to say, while the subjects of their attacks varied (for example, they once skewered me overusing she/her pronouns to refer to God), the tone did not.

At first, the spirit of smug superiority dripping with contempt shocked me. I couldn't square how Christians expressed such loathing for others in their own spiritual traditions. But looking back, I think the tenor of these rags was predictable. The purpose of tabloid scandals is power, namely, to allow the authors and audience to experience a sense of superiority. We are drawn to these stories because, frankly, judging others feels good. At its worst, however, the tabloid cycle goes past leveling the playing fields and morphs into hunts for retribution. The truth is that when a scandal leads to tar-and-feathering by way of forced resignations or shunning, it has achieved its purpose.

---

3 - Perhaps it's not a cultural thing so much as it is a human phenomenon. Pick a country from around the world and it would be difficult to not come across local gossip in whatever form.

Here's the thing, though. Not all scandal reveals inconsequential secrets about minute deviations from eccentric moral systems. Just as trash news is scattered with trivial reports, it also is often buttressed by more substantive stories of failures that led the way to criminal acts, injustices, and corruption. Sometimes, what was hidden before the scandal needed to be revealed for the public good.

In the age of #metoo, we especially know this to be true. The scandal revealed by the Spotlight Team at the Boston Globe was not merely about a quirky ethical failure. It wasn't reported because the authors wanted an ego-rush. It wasn't devoured by readers because of their unconscious projections against religion. Much further, the scandal challenged the injustice of a system that had been propagated and empowered by the Christian Church. Hundreds of thousands of children had been harmed, even to the point of death, and it all had been kept secret. And so, in this case, the scandal was a means by which some semblance of fairness could be restored. Make no mistake about it; it is frequently absolutely essential for the cause of justice that the secrets of the powerful must be revealed.

Two things can be said about this kind of revelation. First, it is undeniably good, the primary means of preventing future injury. Second, it is also deeply troubling because of what it suggests about the people we trust as leaders. We may think to ourselves, "If religious clergy are capable of such harm, then what about athletic program directors, congress-people, physicians, educators, and police officers?" Sadly, as we have learned in the 2010s, many of our leaders do not only conceal insignificant facts about their private lives, they also sometimes hide heinous evil. In a sense, scandals of corruption and abuse highlight our fragility as human beings. They can destabilize worldviews that help us feel safe. And on the other hand, honorable leaders might be frustrated by the dynamic for how it implicitly undermines the influence they have worked so hard to develop[4].

Predictably, this second observation gives me pause as a spiritual leader. As I mentioned above, I have been reported at the center of "scandal" in my small religious community. No, I have never been abusive to people in my flock. But I have at times departed from the doctrinal and the cultural party line. In chapter five, I described how the conscientious management of secrets is essential to maturation as human beings. Whether in parenting, giving medical advice[5], or providing spiritual direction, many of us walk the razor's edge between revealing too much or too little. As a pastor, I have often feared causing damage to my church members' spiritual lives by exposing my personal secrets. The bulk of this chapter explores the underlying mechanisms for this.

In what feels like a fluke, I was never forced to read Herman Melville's epic novel *Moby Dick* in school. The suffering that so many of my older friends and acquaintances describe regarding the long and dense (and yet classic) book wasn't something to which I could relate. Until very recently, that is. Well into my 30s, I decided it was high time to take the plunge[6].

One of my biggest takeaways from the book is how simple the story is. It is one that can easily be summarized in just a few sentences. But this is classic literature. As might be expected, Melville's style is to leave no stone unturned, to explore every nook and cranny

---

4 - I think about a situation like that which was presented by the COVID19 pandemic. Large swaths of the country chose NOT to become vaccinated despite the recommendations and examples of 99% of physicians. Perhaps trust in authority has been eroded by too many scandals.

5 - There's a story from my life in chapter nine that touches on this.

6 - I've since learned that Melville's work is lauded by some LGBTQ people for its covert celebration of queer love.

of this simple story. All in order to set up the great final battle between Ahab and the White Whale. As a consequence of these painstaking details, 17-year-old captive readers have had to wade through endless chapters on the taxonomy of whale species, the intricacies of sharpening harpoons, and methodologies for preparing hunting rigging.

As an adult, I was shocked that it takes 20 chapters just for the narrator, Ishmael, to even get to the ship, Pequad!

Melville's language is remarkably well crafted, even if thorough. One passage that struck me for its beauty is nestled among some of the author's generous contextual details early in the book. It is the colorful description of a preacher in Nantucket and the worship service he leads before the fishermen sail away. In poetic propriety, the subject of Father Mapple's sermon is Jonah from the Bible. Melville writes the pastor leading a hymn that was in reality inspired from an actual old Dutch Methodist tune. In *Moby Dick*, a few of the lyrics go like this:

> *The ribs and terrors in the whale,*
> *arched over me a dismal gloom,*
> *While all God's sun-lit waves rolled by,*
> *and lift me deepening down to doom.*
>
> *I saw the opening maw of hell,*
> *with endless pains and sorrows there;*
> *Which none but they that feel can tell —*
> *Oh, I was plunging to despair.*
>
> *In black distress, I called my God,*
> *when I could scarce believe him mine,*
> *He bowed his ear to my complaints —*
> *No more the whale did me confine.*

For someone unacquainted with the Biblical[7] account of Jonah's fantastic tale, Father Mapple's hymn might come across as oddly dark. But for those familiar with the prophet[8] famous for being swallowed whole by a monstrous sea creature, Melville's choice makes more sense. The song's poetry communicates the despair and hope of a flawed but earnest man's fateful and unique experience. In the belly of the beast, Jonah considers the arc of his life and the harm he has caused. His is certainly a story relevant to the whale hunters of *Moby Dick*, but it is also relevant to our discussion of secret-keeping leaders.

In the short Old Testament of Jonah, God calls the Israelite seer to give words of warning (and ultimately salvation[9]) to a despised inland people group in Ninevah[10]. The prophet balks at the order, conceivably outraged that his God might include the capital of the large, wealthy, and arrogant Assyrian empire with divine wisdom and salvation. Perhaps Jonah was outraged due to overt racism, religious superiority, or even pert laziness. But regardless of what drove him, the story reads that Jonah ran away, boarding a sailing ship that obviously could never arrive at the land-locked city of Ninevah!

The reluctant leader's de-facto porters were none the wiser of

---

7 - The same story with few significant differences can also be found in the Qur'an.

8 - In the Judeo-Christian tradition, a prophet is someone through whom God speaks.

9 - According to the longer Biblical story, rather than abandoning the planet in its brokenness and dysfunction, God entered in and stayed present, pledging to heal, restore, and recreate. Some of this work, he would accomplish through prophets. A common misconception is that God's judgments through prophets are all about terror and fear. Missed in this surface-level interpretation is how the warning or even condemnation is almost universally followed by affirmations of grace, rescue, and new life.

10 - Believed to be 700mi from Israel in what is present-day Iraq.

this backstory as he joined them for the voyage westward across the Mediterranean. But when a violent storm erupts, threatening the sailors and their ship, Jonah is faced with a reckoning. As the crew frantically raced to secure their vessel, throwing cargo into the sea to lighten the load, Jonah slept peacefully in the hold. According to the narrator[11], it was Jonah's secret that was responsible for the chaos falling upon the small seafaring band.

Tension grows to a breaking point before the prophet's guilt before the sailors' inquiries draw him to confession. The tale implies that the crew was aware of the Hebrew God and the many miracles credited to him. Jonah's concealment put the whole community at risk. The only solution is immediately obvious to all: the prophet must go overboard.

Melville's "opening maw of hell" was there in the waters to greet him; Jonah was swallowed by a "great fish." Immediately the storm is said to have stopped. Indeed, it had been the substance of the prophet's secret that had caused the gale. After three days in the belly of the fish, Jonah is deposited alive on land. Convinced of his error, the book of Jonah reads that the prophet is deposited on the shore (alive). Finally, convinced of his error, he obeys the original command delivering an effective message of warning and grace, transforming[12] the lives of Ninevah's inhabitants.

---

11 - The text reads that it was God who sent the storm as incentive for Jonah to follow his original command to go to Ninevah. (Jonah 1:4-6)

12 - One of the most ironic and humorous details of the story is Jonah's ANGER at God for not following through on the prediction, "Forty more days and Ninevah will be overthrown." Instead, after the people heeded the warning and re-prioritized their lives, God chose not to make Jonah's prediction true. In outrage, the end of the book describes Jonah complaining about this lack of vengeance to which God responds with a reminder that his heart is for people rather than esoteric ideals.

Jonah's secret is an interpretive key[13] to the story. As a spiritual leader, his hidden disobedience put every soul on the ship in peril. Whether he recognized the latent energy contained in his concealment or not, it was undeniable in the storm. But as a spiritual leader, his lie also threatened the reputation of Israel, people who believed they represented God in the world. Even further, Jonah's failure to reveal his hidden truth (for a time) deprived the Assyrians in Ninevah from hearing a good word from the divine.

When spiritual leaders keep secrets today, even if the subject has nothing to do with a moral failing per se, there is an impact both to the collective organization and on the individuals forming it. Part of this has to do with the nature of spiritual conversion itself.

When we're young or immature, the process of aligning ourselves to a new spiritual worldview can be thought of as "enchantment." We learn from a new leader, idealize them or their teachings, and revere their way of moving through the world. This is normal. We humans inspire one another to reach forward and become better versions of ourselves. The glamorized relationship is a useful device for spiritual growth and has blessed countless generations through the millennia. It's what we see between Jesus and his students. And just as in that Bible story, when we go through conversion, our souls become attached to our mentors, gurus, and teachers.

Because enchantment feels so wonderful, it is easy to miss how fanciful it is. In spiritual conversion, part of our thinking is magical — not unlike a child writing letters to Santa Claus or Dorothy chasing the Wizard of Oz. They are under a spell if you will, and it's beautiful to behold. But the enchantment is based on assumptions that are more nuanced than the blunt "Truths" that

---

13 - We can read and understand Biblical stories in myriad ways. While my fundamentalist fan-club might insist on exclusively literalistic readings, I often find allegorical or anagogical readings useful (as in this case).

support them.

Because of this, in healthy arcs[14] of spiritual growth, there is inevitably disillusionment. This is where secrets come in. Somewhere along the way, we realize that our guru isn't as perfect as we had imagined. Perhaps they disappoint us with an unexpected reaction, an unexamined belief that doesn't fit the model, or an unexplored behavior pattern. We might realize that Santa Clause is really Uncle George or that the Wizard of Oz is a humbug hiding behind smoke and mirrors. Whatever the discovery, it breaks the spell resulting in disenchantment. The idealized relationship becomes a threat when the student has outgrown the teacher's maturity. Still, this is normal.

Sometimes, disenchantment is where the process stops. Many people throw the baby out with the bathwater and pledge never to become enchanted again. Others double-down, insisting that their mentor's secret isn't, in fact, a problem—this yields fundamentalism of many stripes. But spiritual growth finds its path through disillusionment, not avoiding it.

Deconstruction[15] is the next phase. It is the process of breaking apart the essence of beliefs, culture, and traditions — coming to understand their sources and searching for that which is indispensable. The hard work of deconstruction leads us to (for example) consider different ways that one might read the book of Jonah. It might even help us to discover that the most important question is not "Did Jonah really get swallowed by a fish?" but instead something like, "How have I been swallowed by the consequences of my secrets, like Jonah?" Deconstruction leads us to consider why a people group might have created and

---

14 - Again, this is excepting the kinds of situations involving abusive harm as in the Catholic Church's coverup of molestation.

15 - A term coined by Jacques Derrida, and almost certainly under appreciated by me here.

handed down the tradition of Santa Clause in the first place and why Uncle George goes through the effort. We might even come to see that experiencing joy and wonder through a child is worth a great amount of expense. In deconstruction, we learn that just because the Wizard of Oz isn't magical in the way Dorothy had believed doesn't mean that getting home to Kansas is impossible.

Remaining present in the face of disillusionment and honestly facing the humanity of our mentors is hard. But it's worth it. The reward on the other side of a deconstructed faith-wall is not a better-made structure. Instead, it is a river in the form of a mature, knowing peace. If we're lucky, we will float away in the joy of experiencing re-enchantment: where we become friends with one another's flaws, mutually celebrate our humanity, and embrace the mystery that is existence. This phase allows us to hold on to that which is beautiful, whatever its source while releasing the chaff. Re-enchantment is the source of wonder and the birthplace of grace. I'll return to this at the end of the chapter.

The truth is that spiritual leaders keep secrets because they must. It is what allows for the possibility of enchantment, disillusionment, deconstruction, and re-enchantment in the first place. But just because it is necessary doesn't mean it is easy. The potential threats it presents for communities and the power structures that shape them are a very real weight to bear for any conscientious spiritual leader.

———————

I've already hinted at what I believe to be the solution for the problem of self-concealment in leadership. But that route is much harder to navigate than several other more commonly chosen paths. We'll look briefly at three (poor) alternatives.

The first is refusing to follow anyone at all. After going through a painful disenchantment or seeing someone we love to experience the same, some people throw up their hands, pledging total independence. "I will never be disappointed like this again," is the implicit mantra.

In one sense, this is what the Christian protestant tradition has tried to do since the reformation, pressing back against the authority structures that the church had come to rely on for centuries. "Sola scripture" can be a covert way of saying, "I don't want to follow anyone other than myself."

This also happens on an individual basis. As a pastor for more than a decade, I've known countless people who have outgrown their conservative faith and chosen to leave. But it's heartbreaking to see some replace their rigid religion with an equally rigid worldview. Deconstruction is painful. So it's natural to run from it. But fleeing into the arms of a self-referential isolationist philosophy (or a new unyielding fundamentalism[16]) isn't the answer.

I've got to be honest, though; this strategy actually works for avoiding disillusionment. But this tool for preventing disappointment is also the bluntest. Sadly, it also largely eliminates the possibility for joy. I discussed at some length the problems of isolation and unappreciated secret wisdom in chapters four and five, respectively. Obviously, when an individual decides to go it alone, ostensibly becoming their own frame of reference, there will undoubtedly be negative consequences. Shunning all leaders or mentors is a recipe for an austere and gloomy life.

A second poor alternative to the problem of the enchantment-disenchantment-deconstruction-re-enchantment cycle is to insist that every leader surrender their entire private lives in exchange for influence. The underlying line of reasoning here goes, "As long as my mentor never holds a single secret, I'll never be surprised by something new about their beliefs or behaviors." Of course, this blunt solution likewise "works." But its substantial consequences

---

16 - Sometimes leaving involves swapping out one absolutist leader for another.

outweigh the benefits[17]. Specifically, while preventing leaders' privacy guarantees a faith system's apparent stability, it likewise short-circuits the natural path of blooming maturity (which always involves change). This is not to mention its incredibly detrimental impact on individual leaders themselves!

As a young pastor on my first church assignment, I had a mentor who gravely instructed me to be careful about what I put in the garbage can at home. Confused, I asked, "Why could that be?"

He went on to explain that as a young minister himself, he had been in the habit of throwing empty ice cream containers into trash cans that would be collected by the city waste disposal division. Apparently, a staunch elder of the church had been rifling through his garbage bin each week in hopes of "holding him accountable" to the church's ideals[18]. When the elder discovered evidence of contraband in the associate pastor's trash bin, she collected and delivered it to the senior pastor. She expected immediate punishment of her erring young clergy. And the church didn't disappoint! Questions about his character were the first items on the agenda at the ensuing board meeting. My mentor was nearly fired over the "scandal"! Even though he continued on through a long career, the experience had stuck with him, keeping him anxiously on edge for decades to follow.

Organizations must build structures and establish boundaries[19] in order to exist. This is what defines them in the first place. It is

---

17 - Spiritual leaders logically give up some privacy in order to lead; authenticity is the name of the game as I suggested at the beginning of the chapter. And again, this doesn't apply to matters of abuse and corruption in, say, political leadership.

18 - For many conservatives in my spiritual tribe, dairy foods are an explicit sin.

19 - Again, I am indebted to Richard Rohr's work in "Faling Upward" for a model of organizational dynamics that helped me thrive as a minister.

normal. The problem comes when the list of rules and regulations is unsustainably long, demanding an ever-increasing pool of items requiring inspection. If an entire worldview hinges on ice cream, the problem is not the people who predictably transgress the rule but rather the rule itself! It's natural for institutions to expect official representatives to embody their values. But when those values encompass every aspect of life, the sphere for individuality, creativity, and innovation shrinks out of existence. This touches back to the introduction of the book and the principle of differentiating private from secret. When that which is private is demanded to be exposed, resistance renders the thing a secret.

A third and final poor solution to the problem walks hand-in-hand with the second. If absolutely everything in leaders' lives is fair game for the cruelest of public critique, then the unbearable standard of perfection becomes the benchmark for continued influence. Again, this strategy would "work," except for the fact that no one is perfect. As a result, many leaders in exacting cultures are compelled to hide incongruities in order to protect their legitimacy, only upping the ante for the potential impact when errors are inevitably exposed.

This dynamic is why "the world[20]" tends to judge fundamentalists harshly. It's not that they are flawed like everyone else. It's that they project a lie of superiority while in reality being the same (and often worse)! People roll their eyes at fundamentalist leaders because they're fundamentally[21] dishonest, using strategic secrets to manipulate followers' allegiance. Fundamentalism isn't about virtue. It's about power and control.

In the 1980s, when the televangelist Jimmy Swaggart was discovered to be hiring sex workers, most people were outraged not so much about his intimate preferences but because he was

---

20 - To borrow the term so commonly employed by conservative evangelicals.

21 - See what I did there?

a fraud. As an evangelical zealot, he had demanded perfection from his myriad flocks for years, amassing a fortune by squeezing the consciences of his faithful. But all the time, Swaggart conveniently kept his departures from the ideal hidden from public view. "The world" was not surprised when he was exposed or even disappointed in him. Instead, they were outraged that this charlatan had used a totalitarian worldview to lie his way into a media empire!

A colleague once told me about a prominent church elder who had been involved in an illicit relationship with another man in town. According to the story, the elder's not-straight sexual orientation was well known in the area. Folks who were not part of the church clucked condescension over his hypocrisy. But inside the church community, the elder's secret was entirely unknown (save for gossipy whispers). Even the man's wife (who was employed by the denomination) knew about his relationship, remained married to him, and was apparently hypersensitive about confidentiality. For my colleague, this convergence of details was both confounding and outrageous. As he shared the story with me, I could also hear contempt seep through the cracks. As a pastor, his organizational loyalty led my colleague to resent how the elder's behavior reflected on their congregation. In fact, the "negative impact on mission" secrets can have for churches was the reason he told me the story in the first place.

But while it's technically true, let's step back for a moment. Here we have a man and his wife whose reputation and livelihood rely upon secrecy. They are working within a system that demanded perfection and also granted no privacy. Like me, you might be thinking, "Well, of course then, what other options did they have?!?!" The maligned elder and his wife opted for hiding as a coping mechanism. It's easy to judge leaders when scandals arise, but could a little compassion sometimes[22] be a better response?

---

22 - Obviously in the case of secret abuse and corruption, correct judgment, appropriate accountability, and restoration of justice is non-negotiable.

When organization lays claim to an ever-increasing portion of their leaders' lives, the least they can do is have a gracious spirit about accountability. Sadly, perfectionism and encyclopedic moral systems tend to run together in religious circles. The remaining options for leaders are few. Most[23] follow Jimmy Swaggart's example: hide the dirt.

Every one of us needs leaders to show us the way. And the guides we trust have needs as well. Leaders require privacy for their own dignity and for the sake of their followers' maturing process. Leaders need their students to accept our mutual humanity and the impossibility of perfection. These realities inherently contradict the three most common means for dealing with the tension of leaders keeping secrets. In the final section of this chapter, I will share a poignant story from my ministry. It suggests a kinder, more nuanced posture we might adopt moving forward.

––––––––––

Not long ago, I slipped into a season of despair. I suppose this unpleasant experience had come up before, but this was the first time I consciously said "hello" to it. For me, despair was a combination of feeling trapped, hopeless, and dispassionate about life. Its tangible symptoms included reactivity, gross procrastination, and over-indulgence. The dawning awareness that this amalgamation of sensations amounted to despair was deeply troubling to me (not to mention its possible impact for me, a pastor). In fact, my reaction was, at first visceral. I remember the hot summer afternoon. My hands and feet fidgeted restlessly. My body nervously moved from task to task, to task, never really completing anything. Agitated, my mind buzzed with thoughts seeking solutions. Disconcerted, I felt frantic.

As a leader of a church, I intuitively sensed that admitting such

––––––––––

23 - Like every pastor I've ever known, my elder friend and his wife, as well as myself!

experiences would be as disruptive as the feelings themselves. My denomination tended to teach that habits like Bible study and church attendance are the best possible treatment and prevention of any mental illness. Not unlike many Christian tribes, Adventists often implicitly communicate, "Good people don't feel despair." But even across the arc of church history, Christianity has frequently taught that despair is a sin unto itself; a form of sloth, one of the seven deadly sins. So by consciously noticing my despair in that context, I was also admitting failure. What's more, I intuitively knew that in my leadership context, such a sin hung menacingly over my head. Despair was putting my whole world into peril.

That's scary!

The underlying reason for my troubling emotional state is the subject of another book (and frankly, it's still private). But it was directly connected to my abrupt resignation from full-time professional ministry in the summer of 2021. But the complex circumstances that led to it were not unique. Many millions of people every year in America alone tangle with depression and its debilitating effects. Suicide is the most severe outcome of this disease and is one of the leading causes of death across the board. Graciously, I was able to confidentially access help, community, and resources. I survived my mental illness, but not everyone is as fortunate as me.

Unsurprisingly, pastors suffer from depression at significantly higher rates[24] than the general population. Job stress is an obvious culprit. But the realities of forced secret-keeping under the demands of leadership is the elephant in the living room. Spiritual leadership is an incredibly lonely road.

The weight of self-concealment only multiplies when conscientious

---

24 - According to a Duke University study in 2013, clergy suffer depression at nearly double the rate of the national sample.

pastors consider how it threatens the very communities they serve! Spiritual leaders see how their students sometimes react to the scandal of moral defect. We have witnessed countless individuals lose their faith systems because of their mentors' shortcomings. Spiritual leaders also know the combined pressure of expectations of perfection in the context of little privacy. The high demand adds up to stunningly heavy loads. Isolated and trapped, it's no wonder that ministers end up depressed!

None of this is to minimize the negative impact spiritual leaders have had on our lives. The pain is real. Your suffering is valid. And it's possible to have compassion not only for yourself but for your mentors as well.

In fact, that's the alternative path. The extent to which you have mercy on your own failures defines the magnitude to which you can be merciful to others. Interestingly enough, the solution to the problem of leaders keeping secrets isn't found in our leaders or organizations. It's found in ourselves! The training grounds of empathy is your own soul.

Brian Stevenson, the esteemed author of *Just Mercy*, writes on this principle from the legal realm:

> *I believe that each person is more than the worst thing they've ever done. What's ironic is that we all want rehabilitation when we make mistakes. None of us want to be judged by our worst act. When we make mistakes, we want a chance to show that we are not just that mistake. And yet, we have created this system that is so unforgiving, that is so judgmental. And it's intoxicating to imagine all of these evil people that we can all organize, and beat up on, and go to war against. But it's dishonest.*
>
> *One of the great challenges that I think we have in this country is to revive a conversation about what it*

means to recover. We don't give justice to people just because we want to be fair to them. We give justice to people because we want to be just. We don't give mercy to people because some people need mercy. We give mercy to people because we want and need to be merciful. Our strength, our humanity, and our dignity turn on how we treat other people. Including people who have committed crimes, who have fallen down.

We can do better, not only for our spiritual leaders but for ourselves. We can see the humanity in one another and love unconditionally. We can hold each other accountable while acknowledging the essential role those mistakes have in our subsequent flourishing. We can accept the realities of the enchantment-disenchantment-deconstruction-re-enchantment cycle of faith formation instead of running from it. We can be gentle while also confused. We can be merciful while also strong. We can live in grace.

QUESTIONS FOR DISCUSSION:

1. Do you enjoy tabloid media (on any subject) or water-cooler gossip? Why or why not?

2. Think about a time you learned something about a teacher, mentor, or leader that you hadn't expected. How did this revelation affect you? What might account for someone's differing reaction to the same information? Explain.

3. In the story of Jonah, he is said to have been thrown "into the belly of the beast." Have your secrets (or the secrets of a mentor) ever placed you in such a metaphorical place? If not, describe a time when you've seen it in someone else.

4. The author presents a model for spiritual growth involving enchantment, disenchantment, deconstruction, and re-enchantment. Which of these phases have you experienced in your life? (Note that you may have gone through the cycle multiple times, or not even one full time. It varies according to every person's experience.)

5. Which of the three suggested "poor solutions" to the problem of secrecy in leadership have you witnessed or used? Do you resonate with the author's criticism of them? Why or why not?

6. Describe a time when you gave yourself mercy, unmerited favor. Likewise, describe a situation when you did the same for a leader in your life. What led to these responses?

9 | GIVING AND RECEIVING TRUTH

"You can't handle the truth."

-Jack Nicholson, A Few Good Men

Up until I was in 6th grade, my home context resembled a standard American nuclear family complete with three kids, two parents, pets, and a rural farmhouse. But underneath, circumstances were not as idyllic as they might've seemed on the surface. My stepfather, while somewhat present in my and my siblings' lives, parented with an iron fist. As an adult, I realize that the cycles of dysfunction and abuse he inflicted stemmed from his own wounds.[1] But despite my forgiving him, the injuries he inflicted on my soul have left scars that still affect me to this day.

The most detrimental child-rearing techniques he employed were not his physical violence, toxic masculinity, or even tirades of shaming over the tiniest of household infractions. Instead, it was the way he used judgment against me. While his critical evaluations may have been" the truth" at times, he used them as

---

1 - Talk about "keeping secrets from oneself," I have little doubt that many repressed secrets drove much of the culture I lived under as a child.

weapons to exert control.

This chapter is about the importance of truth-telling and truth-hearing. And really, it deserves its own book. But instead, I've distilled down a few key teachings that interact with secret-keeping. By the end of the chapter, you will walk away with three tools for giving and receiving the truth in ways that are life-giving instead of destructive.

When my mother made the aching decision to file for divorce, I was 12-years-old. Despite its reputation, the news came to me as a relief. A huge weight had been lifted. Peace in our home had won out. For the first time I could remember, I felt freedom in the absence of fear (I've since learned that this emotion is often named "joy"). But even as I experienced the ecstasy of liberty, something was yet missing.

I don't remember my mother calling me "the man of the house" after separating from my step-dad. But I subconsciously took on the grave mantle as an obligation. Our idyllic rural farmhouse was situated on 8 acres of land, which required a significant time investment in upkeep. In reality, I didn't do very much. But at the time, I considered my very amateur lawn-mowing, weed-pulling, sprinkler-fixing, appliance-tinkering, and house-painting essential. I was proud of my "adult" contributions and felt ethically bound to help out my mom.

As I grew into my teenage and young adult years, my mother continued to be generous with praise regarding my basic home repairs. She encouraged me to try and fail and almost delighted in my mistakes[2]. "It doesn't have to be perfect," I can still hear her say in my mind's eye. The truth, as it were, is that my work was

---

2 - I remember one such error that by pure luck didn't result in serious injury. During a particularly snowy winter in Washington, the back-patio-cover I had constructed collapsed under the weight of ice and snowfall. Mercifully, everyone was inside when it happened.

frequently shoddy. But at the moment, that truth was unimportant. Her kindness fueled my experimental resourcefulness, a value I cherish to this day.

As the years went by, my enthusiasm to try new things led me to confidently take on larger and larger home improvement projects in adulthood (for example, my wife and I added a master bathroom to our first home). But eventually, I predictably ran into problems that optimism, curiosity, and the local Home Depot salesperson couldn't overcome. These were the days before YouTube became a catch-all training ground for novice do-it-yourselfers. My only option as a newly married fix-it man was to turn to my community of friends and family who served as would-be experts. Now, this impulse of turning to one's human network for wisdom in times of confusion became a habit for me as I grew into my 30s. And I applied it in almost every sphere of life: from parenting to money management and from career crafting to boundary-setting. Repeatedly throughout my life, I have found myself asking my community, "Is this normal?" Or, "What's the best practice here?" Or, "What is the truth?!?" I'm not alone in this.

My therapist once observed that some of my psychological friction-areas as an adult resembled well-known patterns observed among those raised in families where addiction was present. She led me to "Adult Children of Alcoholic Parents" (ACOA)[3], an organization whose mission is to help folks negatively impacted by family systems like mine. I learned through ACOA that children raised in environments marked by chemical dependency (or the emotional ghosts left by it) have a difficult time discerning what "normal" or "the truth" is. Rules change so often for children of alcoholics that they have little sense of a stable family culture to operate from in forming their own values. In my case, I felt frozen by my stepfather's judgments, terrified of making a mistake. As

---

3 - The ACOA "Laundry List" was a very helpful resource for me in the weeks and months my therapist and I worked through this material. Learn more at: http://www.adultchildren.org/lit-Laundry_List.

adults, people like us are frequently flummoxed by what might otherwise be experienced as everyday happenings for everyone else.

But besides people who resonate with the ACOA phenomenon, almost everyone at some point runs into circumstances where we need advice. It's common to reach out to others we consider wise or who have, as we say, "good judgment." We have already discussed in chapter four how isolation is risky, and in chapter five, how correct timing and motivation are essential when unveiling secrets. Here in chapter nine, we will explore how giving and receiving "good judgment" is essential to making our most meaningful impacts in the world. I need your good judgment to become the person God created me to be. And you need mine. Full stop.

Usually, the word judgment brings up negative stories, such as my stepfather's attacks against me. But the term is multifaceted. It surely can refer to knee-jerk prejudice based on stereotype, rancid gossip run amok, or even the Christian apocalyptic motif that damns sinners to eternal judgment. But in this chapter, we will contrast poor uses of it (e.g., "judgment as a weapon") with life-giving uses (e.g., "judgment as wisdom"). The reality is that judgment is both good and bad, helpful and unhelpful, principled and arbitrary.

The double-edged nature of judgment is well attested in the Bible. The Old Testament book of *Proverbs* teaches, "Plans fail for lack of counsel, but with many advisers, they succeed.[4]" At the same time, the same book also says, "Even fools are thought wise if they keep silent, and discerning if they hold their tongues.[5]" Jesus famously preaches in his Sermon on the Mount, "Do not judge, or you too will be judged. For in the same way you judge others, you

---

4 - Proverbs 15:22

5 - Proverbs 18:21

will be judged[6]..." But Jesus also vociferously chastises religious leaders of his time for their hypocrisy (see Matthew 23). The enormous value of judgment is undergirded in the scriptures by stories of prophetic critique from the likes of Isaiah, Jeremiah, Hosea, and Jonah. But its danger is likewise highlighted by Job's (unhelpful) friends, and even in the temptation of the serpent in Genesis who's judgment about the Creator's benevolence influences the new humans' decisions for the worse.

One of my favorite bits in the Christian scriptures that points to the latent energy contained in judgment is the Apostle Paul's letter to a small early church in Ephesus, a town in located in what is now Turkey. In it, he defines spiritual maturity: "we're all moving rhythmically and easily with each other, efficient and graceful in response to God's Son, fully mature adults, fully developed within and without, fully alive like Christ."[7] He goes on, "[by] speaking the truth in love, we will grow to become in every respect the mature body of him who is the head, that is, Christ" (emphasis mine). For Paul, "speaking the truth in love" (i.e., offering judgment) is the pathway to the best that life has to offer. In order to become the person you were born to be, you need the insight and wisdom of people around you — and they need yours.

And so here's the punch line about judgment in a book about secret-keeping. When my good judgment ("the truth" as it were) is hidden, withheld, unheard, covered up, or otherwise kept effectively secret, its potential for producing transformation is lost.

———

The first tool for constructively giving and receiving truth I learned

———

6 - Matthew 7:1-2

7 - From Eugene Peterson's magnificent paraphrase of the scriptures called *The Message*.

at a David Sedaris show. A dear church member introduced me to his prose during my second year of pastoral ministry. I've been a fan of his poignant humorous essays about the banal ever since. When Sedaris' website announced that his 2014 book tour would include Whitman College in my hometown, my wife and I jumped at the chance to attend. We had long heard him announce, "I read out loud for a living," and wished nothing more than to contribute to his life's work.

As expected, "the show" consisted of David Sedaris reading several essays punctuated with dexterous commentary on the city, the venue, and its people. Towards the end of the program, he offered several minutes of unmoderated Q&A with the audience. Before that moment, I hadn't realized this would be part of the program, and because I do not often get a chance to "talk" with my favorite authors, I decided to throw my hat in the ring. I stood up, and after being called on, I shouted my question from the back of the 1,500 seat performance-arts auditorium.

"HAVE YOU EVER REGRETTED REVEALING TOO MUCH ABOUT PEOPLE IN YOUR PUBLISHED WORK? HAS YOUR HONESTY ON THE PAGE EVER CAUSED FAMILY CONFLICT?"

If you're familiar with David Sedaris, you know that his claim to fame is his unflinching transparency about his inner assessments of family and friends, always delivered with delightful wit and wry abrasiveness. In essence, I was asking him if his personal judgments about these people, aired in books and magazines like GQ, ever created any tension in those relationships?

Sedaris' response was instructive, and it has stuck with me to this day.

First, he gently teased me about projecting my relationships onto his writing. Then, he earnestly confessed, "I've never published anything about anyone without their prior approval."

He went on to describe how no matter the ultimate destination of his manuscripts, each one is vetted and edited by the relevant friends or family members. In other words, every bit of seemingly private information Sedaris releases to the public has been approved by those to whom it refers. Thus, the author's jokes and judgments are (necessarily) well-aired with their targets before being consumed by the masses. I sat dumbfounded.

My imagination turned immediately to the many forthright conversations he must've had in his life. I couldn't relate. My recipe, when it comes to "speaking the truth in love," tends to be marinated in avoidance rather than seasoned with frankness. Sedaris' style of generous sharing places him on the other end of the spectrum. Perhaps my question from the back of the auditorium that night did, in fact, say more about me and my family culture than his writing! Perhaps you can relate.

Many of us sidestep confrontation at almost any cost. Instead of letting our good judgment be known, we withhold it. Taken to the extreme, the consequences of this avoidance can be just as stark as harsh condemnation. Triangulation, coalition-building, playing the victim, sullen pouting punctuated by angry outbursts, and other dysfunctional relational dynamics can be downstream repercussions of dodging giving voice to our truth.

Now, avoiders like me are motivated to keep quiet for as many reasons as there are people. We might hear Jesus' voice echoing in our ears, "It's my job to love, not judge." Our personalities may tend toward people-pleasing over principles. We may have been raised in family cultures where our role(s)[8] determined forthrightness to be undesirable. Some of us even withhold judgment as passive-aggressive retribution for some real or perceived slight.

Ironically, some of us would rather tell the truth, so to speak,

---

8 - Such as being female in a patriarchal culture.

to everyone except the person about whom it explicitly pertains. Colloquially, we call this gossip a frequent means by which secrets are exposed. In this sense, some of us avoid telling our own secrets (as good judgment) by means of telling other people's secrets (as gossip).

Back in high school, I heard a sermon in which the speaker talked about how gossiping is a form of debt-collecting. When we're wronged in some way, a figurative liability is created. By harming another person, the wrongdoer has taken something, and as such, owes it back. While forgiveness is ultimately the most healthy way of releasing these sorts of interpersonal debts, there are hundreds of other options. Gossip is just one option. And when we use it in this way, gossip becomes the selfish expenditure of good judgment. Of course, it doesn't solve anything. But the quick ego-zing from spurting out our truth gives just enough warmth and superiority to keep us coming back again and again.

Regardless of how or why any of us avoid confrontation (whether by the path of gossip, genuine love, or even fear), the consequences to those in need of our good judgment are the same. Rather than benefiting from what we might have to offer, the truth is kept secret; its potential for life transformation locked in the closet.

_____

The second tool for giving and receiving truth lies on the opposite end of the spectrum from the first. Just as avoidance turns our good judgment into secrets, so too can overly zealous declarations of truth. If we want our wisdom to be useful, it is essential that we pay attention to the way in which we deliver it.

In 2015, I attended a lecture[9] by the author and pastor Rob Bell at a theatre in downtown Spokane, Wash. As my friends and I stood in

_____

9 - Tell me about it! Two stories from public speaking events in the same chapter!

line to enter the facility, we couldn't help interact to some degree with "the greeting committee" (as Rob dubbed them in good nature during the show). The crowd consisted of about a dozen protestors holding signs, shouting in megaphones, and passing out pamphlets decrying the evils of Rob Bell. The evocative terms heretic, hell, and sin emblazoned on their paraphernalia were difficult to miss.

Few attendees stopped to engage with the hospitality team. As far as I could tell, no one turned around to go home because of the vitriol. By all indications, their" truth-telling" fell on deaf ears. It was as if the protesters took on the role of the "boy who cried wolf" from Aesop's fable[10]. Like me, Rob Bell's fans had apparently been so fatigued by years of such oral assaults and inoculated from that kind of verbal venom that they no longer "had ears to hear.[11]" Good judgment spoken at the wrong time, in the wrong way is as ineffective as total avoidance. In fact, practically speaking, the manner of delivery is the difference between our opinions being true or untrue to their recipients.

One last time, I'll point to Jesus in his "Sermon on the Mount." Immediately following his command against judging, the master teacher instructs, "Do not give to the dogs what is sacred. Do not throw your pearls before swine." In other words, your truth is too important to waste. It's as valuable as fine pearls, don't squander it by incessant spluttering from street corners. The question for each of us is, "Do you want to be right, or do you want to be

---

10 - If you are unfamiliar, the general arc of the old fairytale is that a young shepherd boy in a remote field repeatedly calls in the town watch to defend he and his herd from wolves. But at each summons, the boy is shown to have been lying about a threat. Perhaps he was bored or otherwise lonely, we are not told. Regardless, his calls for help eventually begin to weigh down on the ears of his fellow villagers. He's calling out "wolf" so frequently, that they begin taking him less and less seriously. Finally, when a wolf really does come to ravage the boy's flock, no one at all comes to his aid when he cries for help.

11 - To borrow an apt phrase from Jesus.

heard?"

In the context of postmodern American culture, excessive truth-telling tends to breed defensiveness, entrenchment, and even extremism. Rather than inspiring changes in belief, endlessly shouting down good judgment gilds people into their already chosen positions. In seminary, my classmates and I studied the Likert scale, which is sometimes used in marketing circles to evaluate strategies in advertising. In our context, we studied it to learn more about how to influence organizations as leaders. The wisdom I still hang on to from those days is that nuanced conversations are more useful for influencing long-term change than hardline argumentation.

Americans witnessed this dynamic during the presidential election of 2016. We saw candidates frantically one-upping each other with extreme rhetoric. The ultimate winner, Donald Trump, was famous for his eagerness to Tweet his unedited judgments, seemingly stream-of-consciousness. But instead of helping people to change viewpoints, this style of public discourse primarily served to push entrenched followers further apart. We already know this. No one is growing more mature via unanchored rants on Internet message boards or slanted cable-TV news commentary. As a culture, we are too saturated by such media to be positively influenced. The vast majority of it falls on deaf ears—pearls before swine.

David Augsburger, author of *Caring Enough to Confront* summarizes the principle well, "Being heard is so close to being loved that for the average person, they are almost indistinguishable." In a sense, the truth doesn't matter. The truth spoken in love is what matters. If we love our good judgment more than we love people, it'll inevitably show. If you are someone who finds yourself speaking freely and quickly, it might just be that you often treat your friends as opponents instead of image-bearers of the divine. Speaking the truth in love calls us to slow down, listen, and practice patience. This leads us to the final tool we'll explore in this chapter.

––––––––––

The third and final tool for beneficial giving and receiving of truth is rooted in emotional awareness of social contexts. The single greatest predictor of whether or not people receive needed judgment is not a title, authority, education, wealth, or fame. Instead, it is a trusting relationship. This circumstance, more than any other, earns the right to be heard[12]. The greeting committee's pronouncements outside Rob Bell's lecture fell on death ears because of the absence of a relationship. In fact, most of us received their antics as the antithesis of love because they hadn't earned the right to speak! Conversely, it was the presence of trusting relationships that allowed for David Sedaris to vet his essays with family members in the first place. In the context of love, his humorous observations could be aired without disintegrating the relationship.

––––––––––

12 - There is at least one narrow exception to this rule that is worth footnoting. Those having been called to give a prophetic voice in some ways shortcut their way around intimacy-building before speaking up. As the prophet Jonah learned, when God gives a message to be delivered, a servant best do it.

Christians often think of "prophecy" as something akin to fortune-telling or predicting the future. But in the scriptures, the most common role of a prophet is to be a mouthpiece of God - to deliver His message to a person or people. While there are examples of apocalyptic prophecy (Revelation, Daniel, etc.) in the scriptures, there are far more of prophecy as contemporary confrontation (see Jesus, Paul, Hosea, Isaiah, Jeremiah, Micah, etc.).

While claiming the prophetic role might seem like a free pass to those with a more David Sedaris-like personality bent, I think taking on that mantle is a grave and weighty matter. Claiming oneself to be speaking with a prophetic voice isn't something to just willy-nilly fall into. We can't call ourselves a prophet just because we want to be a jerk. I believe there are moments when God communicates good judgment through the prophetic voice (think Martin Luther King Jr.), but I'm doubtful that Aunt Mary can claim it when she wants to wax eloquently about financial responsibility to the panhandler on the corner.

I will close this chapter with a story about how this dynamic has played out in my life. As I indicated in the chapter on shame, I've struggled with elevated body weight since early childhood. The voices of judgment still echo through my head. The feelings of inadequacy and unworthiness because of my size still bubble to the surface when I see myself in a mirror. They still come calling when I take a bite of dessert.

While I was heavier than most of my peers through grade school, it wasn't terribly noticeable until Jr. High, in the years following my mother's divorce of my abusive stepfather. And even then, I really didn't begin to put substantial weight on it until after the death of my brother[13] during my senior year in high school. From that traumatic season and throughout the fifteen years that followed, my weight gain took on a gradual march up and to the right. This trend hasn't been entirely unconscious either. I can't count the number of times within that fifteen-year window that I lost 20 or 30 or 40 pounds. I've been on more diets and exercise kicks than I can shake a stick at. But each and every time I've adopted new patterns, I would wind up gaining the lost mass back (and then even more).

A few years into my marriage, at one of the many times when my weight had arrived at an all-time high, my new wife urged me to get established with a physician. She was concerned about my health. I really hadn't ever really sought out a regular doctor beyond my childhood pediatrician. It was a new concept for me at 27 years old, but I never-the-less dutifully sought a doc out and made an appointment.

What ensued in my first visit was an awful experience for me. After evaluating my blood-work and other vitals, this new physician laid into me with what felt like very harsh and very

---

13 - If you're not reading in order, I describe the story in more detail in the chapter four.

personal comments: "You're too young to be this heavy and have these kinds of problems," "I just can't believe someone like you would be in this state," "I thought you people were supposed to be health-minded" (referring to Adventist Christians), and "What you really need to do is stop eating so much. Just put the fork down, man!"

Hearing these same sorts of unvarnished judgments became commonplace for me as a young adult in subsequent medical settings. After physical examinations, my doctors, filled with concern, would eagerly press me toward greater health. But as I've indicated, the manner by which they would attempt to help was alienating at best.

What I typically heard in their well-meaning judgments was rarely what they actually meant and frequently demotivating. For example, when they asked about my weight or encouraged me to eat cleaner, or exercise more, etc., I often heard: "You're really a strange cat, fatty. You're the only person I've ever seen who has screwed up his life this badly and in such a short amount of time. Congrats, loser!" Or, "How can you possibly claim to be a spiritual leader when your personal life is such a disaster!? You're a fraud! We all know it. Just go take a bath in Alfredo sauce and die." Or, "You need to know that your weight clearly indicates that you're a pathetic excuse for a human being. If I were your spouse, I'd have already left you." Or simply, "You should feel ashamed of yourself."

Clearly, for me visiting the doctor became a painful exercise as time went on. I learned to dread it. And each year, as I showed up for my appointment, I'd shrink with defeatism as I succumbed to what felt like another tongue lashing. Over the years, time intervals between my visits gradually increased. I didn't want to hear what they had to say. I wanted to avoid medical people. I grew reciprocally judgmental of them myself. I switched doctors after particularly scornful lectures. I quit attending my employer's health screenings because of how awful I felt about myself when

I finished. My health only grew worse. The truth was available to me, but not in the context of a loving relationship.

When I moved to Walla Walla, Wash., in 2010, I established a relationship with a new doctor in town (again, at the urging of my wife). I didn't realize at first how different this new Doc was from some of the others in my past experiences. While they had usually cut right to the chase when it came to my obesity, this new fellow was slow to make pronouncements (or offer recommendations).

"How do you feel about your weight right now?" I remember him asking in one of our first appointments together. I was shocked by what seemed like a remarkable way for a physician to enter a conversation. "Is your health something you've given attention to in the past years?" was another line I can recall. How enlightened! I felt intentionally humanized as a real person possessing intelligence, a history, feelings, and value. For me, this was a novel experience. My new doctor seemed more interested in me as a human being than in my condition(s). He wanted to know what made me tick, what I thought, and where I was headed. In short, he seemed interested in having a relationship with me.

My doctor's approach allowed me to start trusting him little by little. In life, every threshold of growth requires some sort of confrontation. That's part of why judgment is so scary. When it comes in the absence of a loving human connection, it can feel like an attack. For me, truth-telling in the context of trust changed everything.

It's probably reasonable to say that in today's medical-industrial complex, intentionally forming connections like this is not often a financially wise decision for medical professionals[14]. Some doctors might even say that the system prohibits such interpersonal

---

14 - And perhaps that's part of why my doctor didn't live in a fancy gated community whisked away from the ordinary folks. Perhaps it's why he dresses in regular clothes and drives an old Honda Accord instead of a BMW.

connection. In any case, I couldn't be more grateful for the way in which my physician took the risk to make a bond. Today I feel as though his financially imprudent tack saved my life.

By the spring of 2015, I weighed in at an all-time high, more than 315 pounds. Under the care of my doctor, I had lost 20-40 pounds five times, if not more, over the preceding five years. And each time, I had regained even more weight back. Together we had examined my diet, sleep patterns, exercise habits, psychological ruts, and quite a number of medical realities, including blood tests relating to the lymphatic and metabolic systems. While some treatments or plans were helpful for a time, I couldn't seem to get to a place where the weight stayed off more than a couple of months before creeping back on.

Because I am 6'1" in height, the added poundage spread all over my frame in such a way that few would've believed I had become as heavy as the largest guys on professional football fields. "I carry it well," I learned to say when my high weight came up in conversation. Close friends all but gawked when I let it slip that I had eclipsed 300 pounds. They did -- and yet they did not -- see me as a person potentially eligible for those weight-loss-extravaganza reality TV shows.

More significant than the scale number, however, were my negative health indicators growing under the surface. While I could've (and often did) made an argument that I was happy at my weight, that it's possible and even desirable to have peace with oneself regardless of shape or size, the truth was that I had developed additional conditions beyond high blood pressure. Metabolic syndrome, fatty liver, high cholesterol, high triglycerides, pre-diabetes, sleep apnea, joint pain, the list goes on.

At the time of my annual physical exam that spring of 2015, I was pretty disheartened. My hope was fading. I had begun to feel resigned to the seemingly inevitable onset of adult-onset type-2 diabetes. While I was thankful to be alive: more sound emotionally than I had been in years, excited to be a father of two boys and a husband of an unbelievable wife, and honored to be working in a career that lends itself quite handily to my personal sense of calling; I knew my health was threatening to take it all away and I felt powerless to stop it. No matter the medical treatment, diet plan, exercise regime, or state of mind, it seemed as though the damage to my metabolism had been done; I was doomed to fight it forever.

When I expressed this sense of discouragement to my new physician in Walla Walla, like any good mentor, he didn't succumb to my set of negative emotions. Even if he had his doubts about my ability to stop the trend of poor health indicators, he didn't show it. Instead, he offered some encouragement saying that he knew I wasn't at the end of the road, as demonstrated by all my hard work in years prior. "I have no doubts you can get to a better place," he said, "I've already seen you do it; we just need to get the right set of tools in your hands."

Then, this physician did something that surprised me. He started talking about a treatment method he had up until that point, never suggested or even hinted at bariatric surgery. I immediately felt incredulous by the suggestion.

"Bariatric Surgery!? I'm not that fat!" I thought to myself. "And besides, the only people who do bariatric surgery end up gaining all the weight back anyway - they're just looking for the easy way out. He doesn't think that's ME, does he?!"

I felt visceral shame at his suggestion. "Is this really where I've sunken to? Am I that desperate now? What have I done to myself? I really am a failure!" My inner dialogue betrayed the fact that I had little concept about the high effectiveness of bariatric surgery for treating morbid obesity. Not unlike when I was a child, I didn't know what "normal" was when it came to getting to a healthy weight.

My mind churned with possibilities and fear. My doctor's truth-telling had jolted me. But because we had built up a rapport over the previous years, I didn't write him off due to this painful vestige of confrontation. Although it felt surreal to be in such a conversation, I remained present and interested. I verbalized some of the above reactions coursing through my head, and he responded with clarity and compassion.

He explained that, in fact, I had already been a good candidate for surgery for a couple of years, not just at that moment after arriving at my all-time-high weight. He said that he wanted to wait to suggest it to me until he thought I was ready to hear it, that he knew I had been committed to finding a way with another lifestyle 'treatments.' But, he elaborated that he thought it was time for me to seriously consider surgery as an option.

I was dumbfounded. I certainly had felt some desperation and even a sense of defeatism over my situation at the point. I had worked so hard and tried so many other treatment programs that had provided only temporary success. It wouldn't be unreasonable for me to feel a little jaded. In order for me to fully embrace hope, I would have to submit to what I now consider to be the truth that my doctor was speaking into my life at that moment.

The story about my experience with going through bariatric surgery is its own tale.[15] A year after my doctor's confrontation of me that spring morning, I had lost 80 pounds (almost 1/3 of my total weight). My health indicators (blood work, blood pressure, etc.) had all normalized. My energy levels had lifted, as had my sense of hope for the future.

Today, I couldn't be more grateful for my doctor's careful

---

15 - The story detailing the lessons I learned from my experiences with weight-loss surgery can be accessed for free on my website: krisloewen.com. These blog posts form a type of confession, and seem appropriate to share in a book exploring the personal liabilities of secret-keeping.

stewardship of his good judgment. Because he managed it well, grew with me in a relationship, and conscientiously considered the right timing for telling the truth in love, he changed my life.

You can do this too. Your truth doesn't have to remain secret, stuck in cycles of disempowered avoidance or unloving shouting. You don't have to squander your truth where it won't be valued outside the context of relationship. Your good judgment is a gift to this world, and as long as it's hidden, it's worthless to those who need it. May you have the courage and attention to transform your truth into a blessing for the world.

QUESTIONS FOR DISCUSSION:

1. In this chapter, the author talks about feeling confused defining "normal" in everyday life situations. This experience is sometimes identified as "Gaslighting" and is not uncommon for people having gone through abuse. Talk about a time in your life when you suspected that you yourself had been deceived and began questioning what before seemed natural. What led you to that awakening? What factors helped or hindered you in that process?

2. Tell a story about when you were grateful for someone else's "good judgment" in your life.

3. Consider the spectrum the author highlighted in talking about David Sedaris. Which end of the spectrum do you tend to fall on when it comes to truth-telling: avoidance or enthusiastic engagement? For you, what does it feel like to have a forthright conversation about a difficult topic with someone you love?

4. Have you ever participated in a protest? If yes, what do you think it accomplished? If no, explain why not.

5. In the final section, the author discusses how a trusting relationship with a physician gave him access to the truth. Is it easy or difficult for you to trust the advice of others? Do you find that you tend to listen to the judgment of strangers over trusted allies, or vice versa? Why?

10 | DISCLOSURE

"Being vulnerable is the only way to allow your heart to feel true pleasure that's so real it scares you."

-Bob Marley

Felix Bushaloo Brazeale ("Uncle Bush") earned fleeting notoriety for pulling an eccentric stunt in his home in Roane County, Tennessee. In 1938 at the age of 74, Uncle Bush solicited a local newspaperman and friend to help him advertise for his own funeral — before his death!

Improbably, the journalist agreed to cover the story as a personal favor. The rest is history. After promotion by the Associated Press, "guests" traveled the rough, dusty roads in droves to attend Uncle Bush's funeral. Nearly twelve thousand people showed up, one of the largest crowds ever in that small county! For his part, the guest of honor hand-crafted his own (empty) walnut casket and hired a minister from Illinois to preside over the event. Uncle Bush even provided refreshment stands for the visitors on the hot summer day.

In *Get Low*, Aaron Schneider's film adaptation of the story starring Robert Duvall, the writers add a captivating yet spurious twist to the tale. Instead of being motivated by a peculiar curiosity to hear his own eulogy, the film paints Uncle Bush as a man in old age plagued by the weight of secrets carried for decades. Duvall's character lives a life colored in the heaviness of blues and grays. He plans his own funeral because deep inside his soul, he knows he needs to tell the truth before he dies. The fictional Bush can't bear the thought of being misunderstood in death.

Get Low climaxes during the Illinois minister's homily as Uncle Bush pads across the raised wooden stage and steals the spotlight. In a confident and yet shame-tinged soliloquy, he confesses his secret publicly.

As a younger man, Bush and a married woman had fallen in love. The two had planned to button up their illicit relationship by running away together. But when his lover didn't show up to the agreed-upon meeting place, Uncle Bush knew trouble was afoot.

His story before the silent crowd continued. At his lover's home in the middle of the night, Bush found her beaten to the point of death by her raging husband, who opened the door covered in blood. The two fought each other viciously until the husband broke a kerosene lantern on the wall, setting the two-story house ablaze.

With a creaking but determined voice, Uncle Bush described how the next thing he remembers is being outside the home, laying on the grass helplessly watching it burn. Neither his lover nor her husband made it out alive.

"This was all my fault," he reports saying to himself in the wake of the fire. "I didn't want forgiveness. I didn't want absolution," he says to the silent throng. The film portrays his disgrace palpably. His silent shame had stuck with him for decades. "I needed to hold on to what I did to be sick from it...so I told no one..." he says in the film.

But as he continues to speak, something amazing happens.

230

Uncle Bush's confidence grows before our eyes. His confidence increases as his shoulders push back, and his chest pokes out. Almost imperceptibly, the aged man's chin rises, his eyes forward and clear. The tiniest hint of a smile appears.

The horrific tragedy that had shut down his heart for so many years was becoming the pathway for healing. Felix Bush knew that it would. It's why he planned the funeral in the first place. The connection between disclosure and healing is built into the fabric of the universe.

Many of us intuitively know it as well. Confessing secrets has the power to lift the weight of stagnation they hold over our lives. Self-revelation has an almost magical property to it, evaporating the negativity holding us back. In the strangest of twists, exposure dissipates shame, interrupts dysfunctional systems, renders isolation impossible, and sprouts intimacy. By the humble act of naming that which was hidden, the best of life becomes possible.

Like Uncle Bush, you probably have some secrets. But you might not be carrying around the kind of life-long closeted stories that threatened to upend his life. Nevertheless, the principle remains true regardless of the secret. Healing and exposure are inextricably linked.

I learned this lesson in part by doing the laundry[1]. While in our egalitarian home, I do the lion's share of the cooking, and my wife Paige does most of the laundry; when our first child was born, all bets were off. The reason was that we chose to use cloth diapers instead of disposables[2] in hopes of a smaller carbon footprint and

---

1 - Our family routinely enjoys a silly song about "Laundry Camp" entitled "Clothes Dryer" by the kids' artist Randy Kaplan.

2 - Apologies if this is TMI, but stick with me, it'll all come out in the wash.

more money in the bank. Because of the large increase in daily laundry production, I had no choice but to get my hands dirty.

For the most part, cloth diapering worked well for us. The market at the time was flooded with many options utilizing modern technology to overcome some of the time-worn problems. But despite the rising popularity, we had difficulty with one underlying problem: stains.

For all our expertise and internet research, some of the worn-in colors on the bright white hemp diapers just wouldn't come out. Of course, these articles of clothing continued to function properly, but their appearance was kind of gross.

One day, my wife and I haphazardly stumbled across the answer to our disagreeable quandary. It was the sun.

Simple old-fashioned UV light from the sky is the best companion to old-fashioned cloth diapering. What might not otherwise launder out in a machine, sunlight handles effortlessly. It was a revelation for my wife and me. Almost like magic, our son's clothes diapers looked like new again.

Metaphorically speaking, our discovery about diaper cleaning is also applicable to human nature. Transformation is next to impossible without dragging our secrets out into the light of day. As with diapers, using exposure as a remedy might lead to the neighborhood finding out (clothing hanging on the line in the sun is a sure sign that there is probably some dirty laundry inside, after all). But public disclosure surely beats keeping things hidden in a wet, smelly, moldy pile in the basement! Like washing cloth diapers, if we want to experience healing, the bright light of the sun is second to none.

A first-century Christian apostle named James[3] wrote a letter that is now found in the New Testament. His message to one of the earliest Christian communities speaks to the mechanism by which secrets are disarmed through confession. Instructing his recipients on the importance of providing spiritual support to those suffering from illness or disease, James writes,[4] "confess your sins one to another, and you will be healed."

To me, this phrase sounds eerily familiar to the wisdom of line-dried diapers. Exposure and restoration are inextricably linked.

Sometimes, when religious people read this Bible verse, their minds go immediately to Roman Catholic confessionals, rote rituals, and shame-tinged penance. In other words, some of us read James' reminder to confess sins understanding him to be addressing individualistic salvation and eternal life. While there may be some truth to that assumption, something deeper and more meaningful is happening here.

James isn't talking about a sort of mystical computer password that guarantees access to heavenly realms after death. He's talking about the here and now[5]. He's describing reality. Confession leads to healing in this life, not just over the way by and by. In James' experience, there is a direct correlation between verbalizing our secrets and physical restoration. "Confess one to another, and you will be healed." Indeed.

---

3 - Many believe the author to be not one of the twelve original disciples, but rather one of Jesus' brothers.

4 - James 5:16

5 - The Greek word the author uses here for "healed" isn't the term we would expect if his intended application was entirely in the spiritual realm. That word is sozo: to save or be saved, to go to heaven, to be counted among the righteous at the judgment, to be cleaned of sinfulness, etc... Instead, he uses iaomai (eee-aaa-oh-my) which is about physical healing in the physical, temporal, present sense. Iaomai implies 'being made whole' or having a disease or infirmity resolved.

The question is, how do we put this power to work in real life? We'll look at that question through the rest of this chapter as well as the next.

––––––

The catharsis available through self-disclosure isn't merely a nifty axiom I picked up by watching movies and washing diapers. I've lived it. The truth of it has changed my life. In fact, my personal discovery of the indisputable link between confession and personal transformation has been among the most significant of my life. In many ways, living this truth initiated this book project!

I'll explain by sharing another story from my life. I've already written about[6] how divorce loomed large in my childhood. This experience is part of why I've taken the prospects of my own marriage exceptionally seriously for about as far back as I can remember. Since I was little, I have longed for a spouse with whom I could enjoy a deep and intimate connection. My earnestness led me to extensive reading on the subject and endless ruminating on who I might end up with. Little did I know that the beautiful cellist I stood behind playing string bass in our grade-school string orchestra would later become my wife. What we inadvertently discovered in our spontaneous, heartfelt conversations on orchestra trips was that disclosure breeds connection. She, like me, grew up in a home marred by the chaos of divorce. And also, like me, she too had similar solemnity regarding marriage. Our common stories eventually proved to be the long-term bass-line of our relationship.

In college years later, when Paige and I were seriously dating, my pensiveness gave way to anxiety. I pressed for the two of us

––––––

6 - See chapter nine for more about my relationship with my step-father. Chapter three explores some of my experiences as they relate to my mom and dad's divorce.

to begin meeting with a family therapist before we were even engaged — in order to dig through "family junk," as I explained it. While I truthfully justified my motive as a desire for us to establish a firm foundation in our would-be marriage, that wasn't the only reason brewing. I intuitively knew that in order for our relationship to be healthy, we needed our secrets to be hung out in the sun (at least in our own figurative backyard). At the time, I didn't yet understand that secrets, like dirty baby diapers, are perfectly normal. I didn't yet realize that they aren't intrinsically dirty or evil — but instead that they carry helpful and not-so-helpful consequences based on how we manage them. But in one of life's many great graces, I instinctively knew that at least in my marriage, my secrets had to be disclosed. Couples therapy proved to be the beginning of some of the most difficult and yet valuable conversations I would ever have.

What was my secret? Well, looking back, there were many layers of hiddenness in my psyche. But from my vantage point at the time, the chief superficial problem was my habitual use of internet pornography. I was dreadfully ashamed of my habit that in those days I regarded as a disgusting addiction.[7] It had grown out of hormone-induced curiosity around the age of 12. I had been too scared to ask for explanations about genitals and sex-acts and pregnancy despite an ever-increasing interest. In the context of a repressive and puritanical conservative religious culture that taught me to fear bodily attraction and sexual pleasure, I felt like a freak for having these curiosities. My questions felt morally wrong. Complicating circumstances further was my family history of abuse. The cruelty, abandonment, and multi-generational patterns I had inherited produced an acute absence of confidence in me as a pubescent teenager. I felt too afraid to speak up for myself, ask for my needs, and ask perfectly natural questions.

---

7 - Today, I'm not convinced that it actually rose to that level of dysfunction. I have come to have more compassion on myself in that situation, under the influence of puberty and a profound amount of pain that I learned could be temporarily medicated by porn.

Instead, I started checking out my step-father's porno magazines that had been left in his ransacked home office after moving out. My hormones kicked into overdrive. As the age of the internet dawned in the early 90s, a whole new horizon of anonymous access to "answers" opened up for me. As the resident computer expert in my single-parent home, I quickly learned how to cover my tracks, erase histories, and ensure my repeated escapades remained hidden. For the better part of a decade, I compulsively consumed pornography in our home. I was never "caught." I was never confronted about it. It remained a tightly kept secret. I felt alone and hopelessly out of control.

I also felt ashamed. Marinated in Evangelical purity culture[8], I didn't realize that the overwhelming majority[9] of my peers were doing the very same thing as me. I didn't understand that my sexual desires were not wrong. My church didn't teach me that having a libido during puberty is normal, even holy. All I received was repeated messages of inadequacy each time I "relapsed" after once again unsuccessfully praying away my "addiction." As a teenager and young adult, I felt utterly lost; wandering alone in the desert, desperate for water, and yet ceaselessly drinking sand. And while today I don't regard porn as a panacea of sexual freedom[10], I likewise don't think people should live in constant disgrace if they use it.

In the wake of my hopelessness, I never contemplated suicide.

---

8 - I enjoyed Beth Allison Barr's history of patriarchal Christianity that cogently also describes purity culture, *The Making of Biblical Womanhood*.

9 - According to a University of New Hampshire study, 93% of boys and 62% of girls access online porn during adolescence (ages ~12-22).

10 - I've appreciated www.yourbrainonporn.com for its unbiased evaluations on how internet pornography can negatively affect the brains of young people. Furthermore, I think that it's self-evident how porn is not a constructive tool for childhood sexual education.

But looking back, I think despair is the best descriptor for my heaviest emotions during that season of life. Overwhelmed by a problem that I presumed to threaten my life's greatest desires, I felt trapped. And yet, as I've said, intuitively, I already knew what to do. I just hadn't realized how transformative it would end up being!

I asked Paige to marry me on a Monday, November night in College Place, the little college suburb of Walla Walla. I made arrangements to use our cavernous church sanctuary for the proposal; six months later, it was the same space in which my wife and I would say our vows. Our engagement proved to be the first circumstance in my life to provide me with adequate motivation to confess. I so longed for a healthy marriage, and I couldn't risk it by continuing to hide. I'd have to go through the valley of the shadow of disclosure. The prospect of making a lifelong commitment to Paige was the push I needed.

A few short weeks after I asked Paige to marry me, we went for a walk on a similarly chilly winter evening in College Place. Strolling the quiet sidewalks, it didn't at first feel much different from the other jaunts that had become our nightly habit. The two of us were in love and also very close friends who spoke freely about the day and our future together. As we talked that night, though, I ruminated about how to initiate the conversation I knew to be essential. When it became clear to me, I slipped into the stream and let go.

Paige and I had worked through a number of pre-marital workbooks over the previous months. One of them included an exercise encouraging us to discuss our sexual histories with one another. At the time, we had both shared. But of course, I had held back. So that December night on our walk, I took a deep breath.

"Remember that workbook we did, that had us share about our pasts...like...erm...in terms of sexuality?" My heart beat rapidly as I plunged into the metaphorical cold water.

"Yeah...," she replied, concerned but also immediately understanding that I had something more to say.

"Well, did you tell me everything?"

She seemed surprised by the question, pausing for a moment before saying without a tinge of shame, "Hmm, no...I'm pretty sure I said it all." She paused, "What about you?"

My moment had arrived. Anxiety swelled to the surface. "Um... well...uh...," I delayed, "...yeah, kinda...I guess."

We continued walking. Paige didn't speak but instead looked over at me with love in her eyes. It was the same look she offered in every other conversation. She didn't appear afraid or triggered. She was "here" for whatever may come. In the 16 years since that moment, that posture of courageous presence hasn't wavered.

I took another breath, and as the words came tumbling out of my mouth, the surreal moment etched into my memory. I remember my voice trembling, face flushing, and skin growing cold and clammy. I continued to stammer, pause, and backtrack as I walked her through my childhood, the magazines, the pictures and videos, and all the private experimentation that I had done over the years. My ongoing training for pastoral ministry flashed across my mind as I talked. I thought to myself, "What would all the people at school or at the church think of me if they heard what I'm confessing tonight?" I thought about my mom and my sister and felt ashamed. The whole thing was terrifying.

But soon, it was done. I said everything I needed to say.

And like flipping a light switch, my secret was out in the wild. I no longer had control of it. I couldn't manipulate the outcome. Paige would rightfully get to shape her future with me in light of the information that I had kept hidden for so many years.

She continued to walk with me but continued in silence for a time before responding. And then something that felt magical happened. Paige didn't freak out. She didn't run away. She didn't ridicule me or suggest that we break up. She didn't even appear disappointed in me. In fact, her behavior failed to materialize any of the fears I had so carefully nurtured in my psyche. Instead, this remarkable woman expressed empathy, asked follow-up questions, listened to my responses, and repeatedly emphasized her unconditional love for me.

My toxic shame began dissolving right then and there. I later learned that likewise, in that same moment, my decadent relationship with pornography also irrevocably changed. Healing had begun the instant I confessed, just as the ancient spiritual leader James had promised in his letter to early Christians. While this solitary experience wasn't the end of the process for me, it surely was the beginning.

In his book on the character formation that takes place through practicing spiritual disciplines, Brian McLaren writes, "Experiencing mercy and grace from you, someone both present and visible to me, I can believe in mercy and grace from God, who is present but not visible to me." In a mystical and yet tangible way, confession had led me into the very presence of God. All of a sudden, I corporeally knew what it felt like to trust the Divine and to be loved by her exactly as I am. In fact, it wasn't until that moment in December of 2004 that I really began to grasp, on a visceral and emotional level, what it's like to be embraced by God's scandalously unconditional affection.

It's no overstatement. The moment was transcendent. Whatever you want to call it: truth-telling, confession, self-disclosure, or spilling the beans. Taking that risk changed everything for me. And it continues to do so to this very day. (And fascinatingly, the more I have shared my experience with others who have similar struggles, the easier time I have had making the kinds of decisions that feel life-giving instead of life-draining.) Courage breeds courage. Trust breeds trust.

You probably have secrets in your life that you intuitively know must be shared with someone somewhere in order for you to reach your full potential. It might feel scary to consider disclosure to those you most fear knowing the truth. It may even seem impossible. But before you write it off, consider this. Every single time I've been daring enough to get vulnerable with people (Every. Single. Time.), I have been blown away by the powerful reply, "Oh, you too?"

Dietrich Bonhoeffer knew a lot about keeping secrets. A German theologian and activist, he eventually lived as a double-agent during World War II, working within the Nazi party while simultaneously working against them. In his seminal work on Christian community, *Life Together*, Bonhoeffer writes, "A man who confesses...in the presence of a brother knows that he is no longer alone with himself; he experiences the presence of God in the reality of the other person. As long as I am by myself in confession...everything remains in the dark, but in the presence of a brother [it] has to be brought into the light."

A few months after getting honest with Paige, I once again mustered up the courage to speak about my experiences with pornography. This time, it was to a group of high school boys at a weekend spiritual retreat. Not unlike the first time, once more, I found self-disclosure to be frightening. There I was, an undergraduate in training for pastoral ministry with a job offer on the table, laying bare my soul before a bunch of people who could use the information to hurt me. In probably overly-melodramatic fashion, I felt as though my career lay in the balance before it even began. I wasn't even an official pastor yet, but I still felt the weight of expected perfection on my shoulders.

But once again, my fears didn't materialize. Instead, just as with my confessions to Paige, I received the byproduct of grace and healing in my own life. I felt stronger and braver than ever! But that wasn't all. Something even more beautiful was born at that moment.

By telling my own story with honesty, I not only communicated a warning about a set of behaviors I had found to be destructive; I also created an open door for further conversation. It felt like magic the first time it happened. To my great shock, many of the boys at the retreat started telling me their own stories about shame related to their sexualities. It didn't seem possible before, but what I discovered is that the majority of young men at the retreat had secret patterns in their own lives. And somehow, my self-exposure gave them the courage to speak up with vulnerability as well. It turned out to be a transformative moment for all of us.

Confession in the context of community multiplies its healing potential.

As an adolescent, my Dad's visits from New York to Washington State had given way to my own voyages across the country to visit him. Sometimes the summer versions of these trips would extend to several weeks at a time. More than a decade after my parents' divorce, my Dad was well into his recovery from addiction. He was back to work, more than full time: as a cancer physician, a musician, and a father. In many ways, he probably felt stretched to his limits. More than a few times during my summer visits, he dragged me along to open Alcoholics Anonymous (AA) meetings in musty church basements, probably having no other choice but to include me. I would only later come to understand how fitting such settings are for the metamorphosis that often takes place in 12-Step groups.

Although, as a guest, I never became terribly familiar with Bill W.'s Big Book or the methodology it taught, I did develop a healthy respect for the process represented in those meetings.

AA continues to help many hundreds of thousands of people through chemical dependency, a beautiful expression of the gracious Divine in the world. By sitting quietly in the circle and listening to authentic stories, I also learned to respect the sense of community AA creates. In just a one-hour meeting, a person could change from a stranger to an ally.

If you've never attended a 12-Step meeting before, you might not know that majority of time is spent storytelling. As a religious person, I am more accustomed to gatherings that feature presentations, lectures, or other instruction. In AA, the focus is much more on self-disclosure. One of the rituals I repeatedly witnessed during those New York summers had to do with introductions. As individuals took turns, each person would introduce themself with something like, "Hi, I'm Jane, and I'm an alcoholic." Each time, this greeting was resoundingly affirmed by the rest of the group, "Hi Jane!"

Even before anything else happens in AA, that simple rite carries a huge weight for those in recovery. In the exchange, the group implicitly communicates: "We see you, Jane. You are welcome here. You are not alone."

In the shadows of the basement, people are seen and loved, even in light of their mistakes. There are, of course, many reasons why the 12-Step process is powerful to many people. I believe that one of the essential reasons has to do with this sense of supportive community built in 12-Step groups. In AA meetings, the secret nature of addiction is gently ushered out into the light of day. Not only is it greeted with uncompromising kindness, but it is welcomed into community.

While many forms of secret-keeping have the tendency of isolating us, self-disclosure very often has the tendency of connecting us. We build bonds of commonality by comparing secrets. When I shared my struggles with porn to that group of young men, I unequivocally learned that I am not alone. And they learned it as well. This magnificent discovery rocked my world. I felt tangible grace in it. The experience set me on a course for trying to learn how to build spaces for others to learn this same truth about themselves.

In vivid colors, this chapter has painted a picture of the beauty that can come when we confess one to another. The possible merits of this personal discipline are endless. There are, however, obstacles to applying it in our lives. As you've read, you've probably already brought some to mind. And so, before I close out the chapter, I want to acknowledge some impediments that commonly prevent self-disclosure.

First, exposing our secrets is inconvenient. As I've highlighted throughout the book, much of the time, we have very strong reasons for keeping things hidden. Often the homeostasis of our careers, reputations, family systems, identities, cultures, and organizations hinge on concealment. And so, by its very nature, telling the truth about these structures threatens to disrupt them.

For many people in American culture, the inherent inconvenience of disclosure strikes at the heart of one of our core values: easiness. Living in Southern California especially, I've learned that there is a huge market for selling convenience. The number of businesses oriented around bringing services to people so that they can avoid the disruption of being forced to go to them is stunning. From mobile mechanics and car-washers to at-home veterinarians and grocery delivery, to even residence-based haircuts or medical treatments, it sometimes seems entirely possible that should we choose, we never will have to leave our homes[11]!

---

11 - Obviously, the 2020 Coronavirus pandemic raised some of these services to a level beyond mere convenience.

Despite this value that many of us have inherited, telling secrets works in the opposite direction. Because we develop them in order to protect the status quo, exposing our hidden truths is necessarily inconvenient. But that's not the only roadblock.

Self-disclosure is also very hard work. As we've seen, confession can be downright all-consuming given the right set of circumstances. People who have gone through intensive treatment for addiction know this to be true. In order to get and stay "clean," folks in recovery work incredibly hard to face past traumas, reorganize their thinking, develop greater self-awareness, and build community. In his TED Talk, journalist Johnathan Hari says, "The opposite of addiction is connection." An underlying theme in recovery is owning and acknowledging that which had been covert. It's hard in part because truth-telling is hard.

Again, let me pick on American culture. Here in the USA, we love transformation. However, we frequently don't want to be bothered by paying the price. We want strong and healthy bodies, but we don't want to have to say "no" to Frappuccinos, french fries, or fondue. We want to finish the marathon, but we don't like having to train for months to get there. We dream of strong retirement funds, but we don't want to delay gratification because of savings plans. We desire to be moral people, but we don't want to be confronted with systemic problems like racism, mass incarceration, climate change, political corruption, or economic inequality. As Americans, we love to imagine what could be, but we're frequently held back by the drudgery that is necessary to create it.

Becoming the person you always wanted to be will not be easy. And as is the case with most things of value, grasping for maturity through shortcuts is unreliable. Instead, we have to put in the hard work. There are no "as seen on TV" solutions to blossoming into the best version of yourself.

So that's two roadblocks so far; we'll close with the third. For most of us, the greatest sources of resistance preventing us from self-revelation aren't inconvenience, or exhaustion, as common as those might be. Instead, the biggest obstacle to self-disclosure is found in its very nature. Confession is a form of death. When we get vulnerable about the hidden parts of our lives, something dies; whether reputation, ego, security, a dream, relationship, a belief, etc. This is why it can be so anxiety-inducing to consider sharing such information. When we do, in a very real sense, we are placing ourselves at the mercy of another human being. Depending on the circumstances, that can feel like a threat to our very existence. Confession can change everything in an instant. Telling secrets is risky business, but that doesn't mean it's bad.

Back at the beginning of the book, I introduced Nathaniel Hawthorne's classic novel *The Scarlet Letter* as an illustration of the weight of secret-keeping. But if you remember, I only highlighted its character, Pastor Arthur Dimmesdale, who suffers under the great pressure concealment until it threatens his physical health and his very life. If you're familiar with Hawthorne's book, however, you know that Dimmesdale isn't the only character in *The Scarlet Letter* who tangled with the power of secrets.

The main protagonist and clear heroine of the book is Hester Prynne. By the end of the tale, she discovers a cognate principle to that which the pastor's life exemplified: the integral connection between thriving and disclosure. After a lifetime of hiding the secret of her illegitimate pregnancy (namely, that Dimmesdale was the father), Prynne finally allows the truth to come to light. Of course, everyone could see what they considered to be her great sin. A pregnant belly and later a baby became just as much a sign of her second-class standing in her 17th century Massachusetts society as the scarlet-colored "A" she was forced to wear on her clothing.

There are no doubt many reasons Prynne resists disclosure for such a long period of time. Certainly, fidelity to her personal promise to the father could have been part of the motivation. Some critics highlight how a prison term for such a crime may have been possible at the time. Others suggest literal physical banishment aside from the figurative one she faced on a day-to-day basis. Perhaps she was scared of even more public ridicule. Whatever the combination of causes, I have no doubt that the perceived threat to the vulnerable woman felt mortal. No matter how you slice it, Hester Prynne's walk through the valley of self-exposure would have seemed like a kind of death.

The more we stand to gain by telling the truth, the more we will (seemingly) stand to lose. Confession is a risky endeavor. But it's worth it.

In the closing scenes of the book, Hawthorne tells us about the beginnings of Hester Prynne's new life in light of her self-revelation. In a moving shift, the young woman's confession paves the way for what will become her personal calling. Ultimately Prynne spends the second half of her life creating a safe home for other women who became mothers outside of wedlock as she once did. As dark and scary as it might've been, living her truth gave way to a greater purpose. Something similar is true for everyone. It's easy to imagine that hard work, accomplishments, and wisdom are the most important factors needed for people to become their best selves. But a lot of times, the opposite is the case. In the care of a universe that is designed to reflect grace, our mistakes, defeats, and embarrassments turn into gold.

This pattern of darkness giving way to light is baked into the fabric of creation itself. We see it in the mysterious life cycle of Eastern North American Periodical Cicadas, who mysteriously and cyclically "come to life" every 13 or 17 years. We see it in changing seasons, in parents sacrificing themselves for their young, and in the planting of seeds for food in agriculture. We even take advantage of it by fueling our cars and homes using chemicals that in millennia past were once living beings. In our world, death gives way to life, sadness to joy, poverty to prosperity, and despair to hope.

In the Christian tradition, this principle is most readily seen in the story of Jesus' death and resurrection. In almost every strain of Christian theology, this central narrative is the anchor point for hope. While there are dozens of theological theories attempting to make sense of this epic account, almost all of them share the same underlying theme: it is only through death that new life is possible. The Old Testament prophet Isaiah puts it this way, "By his wounds, we are healed."[12]

What's more, for centuries, Christians have taught that without the injustice, suffering, fear, and abandonment that Jesus experienced that Friday afternoon, the utter transcendence of Sunday morning wouldn't have been impossible. Reverend Rachel Mann elaborates on this theme in her powerful memoir about gender transition, *Dazzling Darkness*.[13] She writes, "It is the God who operates in the shade who reveals that the places of darkness aren't to be treated simply as negative places but as places of becoming...The Christ who comes to us, who is the resurrected God, also bears the marks of wounds." She goes on, "The hope of new life lay somewhere in the darkness."

Another spiritual teacher who I have valued takes the metaphor a step further, applying it in a kind of road map for spiritual maturity. Father Richard Rohr, a Franciscan mystic from New Mexico, writes about the two halves of life in *Falling Upwards*. According to Rohr, every person has a first half of life, but not everyone completes it. Only some make it to the second half of life. And the only way of making the jump is by way of what he calls necessary suffering.

---

12 - Isaiah 53:5

13 - The book explores the pattern of death and resurrection because it is so familiar to the LGBTQ+ experience. When people come out of the closet and begin living their truth, it is often feels like a passing from one life to another.

"The path of descent is the path of transformation. Darkness, failure, relapse, death, and woundedness are our primary teachers...Heartbreaks, disappointments, and even our own weaknesses can serve as stepping-stones to the second half of life transformation. Failings are the foundation for growth. Those who have fallen, failed or 'gone down' are the only ones who understand 'up.' "

Rohr goes on to describe how no amount of penance, aesthetic deprivation, self-sacrifice, or achievement can do it. It must be utter wilderness: outside our control. It is impossible to learn, train, or win our way into the second half of life. The only path lies through experiences we never would've chosen ourselves. Transformation takes place when we're not looking. New life is first birthed in the shadow. Beauty is formed from the dust of the earth[14].

Sometimes, the powerlessness that comes in the experience of self-disclosure can be the dark valley we need to grow into the people we most want to be. It might be risky, but you can do it. You can trust the nature of the holy universe. You can trust that reality bends toward grace. You can throw yourself into the flow. And after the descent, you will arise who you truly are.

In the final chapter of this book, we will consider some ways in which we might mitigate the unnecessary risks that come along with confession. These safety measures may become some helpful barriers you can use to guide when and where and to whom it makes sense to share your story.

---

14 - Genesis 2:7

QUESTIONS FOR DISCUSSION:

1. Would you wish to be present at your own funeral? Why or why not?

> *As a more challenging exercise, consider spending time writing your own eulogy. Thinking forward to your passing, what do you hope people will say about you? Are you currently living in such a way that is likely to produce those observations? Why or why not?

> This activity can be a way of coalescing your heart around your deepest values and even your overall life path.

2. The author uses the metaphor of light to illustrate the healing power of exposure. What other metaphors seem apt to you for this phenomenon? When have you witnessed exposure being less than helpful?

3. Write down a secret that you intuitively know you need to tell — and who you might consider trustworthy to hear it. Feel free to use code words or other cryptic language if even this exercise feels exposing. Spend some time in prayer, considering when the right timing for this conversation might be.

4. Talk about a time when you thought you were the only one with a certain peculiarity but later discovered that you weren't. How did it feel to embrace the fact that you were not the only one?

5. Think about a time when you felt not in control. What were the circumstances? If this is an experience that still needs processing and integration, spend some time considering and writing about how it may have impacted you to this point. If it is an experience that you have incorporated into your psyche and worldview, explain how it now moves you.

6. Consider the secret you wrote down in question number three from this list. What is at risk if you follow through with sharing it? What is at risk if you keep it hidden?

11 | BOUNDARIES AND TRUST

"Out of your vulnerabilities will come your strength."
-Sigmund Freud

This final chapter of the book considers two sides of the same coin: boundaries and trust. Applied appropriately, both are effective in mitigating some of the risks that come with self-disclosure. But in order to understand how they do this and ultimately promote healthy growth, we need to talk a little about intimacy.

Among the many things that can happen when people see or hear things that aren't for them, awkwardness might be the most entertaining. Unfortunately, I'm a person who repeatedly attracts these moments, leaving me wishing I could crawl under a rock.

The examples are endless. I've unwittingly talked trash about musicians at their own show while standing next to the band in the refreshments line. "That's my coffee cup," I once awkwardly blurted to a family member visiting our home for the weekend. Laughing, he chugged the hot beverage as I tried to take back my nonsensical insinuation that he would take it home with him. There was the time in the mini-mart when I needed to pee; and the road rage incident with a could've-been girlfriend; and the evening at summer camp when I accidentally crashed an erotic rendezvous. My cringe-worthy moments are endless. Each time, they've unfolded before my eyes like a slow-motion sports collision. Helpless to control my mouth, I watch as relational carnage ensues. It's not that I am unable to identify awkward moments — it's that I notice them one moment too late!

Perhaps this personal deficiency is why I venerate Matt Damon's character in the mid 90's film *Good Will Hunting*. The movie tells the story of a young Bostonian who is gifted on the street and in the classroom. Hunting's rare combination of magnanimous social dexterity and academic intellect made him captivating on the screen. His verbal and mathematical skills come off as delightfully effortless. Will Hunting doesn't have recurrent awkward moments like me.

But as the film unfolds, a conflict begins to loom. While Damon's character is charismatic and intelligent, he's unable to be intimate with others (or himself). He can psycho-analyze his psychiatrist, win bar fights, and solve generations-old academic conundrums. But he can't develop meaningful relationships. The contrast between his gifts and weaknesses leaves Will brittle, frivolous, and lacking passion.

The turning point in *Good Will Hunting* is an iconic scene[1] featuring both Damon and Robin Williams, Will's therapist named Sean. The two sit on a park bench as Sean pinpoints the needed prescription:

> *[Sean]: You're just a kid. You don't have the faintest idea what you're talking' about... So if I asked you about art, you'd probably give me the skinny on every art book ever written... But I'll bet you can't tell me what it smells like in the Sistine Chapel.*

---

1 - I quote it at length here because it's brilliant writing and gets at the heart of what this final chapter is all about.

...If I ask you about women, you'd probably give me a syllabus about your personal favorites. You may have even been laid a few times. But you can't tell me what it feels like to wake up next to a woman and feel truly happy.

... You're a tough kid. And if I'd ask you about war, you'd probably throw Shakespeare at me, right, "once more unto the breach, dear friends." But you've never been near one. You've never held your best friend's head in your lap, watch him gasp his last breath looking to you for help.

...If I asked you about love, you'd probably quote me a sonnet. But you've never looked at a woman and been totally vulnerable. Known someone that could level you with her eyes, feeling like God put an angel on earth just for you. Who could rescue you from the depths of hell...You don't know about real loss, 'cause it only occurs when you've loved something more than you love yourself. And I doubt you've ever dared to love anybody that much....

...When I look at you... I don't see an intelligent, confident man... I see a cocky, scared-shitless kid.

But you're a genius, Will. No one denies that. No one could possibly understand the depths of you. But you presume to know everything about me because you saw a painting of mine, and you ripped my fucking life apart.

You're an orphan, right?

[Still silent, Will nods]

You think I know the first thing about how hard your life has been, how you feel, who you are because I read Oliver Twist? Does that encapsulate you?

Personally, I don't give a shit about all that, because you know what, I can't learn anything from you that I can't read in some fuckin' book.

...Unless you want to talk about you, who you are. Then I'm fascinated. I'm in.

...But you don't want to do that, do you sport? You're terrified of what you might say.

...Your move, chief.

If you've seen the movie, you know that Will Hunting takes his therapist up on the offer and begins to self-disclose. By the end, the title character has gone through a total transformation, discovering that he not only wants human connection but desperately needs it. *Good Will Hunting* is powerful because it paints a portrait of what it feels like to share intimacy with another.

The vital importance intimacy plays in human existence is something we all know about. In fact, we were created for it. Turning again to the Christian tradition because I know it best, my mind is drawn to the creation narrative in Genesis 2. After forming humanity out of the mud, the deity pronounces their brand-new design as "not good."[2] This is a striking declaration, given that the solitary human was surrounded by a planet filled with all manner of things that had previously been named "good" by the creator. It's a fascinating turn, if you think about it, full of

2 - Genesis 2:18

theological innuendos[3] that we will not address here.

In the origins story of Genesis, the creator begins by making humans who are alone. It is not good. Isolation doesn't work. We need each other, and we crave connection. It's how we were wired up from the very beginning. And so, the story in Genesis 2 continues by describing God mercifully designing another human, equal to the first. Together these beings could experience intimacy, just as their offspring would for generations.

What's more, it is only by way of intimacy that people experience love, which is the very essence of reality itself. To be loved but not understood is pleasant but ultimately meaningless. To be rejected after self-disclosure is amongst the highest suffering possible. But to be fully known by another human being who loves us we are is strengthening and transformative.

The context of confession between people is always intimacy, no matter the outcome. As we explored in chapters four, five, and nine, telling and listening to secrets is an essential part of growing into maturity. Another way of articulating this summary is that relational intimacy is vital for character formation. Not only were we designed to connect, but our best lives are only available through doing so.

With the remainder of this chapter, we will review a few ways by which intimacy can be damaged, built, and protected.

---

3 - For example, what are the implications of the fact that Genesis records God making something that is not "perfect," so to speak? Perhaps the puritanical impulse to "return to Eden" is more misguided than evangelicals realize!

The Internet makes connection easier than ever. And yet, we already know that it often provides a facsimile of intimacy instead of the real thing. Despite the common 21st century tendency of baring our souls on YouTube, Facebook, Twitter, Instagram, Tumblr, and Snapchat, many of us are lonelier than ever. While the Internet provides a ready platform for a certain brand of self-disclosure, it frequently fails to deliver on the promise of delivering deep relationships. Confession isn't a magical elixir that always improves interpersonal bonds.

Back at the dawn of the modern Internet, a teenage computer programming student named Jennifer Ringley turned on a web camera in her dorm room—and simply left it running, 24/7, 365 days per year. Beginning in 1996, it kept recording nonstop for over seven years.

At first, the setup was simple. A basic camera would take a black and white still photograph of her in her home every 15 minutes and automatically upload it to her web page. Every mundane and private detail of her life[4] was streamed unedited to the masses. Eventually, *Jennicam* expanded to include several cameras around her apartment and included live video (in color). At its height of popularity, *Jennicam's* website was receiving around one million hits per day. That was in the late 1990s, long before the Internet became the staple to American life that it represents today.

While *Jennicam* might not seem out of the ordinary in today's Internet, two decades ago, it possessed incredible novelty — pointing eerily to what the Internet would later become for almost everyone. Ringley's experiment brought her a massive amount of attention. She was interviewed for multiple magazines, newspaper stories, and on TV talk programs, including *The David*

---

4 - (Save for bathroom activities.)

Letterman Show. She even earned a brief role on a television show because of *Jennicam*.

According to a rare recent interview with her on the podcast "Reply All,"[5] Jennifer doesn't necessarily regret doing the experiment, but she is rather firm about her need to shut it down decisively. She says that over time, she witnessed her life taking on more and more the ethos of a performance. At first, *Jennicam* had simply been documenting Jennifer's normal everyday life (which had been her intent). It had been uncensored and rather complete — but it had been true. Over time, however, she says she found herself living more in reaction to the camera — self-censoring and presenting a certain image of herself and life than she was comfortable with. Although society had been given unprecedented access to someone's private life, they didn't really have the truth.

Jennifer goes on to describe how over the years she operated *Jennicam*, she was forced to develop a thick skin in order to deflect a great deal of the criticism (and even adulation). She increasingly distrusted those she didn't know, questioning their motives, and judging them for what they withheld. In short order, this reticence to trust strangers flowed over to affect already established relationships. Ironically, opening the doors for anyone to witness her private life ended up quashing her ability to be intimate with even a few.

Today, Jennifer (now Johnson) does not use any form of social media. In her mind, it flirts too closely with the exhibitionism she flirted with in her past life. But for many millions of Americans, this opinion is not shared. Often, ours is a culture of intense transparency, celebrating baring it all at nearly every turn. Whether love, sex, career, parenting, ethics, finances, hobbies, or food, nothing is too personal for our keen stare.

---

5 - http://gimletmedia.com/episode/5-the-jennicam/

Tell-all autobiographies from Andre Agassi, Tina Turner, Hulk Hogan, and Elizabeth Edwards are enormously popular. The entertainment news cycle has a penchant for the latest gossip — even to the point of causing harm to its targets.[6] From its birth through MTV's *The Real World*, reality television has become a staple source of entertainment, making every aspect of human life open to digestion. We are drawn to know and to be known. Twenty-first-century communications simultaneously quench as well as stimulate that desire.

A 2014 study out of a university[7] in Australia mirrors the discovery Jennifer Ringley made through her *Jennicam* experience. It found that the more self-disclosures of private information a person makes on Facebook, the more likely they are to be lonely. On the surface, it would seem that the willingness to reveal oneself would actually deter feelings of isolation (and, of course, in a way, this is a key argument of the book). But the opposite seems to be the case: when ramped up, transparency in the extremes makes us lonesome instead of attached.

While confession has enormous cathartic potential for growth, it is clear that complete openness or an absence of privacy hurts us rather than helps us. In fact, as we've seen throughout the book, secret-keeping is sometimes actually a good thing for our spiritual development.

In his book *Privacy*, essayist Garret Keizer writes, "The confusion of privacy and loneliness amounts to the Gordian knot of modern capitalist societies, the big blue bow of alienation on our package of consumer goods. It also bedevils the thinking of capitalism's less imaginative critics, who mistakenly assume that by eliminating everything private, they will eliminate loneliness too."

---

6 - I think of Princess Diana of Wales, who was killed in a car accident caused in part by overzealous celebrity gossip photographers.

7 - By Yeslam Al-Saggaf from Charles Sturt University in New South Wales.

He goes on to argue that American's have unwisely traded the essential value of privacy for convenience (and sometimes for the suppression of fear). A poor trade in his estimation because only through carefully cultivated privacy is real power, freedom, and therefore identity born.

Some of these dynamics are brought to life by novelist Dan Vyleta in his evocative book, *Smoke.* In it, Vyleta tries to answer the question: "what would life be like if there were no such thing as privacy and no such thing as secrecy?"[8]

The setting of *Smoke* is a dystopian version of Victorian England that has become stratified socially and economically according to levels of personal exposure. In this parallel world, smoke billows from people when they are unethical in word, thought, or deed. No one's foibles or mistakes are able to be kept private, except, that is, for the aristocracy, who have found ways to control their bodies' smoking.

While the novel is not about secrecy and privacy per se, the power dynamics underwriting them animate the novel. When people are not afforded even basic privacy, it becomes a commodity around which all of society is ordered. The book offers an implicit criticism of those who would throw it away rashly.

The truth is that if we confess our secrets haphazardly or without care, it tends to cheapen our humanity. Paradoxically, even in confession, a carefully cultivated sense of modesty serves to protect intimacy.

---

8 - A less serious answer to this question is depicted in the delightful (and somewhat violent) short western film "The Gunfighter." Accessible at: vimeo. com/79306807.

———————

Since 2004, Frank Warren has received over a half-billion postcards emblazoned with unvarnished secrets. An anonymous community art project, Warren started PostSecret.com as a space for people to confess funny, heart-warming, or shameful details they otherwise felt unable to own amongst a living, face-to-face community. His only rules for participants: mail postcards (or other items) to the specified address, all secrets submitted must be true, and they must have never previously been shared.

The secrets Frank Warren has received over the years since (the project is still going as of 2021) have run the gamut on themes in human life: sexuality, relationships, career, family, religion and spirituality, loss, and any number of trivial preferences and quirks. Some carry intense emotions of fear or shame, others carry joy and playfulness, and still, others carry confusion or withdrawal. In addition to his five books publishing photographs of the postcards he has received; Warren also maintains an active blog that features new secrets posted every Sunday.[9] He also travels the world lecturing about secrets and creating opportunities for people to confess their hidden truth publicly in large auditoriums and theaters.

The first time I encountered it, PostSecret charmed me to the core. It is an absolutely remarkable project—highlighting the power of secrets and teaching people how to take the first step toward authenticity. Undoubtedly, the project makes the world a better place, if not only through the significant way it has helped people experiencing suicidal ideation get help[10]. Because it is so widely enjoyed (the website receives millions of visits each year and has

———————

9 -   His blog, www.postsecret.com, boasts over 573 millions visits since its creation in 2004. I have visited it almost every Sunday for over 4 years.

10 -   One of the partner projects with PostSecret over the years is "To Write Love on Her Arms" a nonprofit dedicated to preventing suicide.

a large regular following of weekly supporters), PostSecret has developed a social media component, connecting people even anonymously with resources designed to help the at-risk survive.

Obviously, PostSecret isn't the same thing as face-to-face community-nurtured disclosure. In a sense, it came about because Frank Warren intuitively realized that people needed to talk about their secrets in order to build relationships. He also saw that for a variety of reasons, many couldn't do it in their existing contexts. His anonymous platform allowed for people to express themselves in safety.

The hallmark of the project is its anonymity, which Frank Warren takes great pains to maintain even with piles of his postcards being put on display at the Smithsonian. As such, it doesn't have the power to create the kind of intimacy that can grow out of the deepest of confessions. The exceptional stories where deeper connections have brewed are universally linked back to anonymity being relinquished along the way. Some of the most powerful stories I've heard from the PostSecret project emerged at live shows where secret-tellers are afforded the opportunity to be seen, known, and heard by their local communities. The breakdown of total obscurity allows for the development of intimacy.

There was a time in which I felt critical of PostSecret because I judged it as a cheap reproduction of the kind of confession, I had found so transformative in my life. However, I no longer see it in such binary terms. Instead, I find it more helpful to praise Warren and his project for what it is: one of many essential steps we must all take in becoming more authentic. It may not be the same as a face-to-face heart-to-heart, but it's not the same as shouting to the wind either.

For many of us, naming our secrets is an incremental process. We begin by wordlessly saying the thing to ourselves in the silence of our own hearts. As we sit with it for a time[11], we eventually may come to the place where we can look in the mirror and verbally say it to ourselves. This is where exercises like PostSecret shine. They give us the ability to take something we've admitted to ourselves and share it with the world, but in a way that has virtually zero risks of harming us. If we are able to expose ourselves successfully without a lot of pain, we get stronger. As such, incognito sharing can be a profoundly helpful way to build the confidence needed to later make more public self-disclosures.

Although the deepest intimacy only happens when secrets are reciprocally shared, prior steps in the process are still essential to the outcome. It's not unlike learning how to swim. A beginner has to first sit on the pool edge, dangling her feet in the water before she can jump off the high dive! But even if the first classes only involve splashing, we still call it "swimming lessons"!

The mutual confession necessary for relational intimacy depends on trust. If we wish to connect, we must both take the risk of trusting and also prove trustworthy ourselves. But as I just discussed with PostSecret, this isn't an all-or-nothing equation. Trust isn't a zero-sum game. Just because I may share some secrets with some people doesn't mean I must share all my secrets with everyone! Instead, careful boundaries are an essential ingredient to setting the stage for the healthy exchange of secrets. The brilliant scholarly work of the psychologist Anita Kelly[12] verifies this impulse. Her research suggests that even patients of mental health professionals are best served by self-censoring in clinical interactions.

Let's take a look at another story from Jesus' life that captures

---

11 - Depending on the secret, it can take decades!

12 - I discuss her work in more detail in the introduction and in chapter 1.

the principle well. The gospel writer Matthew describes the final moments leading up to Jesus' betrayal and arrest. In spiritual preparation under cover of night, Jesus spends quiet time in prayer and meditation in a grove of olive trees near Jerusalem. The place was named Gethsemane, or oil press. Of greatest interest for our conversation here is not so much what happened in the garden but who was present.

The story reads that when Jesus arrived at the garden, he had his eleven closest students with him, all but Judas. This notably implies all his many other disciples[13] and followers were not at the scene, conceivably because they weren't invited. While it is impossible to know for sure, it is reasonable to assume that far more disciples were *absent* from Gethsemane on the fateful night of Jesus' arrest than were present.

But there's more. Throughout his biographies, Jesus is routinely interacting with large throngs of people who wished to eat with, be healed by, blessed by, and be educated through this remarkable prophet. His story reads that throughout his ministry, Jesus touched many thousands of people who never identified as followers. While these people were not enemies, they were not dedicated acolytes either. We have every reason to believe that had these multitudes been invited to have a glimpse at such an intimate moment, they would have been there. The masses, likewise, were not invited to be present at Gethsemane.

It goes even further, however. Also absent (at least at first) were the critics, the haters, and the angry mobs. Even though Jesus enjoyed a streak of fame in the region of Judea during his three years of ministry, he also stirred up a great deal of hatred amongst the religious establishment. Not surprisingly, these ostensible

---

13 - He certainly had other students. In Luke chapter ten, we find Jesus sending out seventy followers on a special missionary quest. In Acts 1, we find no less than a hundred-twenty disciples gathered together in terror in Jerusalem after the resurrection. Several female disciples were the ones who found the empty tomb on Sunday morning after the passover.

"enemies" were neither invited to the garden for prayer on the eve of Jesus' arrest.

This is what I'm getting at. As his life drew to the end, Jesus intentionally only welcomed a precious few to witness his deepest emotions. Believe it or not, however, there were more than just the two categories of "in" and "out." Even among those who were welcomed, we see striation in terms of their access to the master teacher.

Matthew 26 describes how, entering into the garden of Gethsemane, Jesus left eight of his students on the outskirts. The story reads how he invited three (Peter, James, and John) to join him in an even more intimate space, asking them to intercede for him as he prayed. Ultimately, however, even those three were left behind. In Gethsemane, Jesus ended up alone in the presence only of the divine.

The boundaries Jesus set up in the garden are a microcosm of the ordered way in which he lived life. His was full of meaning, love, and consequence in part because he had mastered the dynamics of privacy and intimacy. But my point here isn't to challenge you to reach for some high and lofty ideal but instead to offer encouragement. Jesus arranged his life in this way because of how well it aligns with the fabric of the universe itself.

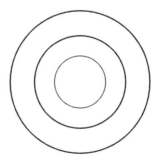

While "circles of trust" is a bit cliché, it captures some truth. Jesus' concentric circls began with only himself at the core, followed by God. At the next ring, we find his three closest disciples, and in the next, we find the eleven. On the outside rings are the crowds, followed lastly by the critics. As was likely the case with Jesus, we should expect our system of boundaries to adapt over time, accommodating changes in trust accordingly. It may make me super nerdy, but global thinker as I am, the circle of trust model helps me conceptualize and apply the concept. The discussion guide for this chapter includes a prompt for examining your personal application of this principle.

But how does setting boundaries in such an intentional way help build intimacy? Well, let's look back at Will Hunting and Jennifer Ringley from this very chapter.

Consider what Will Hunting's circle of trust map might've looked like. Rather than a carefully tended system where some people are highly trusted and intimate, while others are kept at arm's length, Will had just one tiny circle (or perhaps even a minuscule dot)! At the beginning of the movie, he essentially trusted no one with his heart. And that was the problem! As a consequence, he enjoyed zero intimacy with anyone — as well as the myriad of consequences that came with that.

On the other hand, think about what Jennifer Ringley's model might've looked like at the height of *Jennicam*. Hers lay on the other end of the spectrum from Will Hunting: everyone was let into even the most intimate aspects of her life. Hence, Jennifer Ringley's circle of trust map was again one circle, this time extremely large. Yet, as we already observed, her over-exposure likewise didn't create a real community or genuine intimacy.

Together, these stories illustrate how carefully cultivated boundaries actually enhance, rather than hinder, intimacy. You already know this. Not all people are worthy of holding our most tender truths. When it comes to confession, the habits of building, refining, and clarifying who fits where in our lives becomes an extremely useful endeavor. Well-developed systems of trust (rather than wholesale exposure or absolute privacy) counter-intuitively set the stage for the deepest of human connections.

The final question in this chapter is about determining the appropriate levels of trust. "How do I know, for sure, who is trustworthy and who is not?"

The short answer is that you can't. Ultimately, there are no guarantees. Trust always presents some risk; that's why telling secrets is a risky practice. And however we might wisely ease these risks, there is always a point where vulnerability places us at the mercy of another.

But there's hope. Luckily, trust is also cumulative, building upon itself. The more a person proves themselves to be trustworthy, the more we can feel comfortable trusting them in the future. As we learned through the PostSecret project, a small act of confidence naturally leads to a slightly larger act, and so on. Past behavior is a blunt but useful guide for determining who we can count on going forward.

A third aspect to consider is that trust*ing* others and being trust*ed* share complementary principles. People in your life prove they can be trusted in essentially the same ways as you prove your trustworthiness to them! Therefore, the practices or habits we intentionally employ to make ourselves safer to others around us are also excellent indicators to watch out for in determining the safety of someone else. The following list[14] suggests a few things to both adopt and pay attention to.

---

14 - I learned many of these by happenstance through "Wildfire" the young men's retreat I described in chapter five. When I first started working on the project years ago, my team and inadvertently created a context where young men felt safe to be honest. It was absolutely remarkable. And while we couldn't guarantee that attendees would share secrets, we quickly started learning the conditions where it was at least possible. My staff and I became gardeners of trust: tilling the soil, planting, watering, and guarding; all in expectation of what might grow.

1. **Reciprocity.** Intimacy and trust are not a one-way street (unless we're talking about a professional relationship). The most basic way of demonstrating trustworthiness is to show vulnerability ourselves. Brené Brown became famous by teaching this theme. She writes in her book *Daring Greatly*, "Vulnerability is the birthplace of love, belonging, joy, courage, empathy, and creativity. It is the source of hope, empathy, accountability, and authenticity." Perhaps more than anything else, if you'd like to be seen as a safe person, entrust your secrets to others.

2. **Asking for and Receiving Consent.** The principle of consent is incredibly important for navigating sexual contact. But it is also invaluable when considering intimate matters of the heart. Before sharing a secret, ask for the other person's consent. This indicates the level of respect you have for self-disclosure itself and, more importantly, for the needs and feelings of your friends.

3. **Appropriate Time and Circumstance.** I discussed the principle "the right thing at the wrong time is the wrong thing" in chapter five. It applies here as well. When I coached young ministerial students in sermon preparation, I routinely talked about the importance of balancing personal self-exposure with spiritual distance (vis-a-vis the topic of chapter eight). Saying something over coffee with a friend is different than saying the same thing from the stage in an auditorium and is different yet from uttering it at Thanksgiving dinner. A helpful principle[15] for determining suitable times and places is: "Show scars to many; reserve wounds for very few." Applying correct social intelligence to given situations and the content of our self-disclosures is essential to demonstrating our maturity to carry the secrets of others.

4. **Listening.** This may be obvious, but it is worth including because of its impact. Indicators of good listening include appropriate eye contact, remembering past conversations and life details,

---

15 - I learned this from Samir Selmanovic, one of my spiritual mentors, and also an editor of this book.

responding with fitting emotion, minimizing distractions, and refusing inconsequential interruptions (e.g., phone calls). Paying careful attention to those we love is the stuff that intimacy is made of.

5. **Grace First.** As I discussed in chapter nine, there is a place for judgment and confrontation along the path to maturity. But usually, the context of vulnerable self-exposure is not that place. In general, creating safe spaces necessitates gentleness, self-control, kindness, and patience[16]. Tirades about the evils of certain political parties or behavior patterns can feel good and even be true. But they also can mark an environment as dangerous for the way they implicitly press agendas. Donald Miller's book, *Scary Close*, explores the topic of intimacy. Miller says that personal agendas, control attempts, and manipulation are toxic to trust[17]. He elaborates that each one of them is a judgment made manifest in observable behavior.

6. **Gossip.** This habit is absolutely deadly for relationships. You already know it. I mentioned it in chapter nine. Regardless of the motive, gossip destroys safe space unlike anything else. The spiritual author Kahlil Gibran writes, "If you reveal your secrets to the wind, you should not blame the wind for revealing them to the trees." This is indeed wisdom. If I demonstrate myself to be a" windbag" of a person, constantly broadcasting the latest gossip, I also exhibit my unworthiness of trust.

---

16 - My pastor self can't help but chuckle at how Paul's "Fruits of the Spirit" from Galatians 5 overlaps with this list.

17 - This dynamic is part of why I hate it when car-salespeople try to milk me for personal information when I'm shopping for a vehicle. Their agenda to sell me something (at conceivably any cost) makes vulnerability that much more risky for me.

_____

Something[18] profound shifts
the instant we reveal our soul
to those worthy of witnessing it.

A new universe of possibilities emerges:
galaxies specked with the wisdom of ancient stars
and the vibrant enthusiasm of the newly birthed.

Dusty eyes fill with the wetness of hope
rising up against despair.

Shoulders draw back in confidence as hearts swell,
breaking free of fear's prison.

In the moment we surrender ourselves to the
dangers of intimacy, in its wild whitewater flow, we
finally understand.

This is what we live for.

You have the capacity to create cathartic moments for those you love, for those you don't even know, for your clients, and for those you serve. You can identify safe spaces and take the leap into trust by risking authenticity. You know how to create boundaries and how to live in intimate community. You have all you need. May it be so.

_____

18 - Inspired by a piece from the Cuban artist Anais Nin.

QUESTIONS FOR DISCUSSION:

1. Do you tend to be someone who regularly stumbles into awkward situations or pretty much avoids them? What might this say about your personality or values?

2. The author argues that the creation story in the Bible suggests that human beings were designed for intimacy. Regardless of your understanding of human origins, do you agree with this sentiment? Is relational connection inevitable for human beings or more coincidental? Why?

3. How has Social Media served to improve intimacy with others or hinder it? For you, is the Internet, in general, a positive or negative tool for building relationships? Explain.

4. Do you tend to be someone who takes privacy for granted or admires it as a gift when afforded? Consider your culture or context of origin and reflect on the degree to which it values or dismisses the importance of privacy.

5. Have you ever shared a secret anonymously, such as via PostSecret? What impact, if any, did it have on your life?

6. In this chapter, the author introduces the "circles of trust" model for understanding boundary-making. Take some time and draw two maps that represent your life. For the first, illustrate your current actual model of boundaries (remember the stories from the chapter that illustrate the extremes, *Jennicam*, and Will

Hunting). For the second map, illustrate your ideal situation or how you wish you could apply personal boundaries in your life. Is there a large or small difference between the two maps? What do you need to do to bring them into alignment?

7. Which strategy or strategies suggested for building trust most resonate with you? Is there one that stands out as particularly natural/easy? Is there one that stands out as especially difficult? Discuss how you might apply one or more of these in new ways in your life.

ACKNOWLEDGEMENTS

Thank you to Paige, your hidden work that brought this book to life is irreplaceable. I see you. Finn and Sawyer, thank you for your grace when my work limited our adventures. Thank you to my greatest cheerleaders, Mom and Dad.

To all my friends, family, colleagues, and supporters who consulted with me on the project or read early copies, I am forever grateful: Katherine Loewen, Jennifer Loewen, Kandice and Jared Anderson, Suzie Loewen, Tyler Brewer, Alan Newbold, Caleb Henry, Alareece Collie, Troy Fitzgerald, Lois Blackwelder, Jenn Ogden, Alex Bryan, Henning Guldhammer, Dave Thomas, Emily Whitney, Don Veverka, Andrew Perrin, Doug Tilstra, Jon Dybdahl, Paul Dybdahl, Bev Beem, Marc Schelske, Alex English, Blake Englehart, Evan Davies, Casey Bartlett, Karl Haffner, Daneen Akers, Bernie Anderson, Samir Selmanovic, Arlen Farley, Japhet De Oliveira, Jody Washburn, Alden Thompson, and many others.

This project would not have come into existence without

the support of all my backers on Kickstarter, thank you for your generosity and vision. Thank you as well for your grace in accomodating the delayed timeline that *Hidden* wound up following. Eric Sayler, Janet and Ron Wilkinson, Sue Willard, Debbie and Russ Gilbert, Harry Sharley, Lois and Tim Blackwelder, Betsy and Rick Claridge, David and Loralee Thomas, Jeff Kinne, Pedrito Maynard-Reid, Marshall McVay, Ron Hessel, Phil Muthersbaugh, Eric Shadle, John McVay, Bryson Bechtal, Sergio Manente, Emily Muthersbaugh, Terrance Taylor, Paul Dybdahl, Shane Del Vecchio, Mark Weir, Paul Hoover, Jaci Cress, Darold Bigger, Tammy Randolph, Holly Phillips, Doug Tilstra, Jim Wibberding, Yvonne Iwasa, Doug Brown, Ross Donaldson, Jon Rittenbach, Stephen Farr, Greg and Emily Bice, Don and Shirley Mehrer, Glenda and Gary Underhill, Bob Smith, Henning Guldhammer, Michelle Naden, Adina and Clark Pearson, Bill Cork, Mark Witas, Wayne and Gina Pollard, Gary and Julie Wade, Amy Underhill, Robert and Lana Van Dorn, Kraig and Julie Scott, Donna and Richard Worley, Sam Leonor, Brandon Ward, Nikolas Peterson, Lisa Giebel, Dwight Steffanson, Gwen and Darral Payne, Dan Luce, Lauri Rootvik, Connie Maloney, Jackie and Gary Gifford, Shauna Gifford, Scott and Martha Newbold, Susie Crain, Daneen Akers and Stephen Eyer, Alex English, Emily and Nathaniel Whitney, Julia Salerno, Vanessa Becker, Andrew Perrin, Tyler Brewer, Brandon Wade, Justin Knapp, Ron Sydney, Erin Martin, Tye Davis, Casey Barlett, Kevin McGill, Steve and Suzann Rose, Jack and Deanne Hoehn, Rick and Kay Henderson, Caleb Henry, Alan Newbold, Samir Selmanovic, Kandice and Jared Anderson, Japhet De Oliveira, Jon Dybdahl, Sharlene Miller, Alex Bryan, Gregory Loewen, Troy Fitzgerald, Karl Haffner, Jenn Ogden, Arlen Farley, Katie Loewen, Alareece Collie, Kylon Gienger, Bernie Anderson, John T. Mclarty, Conna Bond, Stewart Delony, Timothy Oliver, Nathaniel Malberg, Jared Wright, Alita Byrd, Alisa Williams, Chuck Morrison, Jim Bock, Kathy and Willard Loewen, Melissa Voelker, Caleb King, Troy Walalce, Kati, Jordan Stimmel, Linda Crumley, Donna Coffeen, Kris Catlett, Jay Melashenko, Paul Daker, Bryan, Eileen Greenwalt, A. Beam, Michael Blasy, Jana Cress, Patty Knittel, Bev Beem, Loraine Atwood Ingrasci,

Austin Archer, Sherrie Linebaugh, Matthew Vincent, Herb Sweezey, Nick Peterson, Alexander Wagner, Clint Streifling, Wrandoll Brenes, Ryan West, Matthew Axford, Cheryl De Genner, Nolan Cafferkey, Steve Rose, Walter Cox, Hillary Bigger Catlett, Rudy Scott, Don Veverka, Heather Scherman, Zack Brenes, and anonymous donors.

Thank you to my editors, especially Samir Selmanovic who's expert advice helped me become proud of my work. Thank you as well to E.E. Loewen, who gave me courage to align my writing with my soul. Thank you to my many therapists along the way especially Ms. Susan, Dr. Benjamin, Mr. Oliver, and Dr. M.

I'm ever grateful to Adam Newbold for his generosity of expertise on the cover design. Thank you to Christian Bell of CMBell Company who produced a remarkably well-done marketing video that was used for the Kickstarter campaign. I am grateful for your inventiveness and generosity in financing the project. Thanks to the One Project, Paddy McCoy and Japhet de Oliveira were generous in sharing my work at a San Diego gathering! Thank you as well to Stewart Delony and Jim Bock who welcomed me on their radio programs, Annie Charnley Eveland and the Union Bulletin, Jared Wright and *Spectrum* Magazine, and to Jose Briones who interviewed me on his podcast *Distruptive Adventism*.

Finally , I am grateful to God. They crafted my beautiful soul into existence, and breathe beyond any religion can imagine. I am grateful to the One who makes Herself known through the love of people, in the beauty of music, by scientific inquiry, within vivid dreams, by way of therapists and mentors, at the hands of medical professionals, in the mist of forest runs, through the testimony of truth tellers on Twitter, in the touch of sweet old grandmas, by the person of Jesus, via poets and even pastors. I am grateful for how He has bent the arc of the universe toward grace, how His essence is love, and that He is always more kind than any god or ideology of which we can conceive. I am thankful to be loved exactly as I am, as I was, and as I will be; and that you are too.

RESOURCES AND BIBLIOGRAPHY

The following is a chapter-by-chapter list of resources referenced as well as recommended or influential titles, films, and music.

§ | INTRODUCTION

Avett Brothers. *Weight of Lies*, song. From the album *Emotionalism*. (Ramseur Records, 2007).

Bok, Sissela. *Secrets: on the Ethics of Concealment and Revelation* (Pantheon Books, 1982). I didn't quote this wonderful line, but I did refer to the concept in my own words. "Secrecy is as indispensable to human beings as fire and as greatly feared. Both enhance and protect life, yet both can stifle, lay waste, spread out of all control. Both may be used to guard intimacy or to invade it, to nurture or to consume."

Coehn, Debora. *Family Secrets: Shame and Privacy in Modern*

Britain (Oxford University Press, 2017)

Keizer, Garret. *Privacy.* (Picador, 2013). I reference this directly in another chapter, but it is equally applicable to the discussion on privacy vs. secrecy here in the introduction.

Kelly, Anita. *The Psychology of Secrets.* (Kluwer Academic/Plenum Publishers, 2002). This is an academic title that can be difficult to find. Retailers like Amazon and resellers like eBay or Alibris have it, but it's expensive. I recommend checking out your nearest educational library system if you'd like to get your hands on it.

Nelson, Bradley. "A Gay SDA Play." Heard in person at the Gesa PowerHouse Theatre in Walla Walla, April 1, 2015.

"Radiation Flowed 200 Miles to Sea, Study Finds". (The New York Times. July 17, 1992).

Wright, Lawrence. *Going Clear: Scientology, Hollywood, and the Prison of Belief.* (First Vintage Books, 2013). Also, "Going Clear: Scientology and the Prison of Belief," Alex Gibney, director. HBO Documentary Films, 2015.

1 | THE WEIGHT OF SECRETS

Kelly, Anita. *The Psychology of Secrets.* (Kluwer Academic/Plenum Publishers, 2002).

Corcoran, John, with Carole C. Carlson. *The Teacher who Couldn't Read: The True story of a High School Instructor who Triumphed over his Illiteracy.* (Focus on the Family Publishing, 1994).

Dubner, Stephen J. and Steven D. Levitt. *Think like a Freak: The Authors of Freakonomics Offer to Retrain your Brain.*

(Harper Collins, 2014). *Also, be sure to check out their exceptional podcast, "Freakonomics Radio."

Hawthorne, Nathaniel. *Scarlet Letter.* (Public Domain, 1850).

Uysal, Ahmet*, Helen Lee Lin, and C. Raymond Knee. *The Role of Need Satisfaction in Self-Concealment and Well-Being.* (Personality and Social Psychology Bulletin. 2010 36:187. Sage Publications). And, *Is Self-Concealment associated with acute and chronic pain?* (Psychology, Vol 30(5), Sep, 2011. pp. 606-614. American Psychological Association). *Ahmet Uysal and other colleagues have published a number of good studies on the impact of Self-Conceal-ment. I recommend using Google's scholarly search tool to find up to date research.

Warren, Frank. *PostSecret: Extraordinary Confessions from Or-dinary Lives.* (Regan Books, 2005). *Frank Warren's blog, www.postsecret.com, is updated every Sunday with new anonymous confessions.

Wenger, Daniel. *Paradoxical Effects of Thought Suppression.* (Journal of Personality and Social Psychology volume 53., 1987). Another excellent exploration by a Harvard psychologist who has studied secrets extensively. Wenger is quoted by Anita Kelly more than once in her work.

2 | SECRET SHAME

Baumeister, Roy F. *The nature and functions of self-esteem: Sociometer theory. In Advances in Experimental Social Psychology* (Academic Press., Vol. 32, pp. 1-62, 2000).

Bradshaw, John. *Bradshaw On: Healing the Shame that Binds You.* (Health Communications, Inc., 1988).

_____ *Healing the Shame that Binds You.* (Health Communications, 2005).

_____ *Family Secrets: The Path from Shame to Healing.* (Bantam Books, 1996).

Brown, Brene. TED Talk *Listening to Shame* https://www.ted.com/talks/brene_brown_listening_to_shame. Much of Brown's material explores the theme of shame.

Hastings, Mark E., Lisa M. Northman, June P. Tangney. *Suicide Science.* (Springer Publishers, 2002).

Lewis, Michael. *Shame: The Exposed Self.* (The Free Press, 1992).

Meffert, Harma, Valeria Gazzola, Johan A. den Boer, Arnold A.J. Bartels, and Christian Keysers. *Brain: A Journal of Neurology.* (136; 2550-2562, 2013).

Mettler, Sam. (2005-2013). `. Television Program. Created by Sam Mettler. Aired on A&E.

Pattison, Stephen. *Shame: Theory, Therapy, Theology.* (Cambridge University Press, 2000).

Teroni, J. A. Deonna. *In Defense of Shame: The Faces of an Emotion.* (Oxford University Press, 2012).

Wurmser, Leon. *The Mask of Shame.* (Johns Hopkins University Press, 1981).

3 | FAMILY SECRETS

Augsburger, David. *Helping People Forgive.* (Westminster John

Knox Press, 1996).

Barbing, Kathy. *The Healing Years*, film. (Big Voice Pictures, 2001). http://bigvoicepictures.com/production-3/the-healing-years/

Bly, Robert. *Iron John: A Book About Men.* (1990). Although not directly referenced in this chapter, Robert Bly's influential work helps to inform some of my assumptions about the importance of exploring the shadow.

Bowen, Murray. *Family Therapy in Clinical Practice.* (Rowman & Littlefield Publishers, Inc., 1994).

Bradshaw, John. Once again, essentially anything he's written is very applicable to this chapter. *Family Secrets* has been especially helpful.

Clark, Chap. Lecture in the course Youth Evangelism, Fuller Theological Seminary. Pasadena, Calif., 2012.

_____, *Hurt 2.0: Inside the World of today's Teenagers.* (Baker Academic, 2011).

Glasser, Arthur F. *Announcing the Kingdom: The Story of God's Mission in the Bible.* (Baker Academic., 2003). An influential and helpful book in my graduate schooling at Fuller Seminary.

Howe, Mark, and Lauren Knott. *The fallibility of memory in judicial processes: Lessons from the past and their modern consequences.* (*Memory*, 2015). https://www.ncbi.nlm.nih.gov/pmc/articles/PMC4409058/

Hoyos, Daniel, and Bunee Tomlinson. *No one Knows*, Short Film. 2011. Originally accessed via indieflix.com. Publicly available through the director at https://vimeo.

com/59137646

Napier, Augustus Y. And Carl Whitaker. *The Family Crucible: The Intense Experience of Family Therapy.* (Harper Perennial, 1978).

Parks, Sharon Daloz. *The Critical Years: The Young Adult Search for a Faith to Live By.* (Harper and Row, 1986).

Stoop, David. *Forgiving Our Parents, Forgiving Ourselves: Healing Adult Children of Dysfunctional Families.* (Regal Books, 1991). Another title not directly referenced in this chapter but influential in the development. Recommended for those who choose to do deeper work processing family structure, history, trauma, and unexplainable impulses.

Wilkins, Karl. Learn more about his work by visiting his website: www.worldoutsidemyshoes.org

4 | ISOLATION & MENTORING

Alston, Macky. *Love Free or Die*, Film. Viewed in person with director's interview following at Sundance Independent Film Festival, Park City, UT. January 2012.

Benner, David. *Sacred Companions: The Gift of Spiritual Friendship & Direction.* (InterVarsity Press, 2002).

Bonhoeffer, Dietrich. *Life Together.* (Harper, 1954).

Brown, Brene. TED Talk *Listening to Shame* https://www.ted.com/talks/brene_brown_listening_to_shame.

Buechner, Frederick. *Telling Secrets.* (HarperCollins Publishers, 2000).

Cain, Susan. *Quiet: The Power of Introverts in a World that Can't Stop Talking.* (Random House, 2012).

Carroll, Jonathan. *Bathing the Lion.* (St. Martin's Press, 2014).

Clinton, Bobby and Richard Clinton. *The Mentor Handbook: Detailed Guidelines and Helps for Christian Mentors and Mentorees.* Unpublished, 1991. Digital PDF acquired from authors.

Clinton, Robert and Richard Stanley. *Connecting: The Mentoring Relationships You Need to Succeed.* (Navpress, 1992).

Cloud, Henry and Robert Townsend. *Boundaries Updated and Expanded Edition: When to Say Yes, How to Say No To Take Control of Your Life.* (Zondervan, 2017).

Forward, Susan. *Emotional Blackmail: When People in Your Life Use Fear, Obligation, and Guilt to Manipulate You.* (Harper Collins, 1997).

Gangway, Roberts. *Planes: Fire and Rescue.* Film. (Walt Disney Studios, 2014).

Gladwell, Malcolm. *Outliers: The Story of Success.* (Little, Brown and Company, 2008).
Really, anything by Gladwell is interesting and compelling, including (and perhaps especially) his podcast, "Revisionist History."

Knight, George. Andrews University, quoted from a lecture in the course: History of Adventist Theology, 2009.

Krakauer, Jon. *Into the Wild.* (First Anchor Books, 1997).

Lewis, CS. *A Grief Observed.* (Harper One, 1961).

Stockett, Kathryn. *The Help*. (Penguin Group, 2009). I also recommend the film by the same name, directed by Tate Taylor. Although it (like most film adaptations of books) doesn't follow the written form precisely, is compelling and moving.

Toth, Jennifer. *The Mole People: Life in the Tunnels Beneath New York City*. (Chicago Review Press, 1995).

Williams, Alisa. A Community of Loneliness. Spectrum Magazine. 29 August 2014. http://spectrummagazine.org/article/ alisa-williams/2014/08/29/community-loneliness

5 | SECRET WISDOM

Bell, Rob. *Velvet Elvis: Repainting the Christian Faith*. (Harper One, 2005).

Bradford, James. *The Most Wanted Man in the World*. Wired Magazine, 2014. http://www.wired.com/2014/08/edward-snowden/#ch-1. Accessed November 11, 2014.

Clark, Chap. *Hurt 2.0: Inside the World of today's Teenagers*. (Baker Academic, 2011).

Coelho, Paulo. *The Alchemist*. (HarperTorch, 2006).

Eissenman, R. & Kristsonis, W. *How children learn to become sex offenders*. (Journal of Sexual Behavior, 32, (1), 25-29, 1995).

Kershner, Ivan. *The Empire Strikes Back*, film. (Lucasfilm, 1980).

Krakauer, Jon. *Under the Banner of Heaven: A Story of Violent Faith*. (Anchor Books, 2004).

McDonald, G. Jeffrey. *Adventists' back-to-basics faith is fastest growing U.S. Church.* (USA Today, 2011). http://usato-day30.usatoday.com/news/religion/2011-03-18-Adventists_17_ST_N.htm. Accessed November 10, 2014.

Murray, John B. *Psychological profile of pedophiles and child molesters.* (The Journal of Psychology; Mar 2000; 134, 2; ProQuest Central pg. 211). Accessed November 10, 2014.

Peace, Richard. *Conversion in the New Testament.* (Eerdmans, 1999).

Peck, Scott. *A Road Less Traveled: A New Psychology of Love.* (Simon & Schuster, 1998).

Poitras, Laura. *Citizen Four,* Film documentary, starring Edward Snowden and Glenn Greenwald (Praxis Films, 2014).

Rohr, Richard. *Adam's Return: The Five Promises of Male Initiation.* (Crossroad, 2014).

Ross, Carolyn. *Overexposed and Underprepared: The Effects of Early Exposure to Sexual Content.* (Psychology Today Online, 2012). Accessed November 10, 2014. http://www.psychologytoday.com/blog/real-healing/201208/overexposed-and-under-prepared-the-effects-early-exposure-sexual-content

Schwartz, Barry. *Our Loss of Wisdom.* (TED Talk, 2014). https://www.ted.com/talks/barry_schwartz_our_loss_of_wisdom/transcript

Stollznow K. *God Bless America: Strange and Unusual Religious Beliefs and Practices in the United States.* (Pitchstone Publishing, 2014).

Van Gennep, Arnold. *The Rites of Passage*. (University of Chicago Press, 1961).

Walker, Lucy. *Devil's Playground*, Film documentary, starring Velda Bontrager and Dewayne Chupp (Stick Figure Productions, Cinemax, 2002).

Winn, Mary. *Children without Childhood*. (Pantheon Books, 1981).

6 | SECRETS FROM OURSELVES

Arbinger Institute. *Leadership and Self-Deception*. (McGraw Hill Education, 2005).

Barton, Ruth Haley. *Strengthening the Soul of Your Leadership: Seeking God in the Crucible of Ministry*. (InterVarsity Press, 2008).

Benner, David. *The Gift of Being Yourself: The Sacred Call to Self-Discovery*. (InterVarsity Press, 2004).

_____. *Spirituality and the Awakening of Self: The Sacred Journey of Transformation*. (Brazos Press, 2012)

Bly, Robert, edited by William Booth *A Little Book on the Human Shadow*. (Harper and Row, 1988).

Bradshaw, John. *Bradshaw On: Healing the Shame that Binds You*. (Health Communications, Inc., 1988).

Detweiler, Craig. *Into the Dark: Seeing the Sacred in the Top Films of the 21st Century*. (Baker Academic, 2008).

Fischer, David. *Fight Club*, dramatic film, starring Edward Norton and Brad Pitt. (Fox 2000 Pictures, 1999).

Glass, Ira. *This American Life*, radio show and podcast.

Goleman, Daniel, Richard Boyatzis, Annie McKee. *Primal Leadership: Realizing the Power of Emotional Intelligence.* (Harvard Business School Press, Kindle Edition, 2002).

Gottlieb, Lori. *Maybe You Should Talk to Someone.* (Houghton Mifflin Harcourt, 2019).

Jung, Carl. *The Psychology of the Unconscious.* (Public Domain, 1912).

Loewen, Gregory. *The Unexplored Room.* (Self published, 2018).

Luft, J.; Ingham, H. *The Johari window, a graphic model of interpersonal awareness.* (Proceedings of the western training laboratory in group development, UCLA, 1955).

Merton, Thomas. *The Living Bread.* (Farrar, Straus, & Giroux, 2010).

Nawrocki, Mike. *VeggieTales: King George and the Ducky.* (Big Ideas Entertainment, 2000).

Scarf, Maggie. *Secrets, Lies, and Betrayals: How the Body holds the secrets of a life, and how to Unlock Them.* (Ballantine Books, 2005).

Shermer, Michael. *The Pattern behind Self-deception.* (TED talk, 2010). http://www.ted.com/talks/michael_shermer_the_pattern_behind_self_deception

van der Kolk, Bessel. Interview on "On Being with Krista Tippett". *Restoring the Body: Yoga, EMDR, and Treating Trauma*, October 30, 2014. http://www.onbeing.org/program/restoring-the-body-bessel-van-der-kolk-on-yoga-emdr-and-treating-trauma/5801

_____. *The Body Keeps the Score: Brain, Mind, and Body in the Healing of Trauma.* (Penguin Books, 2015).

Willard, Dallas. *From the introduction for: Gregg A. Ten Elshof's book, I Told Me So: Self-Deception and the Christian Life.* (2019) http://www.dwillard.org/articles/ https://renovare.org/articles/this-pervasive-self-deception

_____. *Renovation of the Heart.* (Navpress Pubslishing, 2002).

The Wachowski's, *The Matrix,* dramatic film, starring Keanu Reeves and Laurence Fishburn. (Warner Bros., Roadshow Pictures, 1999).

7 | SECRET GOODNESS

Barclay, William. *The Gospel of Matthew, Volume 1.* (Westminster John Knox Press, 1956, 2001).

Bishop Briggs, *Dream,* from the album *Church of Scars.* (Island Records, 2018).

Goodrich, Frances, and Albert Hackett. *The Diary of Anne Frank,* stage play. (Public Domain, 1955). Performed on the campus of Walla Walla College, 2004.

Groves, Sara, Produced by Nate Sabin. *This Journey is My Own,* song from the album *Conversations.* (INO Records, 2001).

Rumi. *Masnavi.* (Public Domain). Accessed from: https://thedawnwithin.com/rumi/

Sivers, Derek. *Keep Your Goals to Yourself.* (TED Talk, 2010).

https://www.ted.com/talks/derek_sivers_keep_your_
goals_to_yourself

Theatre for One. https://theatreforone.com/

Willard, Dallas. *Renovation of the Heart.* (Navpress Pubslishing, 2002).

_____. *The Spirit of the Disciplines: Understanding how God Changes Lives.* (Harper One, 1999).

8 | SECRECY AND LEADERSHIP

Cohen, Leonard. *Secret Life,* from the album *Ten New Songs.* (Cohen's and Robinson's home studio, 2001).

Judge, Phoebe. *Criminal Podcast.* Episode 170, Ian Manuel, July 30, 2021.

Glasser, Arthur F. *Announcing the Kingdom: The Story of God's Mission in the Bible.* (Baker Academic., 2003). An influential and helpful book in my graduate schooling at Fuller Seminary.

McCarthy, Tom. *Spotlight,* film starring Mark Ruffalo and Michael Keaton. (Participant Media. First Look Media, 2015).

McLaren, Brian. *Faith After Doubt: Why Your Beliefs Stopped Working and What to Do About It.* (Macmillan, 2021).

Melville, Herman. *Moby-Dick; or, The Whale.* (Constable & Co., 1922; Bartleby.com, 2013).

Rae Jean Proeschold-Bell, Andrew miles, Matthew Toth, Christopher Adams, Bruce, W. Smith, David Toole. *Using Effort-Reward Imbalance Theory to Understand High Rates of Depression and Anxiety Among Clergy.* (The Journal of Primary Prevention: December 2013, Volume 34, Issue 6, pp 439-453).

Stevenson, Bryan. *Just Mercy.* (Penguin Random House, 2014).

The Investigative Staff of the Boston Globe. *Betrayal: The Crisis in the Catholic Church.* (Back Bay Books, 2003).

9 | GIVING AND RECEIVING TRUTH

A., Tony. *The Laundry List: 14 Traits of an Adult Child of an Alcoholic.* (Adult Children of Alcoholics World Service Organization, 1978). https://adultchildren.org/literature/laundry-list

Aesop's Fables. *The Boy Who Cried Wolf.* (Public Domain, 1484).

Augsburger, David. *Caring Enough to Confront: How to Understand and Express Your Deepest Feelings Toward Others.* (Revell, 2009).

Bell, Rob. *Everything Is Spiritual 2.* (Attended live in person at the Knitting Factory theatre in Spokane, Wash., 2015). Loewen, Kris. "How to Lose 70 Pounds." http://www.krisloewen.com/writing-blog/2016/3/25/how-to-lose-70-pounds (2016).

Sedaris, David. *Me Talk Pretty One Day.* (Little, Brown and Company, 2001).

_____. *Let's Explore Diabetes with Owls.* (Little, Brown and Company, 2013).

_____. An Evening with David Sedaris. (Attended live in person at Cordiner Hall at Whitman College in Walla Walla,

Wash., 2014).

Woititz, Janet. *Adult Children of Alcoholics, expanded edition.* (Health Communications, Inc., 1990).

10 | DISCLOSURE

Barr, Beth Allison. *The Making of Biblical Womanhood.* (Brazos Press, 2021).

Bilton, Nick. *Parenting in the age of Online Pornography* http://www.nytimes.com/2015/01/08/style/parenting-in-the-age-of-online-porn.html

Bonhoeffer, Dietrich. *Life Together.* (Harper, 1954).

Breazeale, Mick. *On Jordan's Stormy Banks I Stand: The Extraordinary Last Rites of Felix Bushaloo Breazeale*, blog post. http://www.clanbreazeale.com/UncleBush/

Gungor. *Beautiful Things*, from the album *Beautiful Things.* (Brash Music, 2010).

Hari, Jonathan. *Everything You Know about Addiction is Wrong.* (Ted Talk, 2015).

Kaplan, Randy. *Clothes Dryer* from the audio album *Loquat Rooftop.* (Yellow Thing Records and Books, 2008).

Kelly, Anita. *The Psychology of Secrets.* (Kluwer Academic/Plenum Publishers, 2002).

Mann, Rachel. *Dazzling Darkness: Gender, Sexuality, Illness, and God*, Second Edition. (Wild Goose Publications, 2012).

Mclaren, Brian. *Naked Spirituality: A Life With God in Twelve*

Simple Words. (Hodder and Stoughton, 2011).

Richard Rohr. *Falling Upwards: A Spirituality for the Two Halves of Life.* (Jossey-Bass, 2011).

Schneider, Aaron. *Get Low,* film starring Robert Duvall, Sissy Spacek, and Bill Murray. (Sony Pictures Classics, 2009).

Wilson, Bill. *Alcoholics Anonymous: The Big Book.* (Public Domain, 1939).

Wilson, Gary. www.yourbrainonporn.com.

Yeslam Al-Saggaf, , Sharon Nielsen. *Self-disclosure on Facebook among female users and its relationship to feelings of loneliness.* (School of Computing and Mathematics, Charles Sturt University, Locked Bag 588, Boorooma Street, Wagga Wagga, NSW 2678, Australia)

11 | BOUNDARIES AND TRUST

Al-Saggaf, Yeslam, and Sharon Nielsen. *Self-disclosure on Facebook among female users and its relationship to feelings of loneliness.* (School of Computing and Mathematics, Charles Sturt University, Locked Bag 588, Boorooma Street, Wagga Wagga, NSW 2678, Australia, 2014).

Brown, Brene. *Daring Greatly: How the Courage to Be Vulnerable Transforms the Way We Live, Love, Parent, and Lead.* (Brene Publishing, 2018).

Goldman, Alex. *Reply All Podcast, Jennicam.* (Gimlet Media). https://gimletmedia.com/shows/reply-all/z3hld4

Kissack, Eric, Narrated by and starring Nick Offerman. *The Gunfighter,* short film. (Produced by Sarah Platt, 2013).

https://vimeo.com/79306807

Hauerwas, Stanley. *A Community of Character: Toward a Constructive Christian Social Ethic.* (University of Notre Dame Press, 1986).

Keizer, Garret. *Privacy.* (Picador, 2013).

Miller, Donald. *Scary Close: Dropping the Act and Finding True Intimacy.* (Thomas Nelson, 2015).

Nin, Anais. *The Diary of Anaïs Nin, Vol. 1.* (Public Domain, 1931-1934).

Selmanovic, Samir. *It's really All About God: How Islam, Atheism, and Judaism Made me a better Christian.* (Jossey Bass, 2011). https://www.samirselmanovic.com/

To Write Love On Her Arms. Website. https://twloha.com/

Warren, Frank. *PostSecret: Extraordinary Confessions from Ordinary Lives.* (Regan Books, 2005). *Frank Warren's blog, www.postsecret.com, is updated every Sunday.

Van Sant, Gus. *Good Will Hunting,* Film. (Miramax Films, 1997).

Vyleta, Dan. *Smoke.* (Doubleday, 2016).

Made in the USA
Las Vegas, NV
19 August 2021

28452267R00164